Population Change and the Economy: Social Science Theories and Models

Population Change and the Economy: Social Science Theories and Models

edited by

Andrew M. Isserman

Kluwer-Nijhoff Publishing
a member of the Kluwer Academic Publishers Group

Boston/Dordrecht/Lancaster

Distributors

for the United States and Canada: Kluwer Academic Publishers, 190 Old Derby Street, Hingham, MA, 02043, USA

for the UK and Ireland: Kluwer Academic Publishers, MTP Press Limited, Falcon House, Queen Square, Lancaster LAI IRN, UK

for all other countries: Kluwer Academic Publishers Group, Distribution Centre, P.O. Box 322, 3300 AH Dordrecht, The Netherlands

Library of Congress Cataloging in Publication Data
Main entry under title:

Population change and the economy: social science theories and models

  Bibliography: p.
  Contents: Forecasting birth and migration rates /
Andrew Isserman—Forecasting regional births / Dennis
Ahlburg—forecasting interregional migration / Jacques
Ledent—[etc.]
   1. Population—Economic aspects—Mathematical models—
Addresses, essays, lectures. 2. Population forecasting—
Mathematical models—Addresses, essays, lectures.
I. Isserman, Andrew M.
HB849.41.P67 1985   304.6′2   84-20188
ISBN 0-89838-140-1

Copyright © 1986 by Kluwer-Nijhoff Publishing

No part of this book may be produced in any form by print, photoprint, microfilm, or any other means without written permission of the publisher.

Printed in the United States of America

Contents

Preface — ix

Introduction — xiii

I
Economic Determinants of Fertility and Migration Rates — 1

1
Forecasting Birth and Migration Rates: The Theoretical Foundation — 3
Andrew Isserman

2
Forecasting Regional Births: An Economic-Demographic Approach — 31
Dennis Ahlburg

3
Forecasting Interregional Migration: An Economic-Demographic Approach — 53
Jacques Ledent

II
Regional Economic-Demographic Modeling — 79

4
Economic-Demographic Interactions in the Growth of Texas — 81
Thomas Plaut

5
An Econometric-Demographic Model of New York State — 105
Carol Greenberg and Charles Renfro

6
The Effects of Refining Demographic-Economic
 Interactions in Regional Econometric Models 127
Carol Taylor

III
Interregional Economic-Demographic Modeling 157

7
Economic-Demographic Linkages in an Interregional Model 159
Walter Isard and Christine Smith

8
Multistate Demoeconomic Modeling and Projection 177
Andrei Rogers and Pamela Williams

9
The ECESIS Economic-Demographic Model of the United States 203
*Paul Beaumont, Andrew Isserman, David McMillen, David Plane,
 and Peter Rogerson*

IV
The Challenges Ahead 239

10
Regional Economic-Demographic Modeling:
 Progress and Prospects 241
Jeffrey Williamson

11
Intuition, Science, and the Application of Regional Models 261
William Alonso

Contributing Authors

Dennis Ahlburg, Assistant Professor of Industrial Relations, University of Minnesota, USA

William Alonso, Saltonstall Professor of Population Policy and Chairman, Department of Sociology, Harvard University, USA

Paul Beaumont, Assistant Professor of Economics, Purdue University, and Research Assistant Professor, Regional Research Institute, West Virginia University, USA

Carol Greenberg, Regional Economist, Chase Econometrics, USA

Walter Isard, Professor of Economics, Regional Science, and Urban and Regional Studies, Cornell University, and Adjunct Professor of Regional Science, University of Pennsylvania, USA

Andrew Isserman, Director of the Regional Research Institute and Professor of Economics and Geography, West Virginia University, USA

Jacques Ledent, Professor, Institut National de la Récherche Scientifique-Urbanisation, Université de Québec, Canada

David McMillen, Mathematical Statistician, U.S. Bureau of the Census, USA

David Plane, Assistant Professor of Geography and Regional Development, University of Arizona, USA

Thomas Plaut, Economist, Bureau of Business Research, University of Texas at Austin, USA

Charles Renfro, Chief Economist, C.A. Renfro Associates, USA

Andrei Rogers, Director of the Population Program, Institute of Behavioral Science, and Professor of Geography, University of Colorado at Boulder, USA

Peter Rogerson, Assistant Professor of Civil Engineering and Geography, Northwestern University, USA

Christine Smith, Lecturer in Economics, University of Wollongong, Australia

Carol Taylor, Program Director for Forecasting, Bureau of Economic and Business Research, and Associate Professor of Economics, University of Florida, USA

Pamela Williams, Policy Analyst, Department of the Premier and Cabinet, Melbourne, Australia

Jeffrey Williamson, Laird Bell Professor of Economics, Harvard University, USA

Preface

Population change and population forecasts are receiving considerable attention from governmental planners and policy-makers, as well as from the private sector. Old patterns of population redistribution, industrial location, labor-force participation, household formation, and fertility are changing. The resulting uncertainty has increased interest in forecasting because mere extrapolations of past trends are proving inadequate. In the United States of America population forecasts received even more attention after federal agencies began distributing funds for capital infrastructure to state and local governments on the basis of projected future populations. If the national government had based those funding decisions on locally prepared projections, the optimism of local officials would have resulted in billions of dollars worth of excess capacity in sewage treatment plants alone. Cabinet-level inquiries concluded that the U.S. Department of Commerce should (1) assume the responsibility for developing a single set of projections for use whenever future population was a consideration in federal spending decisions and (2) develop methods which incorporate both economic and demographic factors causing population change. Neither the projections prepared by economists at the Bureau of Economic Analysis nor those prepared by demographers at the Bureau of the Census were considered satisfactory because neither method adequately recognized the intertwined nature of demographic and economic change.

Against this background, the American Statistical Association (ASA) and the U.S. Bureau of the Census, with support from the National Science Foundation (NSF), jointly convened the International Conference on Forecasting Regional Population Change and Its Economic Determinants and Consequences. Participants included leading scholars from Europe, Japan, Australia, and North America, from universities, governmental agencies, international organizations, corporations, and consulting firms. They included demographers, economists, geographers, regional scientists, sociologists, and statisticians. This conference, held in Airlie, Virginia, May 26–29, 1982, was part of a larger ASA/Census program also supported by NSF that included a three-year effort (1979–82) to build ECESIS, an operational interregional economic-demographic model described elsewhere in this book, and an initial fact-finding conference in 1977. That conference had concluded:

> Population projections and migration modeling are, in fact, among the important contemporary concerns in establishing and maintaining an adequate data base for informed planning and programs administration.

The rapid development of the field of economic-demographic population modeling is evident when comparing the papers from the first conference (available from ASA) to those of the second conference only five years later. The papers at the second conference generally were of four kinds: (1) studies of internal migration that help us understand better the nature of the phenomenon being forecast; (2) evaluations of the data available for population modeling; (3) descriptions of economic-demographic models which reflect the emerging state of the art; and (4) essays regarding the state of the art and prospects for its improvements. The chapters of this book generally are revised and extended versions of papers from the third and fourth groups.

Other papers from the conference and ECESIS project are found either in the *Review of Public Data Use*, Vol. 10, No. 4, and Vol. 11, No. 1, published by Elsevier-North Holland or in a special issue of *Socio-Economic Planning Sciences*, Vol. 17, No. 5–6, published by Pergamon Press under the title "Forecasting Population Change and its Economic Determinants and Consequences." The issues of the *Review of Public Data Use* include papers on migration data by Richard Bilsborrow and John Akin, Douglas Norris, and Andrew Isserman, David Plane, and David McMillen and comments by Richard Morrill and Robert Nakosteen. *Socio-Economic Planning Sciences* contains papers on migration by Anne van der Veen and Gerard Evers, David Plane and Andrew Isserman, Matthew Black, John Long, Anthony Warnes, and Curtis Roseman, and on forecasting models by Peter Batey and Moss Madden, Takao Fukuchi, Masahiro Chuma, and Makoto Yamaguchi, Richard Joun and Richard Conway, Anthony Redwood, Steven Caldwell, and Peter Rogerson. In addition, parts of Chapter 1 of this book appear in *Environment and Planning A*, Vol. 17, No. 1, published by Pion.

PREFACE   xi

Helpful comments by the discussants and moderators at the conference are gratefully acknowledged. They include (in order of appearance): Ray Grimes, Donald Pittenger, William Milne, James Kau, Swarnjit Arora, Uwe Schubert, Roger Bolton, Norfleet Rives, Shelby Gerking, Peter Morrison, Richard Morrill, Robert Nakosteen, Richard Engels, Signe Wetrogen, David Gleave, Frank Porell, Al Tella, Anthony Yezer, Ann Miller, Calvin Beale, Larry Long, Michael Greenwood, Thomas Espenshade, Mark Rosenzweig, Jacob Siegel, William Beyers, Roger Herriot, Ken Johnson, John Long, and Shirly Goetz.

Fred Leone, Ede Denenberg, George Tiao, and Arnold Zellner of ASA, Murray Aborn of NSF, and Barbara Bailar, Richard Engels, Roger Herriot, Al Tella, and Kirk Wolter of the U.S. Bureau of the Census gave their strong support to this conference and the ECESIS project. Without their vision and dedication this rather remarkable conference and ASA/Census program would not have taken place.

Introduction

Population change is affected by economic conditions and has an effect on economic conditions. Young migrants are attracted to a region by employment opportunities, but migrants also cause employment opportunities when, for instance, elderly migrants retire in an area and spend their retirement incomes there for goods and services. The number of births in a given year also is determined, at least in part, by economic conditions, and those births, in turn, have an immediate impact on the economy through their effects on female labor-force participation and consumer demand. More generally, changes in an area's population size and composition affect the size of its labor force, salaries and wage levels, per capita income, employment, unemployment, and other indicators of economic well-being and potential. The debates in many countries over national immigration policy are testimony to a general awareness that population change and economic conditions are intertwined.

Interest in population change and its economic determinants and consequences has received recent impetus from the apparent breakdown of long-established patterns. Net migration into the core metropolitan regions of most developed nations has slowed down or even ceased. In the United States there has been net migration *into* nonmetropolitan areas—a reversal in the direction of net movement. Manufacturing jobs also have decentralized, moving into suburban and nonmetropolitan areas. Changing conditions in energy markets have caused population movement, too, as people moved into energy-rich regions. When the comparative advantage or relative prices that spurred this migration sometimes turned out to be short-lived, the resulting quick change from boomtown to bust and the dashed aspirations and hopes accompanying it again focused attention on the interrelationships of demographic and economic change.

This book is concerned with quantifying those interrelationships. It reflects the state of the art in our ability to model economic-demographic interrelationships mathematically using computers and real data. Such models are used to forecast future population levels and economic conditions and to conduct impact studies. (For example, what would be the economic and demographic consequences of changes in tax policies or oil prices?) Since constructing these models requires confronting social science theories with actual data, economic-demographic modeling is a research undertaking involving hypothesis testing and learning.

Emphasis in this book is on models for parts of a nation: regions, states, provinces, or metropolitan areas. Economic-demographic modeling on that spatial level is more difficult than national modeling because of trade and population flows within the country. For example, national models can focus on natural increase (births and deaths) in explaining population change because foreign immigration tends to be a small part of the total change; immigration in such models usually is treated as a fixed number determined by governmental policy. On the other hand, subnational models must consider births, deaths, and internal migration, with the last typically being far larger a component of population change than natural increase. To compound the difficulty, data available for national modeling efforts often are not reliable or tabulated on the subnational level; many key variables only are available every ten years, such as unemployment by age and sex, or not available at all, such as the cost of living for every state and its domestic exports and imports. Consequently, modeling strategies and methods must be invented that recognize and compensate for these data limitations. Thus the models themselves are the product of an intricate interplay of theory, data, and method.

The nature of the economic-demographic interrelationships and the way they are modeled by various social sciences can be summarized with the aid of figure I-1. In brief, population change has both supply and demand effects on the economy. More people means an increase both in the size of the labor force and the demand for goods and services. These labor-force supply and demand effects interact to determine wages, employment, and unemployment. In the case of population growth, employment will increase, but only if the demand effect dominates will wage levels increase and the unemployment rate fall. Whatever effect dominates, the resulting economic conditions will affect both migration and fertility. Hence the initial population change leads to further population change through its economic impacts. Details of each of the relationships shown in figure I-1 and their simultaneous, interlocked nature are discussed further in subsequent chapters of this book.

INTRODUCTION

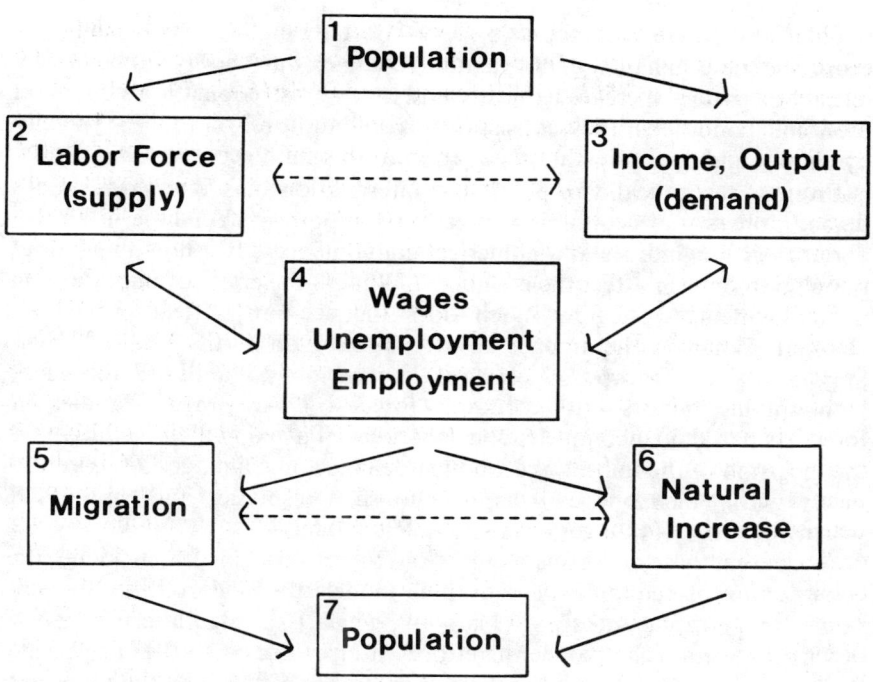

Figure I-1. Population change and its economic determinants and consequences

Although the existence of these economic-demographic interrelationships may seem obvious, demographers and economists very rarely model population and the economy as if they were interconnected. Demographers generally have ignored both the economic consequences and determinants of population change in favor of extrapolating to the future carefully measured age-, sex-, and race-specific rates of fertility, migration, and mortality. In terms of figure I–1, demographic models of population change have focused almost exclusively on the lowest portion, boxes 5, 6, and 7. The models built by economists mostly are incomplete also. They vary in their approaches. Some economic models ignore population entirely; they contain only boxes 2, 3, and 4 from figure I–1. Other models treat population as exogenous, meaning they consist of boxes 1, 2, 3, and 4 and incorporate the consequences of population change but not its causes. Still others ignore the causes and only partially model the consequences of population change; they incorporate boxes 1, 3, and 4, the demand effects of population change, but not its supply effects. Finally some include the economic determinants of population change, but they do not model fertility or natural increase explicitly and they ignore population's effect on economic conditions; they consist of boxes 2 and/or 3, 4, and 7, typically by simply adding a population equation to the main economic model.

From a theoretical viewpoint, the interrelationships ignored by both demographers and economists seem very important. Yet little is known about their magnitudes and numerical consequences. Just how much does population change affect the economy? What is the effect of migration on unemployment? Just how much does the economy affect population change? What is the impact of a recession on fertility rates? How important is it to incorporate economic factors into population forecasts or demographic factors into economic forecasts? Are impact studies or forecasts based on incomplete models seriously flawed and misleading, or is the inclusion of the full set of economic-demographic linkages a theoretical nicety with which one can dispense to save resources and time? Is it worthwhile to build bigger, more complete models?

Answering these questions requires careful, empirical work, including the construction of economic-demographic models that incorporate the economic-demographic linkages. This book, which is divided into four parts, describes several such pioneering efforts. It represents a start in answering these questions. Part I contains three chapters concerned with the economic determinants of migration and fertility. Chapter 1 is a comprehensive review of the theoretical literature, and chapters 2 and 3 present methods for forecasting fertility and migration, respectively. Part II contains three chapters dealing with regional economic-demographic models. Chapter 4 presents a model of Texas, and chapter 5 a model of New York. Chapter 6 presents a series of models for six regions in an attempt to address directly some of the questions about modeling strategies posed above. Part III focuses on interregional models. Chapters 7, 8, and 9 each describes a framework for capturing economic-demographic interrelationships within a system of models that recognizes the linkages among regions. Part IV contains two chapters written in reaction to the emerging state of the art and making clear the serious research challenges yet ahead and some of the disadvantages of working with large-scale models.

This form of economic-demographic modeling requires a considerable research effort in terms of data, computer capacity, and, most important, multidisciplinary human skills. Demography, economics, and geography, regional science, sociology, and statistics are all indispensable. Each contributes necessary theories, methods, and insights. For example, the demographer understands the key population disaggregations and the appropriately defined rates of transition; the economist contributes skill in time-series modeling and an orientation toward rigorous development of theory; and the quantitative geographer and regional scientist bring important methods of analyzing and forecasting spatial interaction in the absence of complete sets of reliable time-series data.

Yet traditional disciplinary boundaries are tightly drawn and encroachments on the others' turfs are strongly contested. It is easier for a demographer to criticize the demographic ignorance of an economist working on a population topic than to appreciate the potential contribution to demography of the economist's work. Similarly, it may be easier for an economist to dismiss important findings of demography as petty accounting or unimportant aggregation problems rather than to appreciate and accept the implications of those findings for economic modeling.

Nevertheless, population forecasting and modeling present a rare opportunity in the social sciences to overcome those boundaries and prejudices. Scholars from different disciplines are working on the same problem—the improvement of forecasting methods and the understanding of economic-demographic linkages. Although demography and economics are very, very different in terms of their dominant modes of inquiry and their research approaches, their contributions, insights, techniques, and wisdom are beginning to be interwoven with those of the other disciplines interested in population change. The end result will not be merely a multidisciplinary approach that simply combines methods from two or three disciplines. Instead, new, truly interdisciplinary methods and approaches will evolve and strengthen the disciplines themselves. Toward such broadening and enrichment of the social sciences this book is dedicated.

I ECONOMIC DETERMINANTS OF FERTILITY AND MIGRATION RATES

1 FORECASTING BIRTH AND MIGRATION RATES: THE THEORETICAL FOUNDATION

Andrew Isserman

This chapter presents a review of the social science literature that provides the theoretical foundation for forecasting fertility and internal migration. The methodological and data problems which must be overcome in implementing the theories are explained, modeling strategies are suggested, and some original empirical work is presented. Methods currently used by the U.S. Bureau of the Census are discussed as an example of the standard demographic approach in order to put the economic-demographic approach into perspective. Fertility is discussed first and then migration. Emphasis is on the state level, in part because barriers are even more severe to modeling population distribution on a finer geographical level.

Fertility

The Census Method

The U.S. Bureau of the Census projects the future population of each state using the cohort-component method (see U.S. Bureau of the Census 1979). Births for each state are projected by applying age- and race-specific birth rates to the female population in each of six five-year age groups. The birth rates themselves are projected in a three-stage process:

1. Ratios are formed of the state's and the nation's actual birth rates from 1970 to 1975 by age and race.

2. The ratios are projected linearly to the future under the assumption that they will equal one in the year 2000. In other words, birth rates are assumed to converge. Each cohort defined by age and race is expected to have the identical birth rate in all 50 states. (Any spatial differences in fertility remaining in the year 2000 will stem entirely from differences in population composition by age and race.)

3. The projected ratios are multiplied by projected "Series II" national birth rates to yield the projected state rates. The projected national rates are based on a completed cohort fertility rate of 2.1, which is consistent with birth expectations data (U.S. Bureau of the Census, 1977b).

The projected births are allocated by sex using the 1970–74 actual proportions of male and female births by race. The births are adjusted so that the total of births in all states is equal to the total projected independently for the entire nation using the Series II national rates.

The assumption of converging birth rates and the manner in which the national rates are projected differ clearly from an economic-demographic approach. In the latter, convergence—or, for that matter, divergence—might be forecast as a result of changes in the various determinants of fertility, but univariate trend extrapolations would be avoided whenever possible. The danger in such simple trend extrapolation can be seen from the recent history of U.S. fertility rates. Both the national general fertility rate (GFR or births per 1,000 women aged 18–44) and the standard deviation of that rate across the states declined sharply from 1958 to 1968. Therefore, it may have seemed logical to assume that the GFR and its standard deviation would continue to fall. In fact, the GFR did decline from 1968 to 1979, but its standard deviation increased to its 1958 level (fig. 1-1). The standard deviation of the total fertility rate (TFR) also increased from 1970 to 1975 (Alonso 1980; O'Connell 1981). Thus, birth rates among the states were diverging in the 1970s rather than converging as a simple trend extrapolation made in the early 1970s would have predicted. Ideally, an economic-demographic approach would be able to predict such changes in trends.

Birth expectations data from sample surveys are used by the Census Bureau to project the completed cohort fertility of cohorts currently childbearing, but projecting the exact timing pattern that will be followed by each cohort depends heavily on the forecaster's judgment (just as did the assumption that birth rates would converge in the year 2000). In an

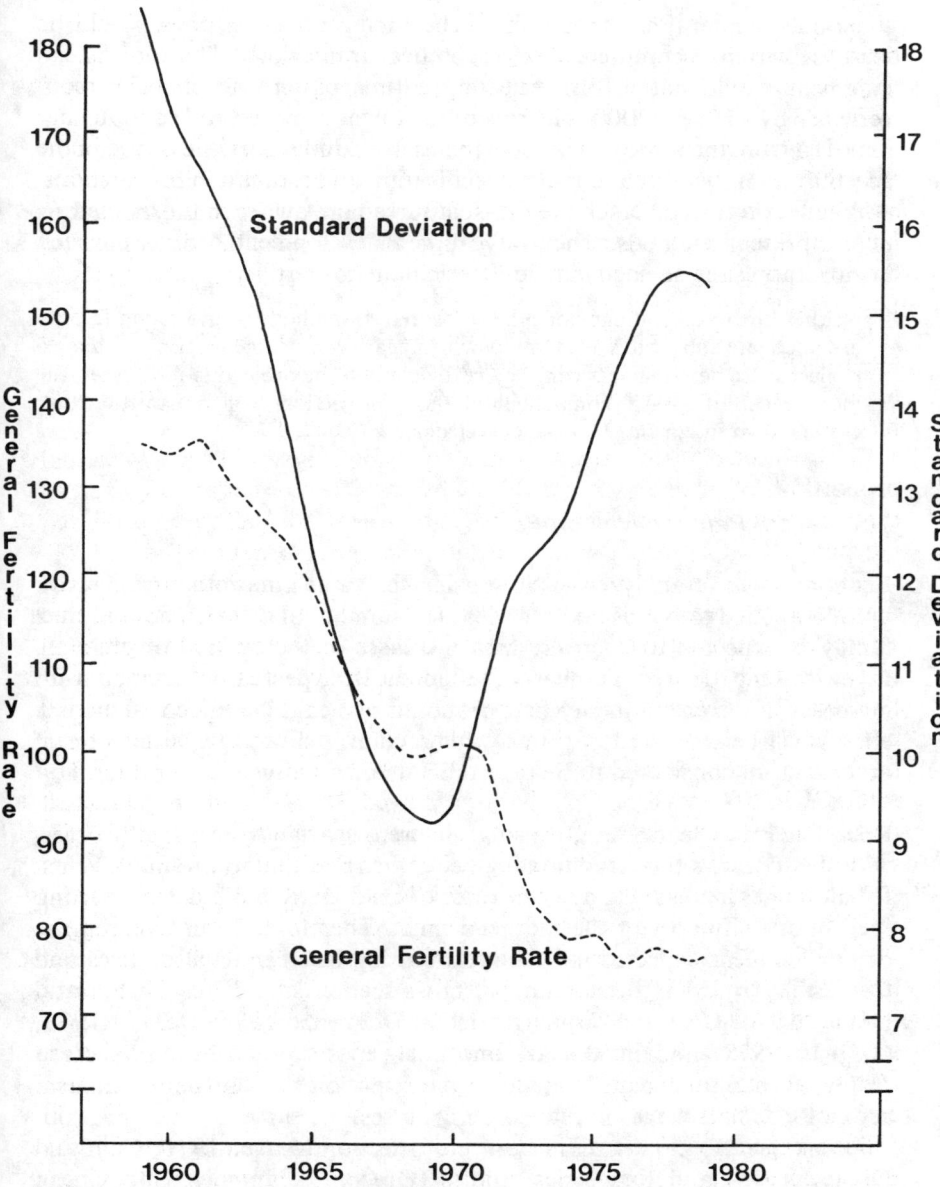

Figure 1-1. The general fertility rate and its standard deviation among the 48 continental states and the District of Columbia, 1959-79

economic-demographic approach to the timing of births, they would be forecast within a comprehensive theoretical framework. The forecaster's judgment would not involve selecting a time pattern or choosing convergence by the year 2000. The role of judgment is more subtle and further removed from the forecast numbers themselves. Judgment is involved in the acceptance of theories and in the specification and estimation of equations.

Population forecasters in the Census Bureau are aware of the limitations of the present methods. They have urged development of an approach incorporating the socioeconomic determinants of fertility:

> Neither birth expectations nor other atheoretical methods of projecting fertility are adequate substitutes.... Only when forecasters are able to discover and to project these determinants can they really claim to be projecting fertility. In the meantime... the basic component of those projections will remain the forecasters' own judgment (Long and Wetrogan 1980).

Theoretical Perspectives on Fertility

Economists have analyzed fertility using the same conceptual framework usually applied to goods and services. The number of children desired by a family is expected to decrease with increases in the "price" of children. Likewise, the desired number of children is expected to change with increases in income, a theory first proposed by Malthus. Price and income effects will be discussed in turn in this section, followed by discussion of other factors considered to be determinants of fertility rates.

Price Effects. Bearing and raising children is a labor-intensive process, with the mother's time traditionally being the most important input. When female wages increase, so does the price of children (female wages reflecting the opportunity cost of the mother's time). Therefore, fewer children are demanded. This expected negative relationship between female wages and the fertility rate has been found in cross-section studies (e.g., Cain and Dooley 1976; Cain and Weininger 1973; DeFronzo 1976; DeTray 1973; Gardner 1972) and in at least one time-series study (Butz and Ward 1979a). When the female labor-force participation rate has been used as a proxy for female wages in regression analyses, the same negative relationship has been found, again in both cross-section (Anker 1978; Cain and Dooley 1976) and time-series studies (Gregory, Campbell, and Cheng 1972). Tabulated data from the Current Population Survey also indicate that working women tend to have smaller families (U.S. Bureau of the Census 1977a).

The price concept has been used to explain observed differentials between urban and rural fertility rates. The higher rural rates have been ascribed to the lower cost of bringing up children in rural areas (DeTray 1973; Gardner 1973; Phillips, Votey, and Maxwell 1969; T.P. Schultz 1973; Wachter 1975) or in areas with lower population density (Joseph 1980). In addition, the net price of children in rural areas is lower because children on farms also are producers and support their parents in old age through continued operation of the farm (Anker 1978; Cain and Dooley 1976; DeTray 1973; Gardner 1973; Phillips, Votey, and Maxwell 1969). Perhaps indicative of many economists' attitude toward sociological and demographic explanations for the urban-rural differential is Phillips, Votey, and Maxwell's argument that the differential can be explained by costs and benefits, not some "mysterious difference in social attitudes and values." (On the other hand, another economist acknowledges the possibility that: "urban individuals have different tastes for children than nonurban families" [Wachter 1975]).

Income Effects. The relationship between income and fertility is complex. Malthus and others have posited a positive relationship. Yet in most countries, declines in fertility have accompanied increases in income, and wealthier families tend to have fewer children. These observations suggest that children are so-called inferior goods (goods whose consumption decreases with rising income).

Other factors which change with income can offset the income effect, however. This possibility permits reconciliation of the theory of positive income effects with the observed negative income-fertility relationships; children need not be classified as inferior goods. For instance, Malthus assumed the price of children would remain constant, but their price increases with the value of human time (T.W. Schultz 1973). Increased productivity results both in rising income and in an increased cost of children because the parental time used in bearing and raising them is now more expensive. Becker and Lewis (1973) posit that the price of children also increases with income because the rich choose higher quality children (which require more time and resource inputs) in much the same way they choose more expensive varieties of cars.

In addition to price, income is thought to affect fertility through other indirect effects. The escalation of aspirations accompanying rising incomes may negate the income effect (Easterlin 1976), as might social pressures leading to higher consumption of status goods (Leibenstein 1975, 1976). In discussing such factors which might offset the income effect, economic models indeed have become "more consistent with the views held by demographers and sociologists" (Sanderson 1976).

Income and price effects are difficult to separate empirically. Willis (1973) presents a model in which the effects of changing income and female wages on fertility may vary even in sign with prevailing levels of income and wages. Most multivariate studies which include factors thought to vary with income, however, do find a positive relationship between fertility and male or even family income (e.g., Butz and Ward 1979a; Cain and Weininger 1973; DeFronzo 1976: DeTray 1973; Gardner 1972).

Other Factors. Another socioeconomic variable with a prominent role in the fertility literature is education, but "too often the husband's or wife's education level is interpreted in empirical work as a good proxy for whatever is of interest to the researcher" (Michael 1973). It has been used to measure the opportunity cost of the wife's time (Anker 1978; Cain and Dooley 1973; DeFronzo 1976), tastes or preferences related to demand for children (Anker 1978; Cain and Dooley 1973), efficiency in child-raising (DeTray 1973), and knowledge and effectiveness of birth control methods (Cain and Weininger 1973; Gardner 1972; Wachter 1975). Empirical support exists for each of these relationships: more educated women have higher earnings; a positive relationship between female education and a very crude proxy for child quality (school system expenditures) was found by DeTray (1973); and data from the 1965 National Fertility Survey show that more-educated women achieve a lower risk of conception (Michael 1973).

Infant mortality rates have been included in empirical studies under the assumption that higher mortality rates induce higher fertility rates by increasing the number of births necessary to attain a desired family size (Anker 1978; Herr and Boynton 1970; Phillips, Votey, and Maxwell 1969). On the other hand, the psychic costs of experiencing the death of a child may lower that desired size (DeTray 1973).

Different fertility levels by racial, ethnic, and religious groups have been observed. Although it is tempting to some to argue that such differences only reflect income and other economic characteristics (e.g., Phillips, Votey, and Maxwell 1969), several economists argue that these groups have different tastes with respect to family size (e.g., Cain and Weininger 1973; Joseph 1980). Empirical evidence does support the latter argument. For instance, the 1970 National Fertility Survey indicates that Southerners want significantly fewer children, even controlling for income and race (Rindfuss 1978).

The studies and theories discussed thus far have focused on explaining the fertility rate itself. A different approach is suggested by the conceptual framework offered by Bongaarts (1978) building on the work of Davis and Blake (1956). He examines the difference between the fecundity rate and the fertility rate. This difference depends on such factors as the proportion of females married, the use of contraception and abortion, the extent of breast-feeding (because of lactational infecundability), and the rate of spontaneous intrauterine mortality. Although Bongaarts' work is essentially an accounting framework or decomposition technique at this stage, it suggests that changes in fertility might be forecast by explaining changes in marriage rates and contraception use.

Migration and fertility. Fertility rates exhibit a definite age pattern, with the highest rates generally observed for the cohorts aged 20 to 24 and 25 to 29. These cohorts, along with those aged 15 to 20 and less than 5 years of age, have the highest cohort-migration rates (U.S. Bureau of the Census 1980, p. 19). Therefore, net inmigration may be expected to have a positive impact on the general fertility rate through its effect on the age structure of the fecund population. When forecasting with methods that use age-specific fertility rates, such interrelationships may be relatively inconsequential unless the inmigrants differ from the remaining population in their fertility rates. Economic–demographic forecasting methods based on annual time–series data, however, often model a general fertility rate or even total births per se because annual data on population by age and sex are not available. When modeling the general fertility rate or total births, recognition of the interrelationship between migration and fertility may be important.

Transferring nationally oriented theories of fertility to the regional level raises some exciting questions because of this relationship between migration and fertility. For example, the countercyclical fertility theory of Butz and Ward (1979a) holds that periods of economic expansion encourage higher female wages and labor-force participation and hence lower fertility rates through the price effect. Yet the same conditions that encourage female labor-force participation during expansionary times also encourage inmigration. Inmigrants, tending to be relatively young, may cause increases in the general fertility rate, offsetting the decrease stemming from changing female labor-force participation. Similarly, during recessionary periods when the employment rates of wives decrease, the expected increase in general fertility rates may be offset by outmigration. Thus, the countercyclical fertility pattern found on the national level may not exist on the regional level.

Easterlin (1976) offers another theory of fertility which becomes more complex on the regional level. If a particular cohort in the labor force is substantially smaller than previous cohorts, its income is likely to be relatively higher as the result of labor supply effects. Data for the United States from 1940 to 1975 are consistent with this hypothesis. The total fertility rate increases with the ratio of males aged 35–65 to males aged 15–34 (Easterlin 1976). On the regional level, however, the cohort size effect may disappear or at least be reduced through migration into areas of labor-market tightness (Alonso 1980).

Birth Expectations. Considerable attention has been given, primarily by demographers, to data on birth expectations. If households can predict accurately the size of their completed families, such information would be of great value in forecasting births. Four necessary conditions must be met. First, stated birth expectations must be stable, i.e., not changed repeatedly as time goes on. Second, couples must exercise birth control sufficiently well to attain their expected births and not have more children. Third, the timing of births must be predictable, and, fourth, the expected births of today's young households must describe accurately the expectations of future young households to be formed during the forecasting period.

Empirical evidence is not encouraging that these conditions will be met. For instance, Butz and Ward (1979b) argue that the decline in fertility during the 1960s is due primarily to the downward revision of couples' expected fertility, and Westoff and Ryder (1977) found that women's intentions to reproduce as stated in 1970 significantly overestimated 1971 and 1975 fertility. In addition, Waite and Wetrogan's (1979) finding that education, labor-force status, and family income do not explain changes in individuals' birth expectations and O'Connell's (1981) finding of no correlation between socioeconomic variables and the expected births across states both suggest that predicting fertility of future cohorts based on socioeconomic characteristics would be difficult.

Forecasting Fertility

Many components and several approaches to forecasting fertility are suggested by the literature. Among the socioeconomic considerations are income, female labor-force participation, female wages, marriage rates, contraceptive practices, infant mortality rates, and population composition, including age, racial, religious, ethnic, and urban/rural distribution.

A useful point of departure in discussing the potential of these theories to

Table 1-1. Cross-Section Regression Results: White General Fertility Rate by State, 1970[a]

Variable	Coefficient	t-Statistic[b]
Male income (100s)	.27	3.44
Female income (100s)	−.76	5.82
Percent rural	.29	4.62
Percent Mormon	.46	9.77
Percent Spanish	.61	5.52
Net migration rate, 1965–70	.34	3.47
Constant	72	9.32
$R^2 = .88$		

[a]Alaska and Hawaii are excluded because of possible inconsistencies in identifying population and births by race. The District of Columbia is included.
[b]All variables are significant at the .001 level.

forecast fertility is an analysis of differences in fertility rates across states. The general fertility rate for whites by state in 1970 varied from 59 to 148 births per 1,000 women aged 18 to 44. A regression equation based on the income and price theory (although with female income as an imperfect proxy for the female wage) and augmented by measures of migration and population composition does remarkably well in explaining the spatial variation in fertility. All coefficients have the expected sign and are significant at the .001 level (see table 1–1).

Despite its good fit, the cross-section equation is virtually useless for forecasting fertility even if its coefficients were to remain invariant over time. Using it to forecast requires forecasts of the independent variables. Unfortunately, the time-series data needed to forecast them are not readily available. Data on percent rural, percent Mormon, percent Spanish, and income by sex do not exist by state on an annual basis. Even if resources were available to obtain or construct some of these data series, however, forecasting the Mormon percentage of the population or changes in female income, for example, might prove even more difficult than forecasting migration. (Further implications for forecasting fertility of the equation in table 1–1 will be considered following a discussion of time-series modeling of fertility on the national level.)

National Models. Three studies have modeled fertility in the United States using time-series data. Butz and Ward (1979a) did so using the female unemployment rate, female wages, and male wages. Gregory, Campbell, and Cheng (1972) incorporated the female labor-force participation rate, education levels, percentage nonwhite, and the unemployment rate. Finally, Wachter (1975) used expected wage, relative wages (expected wages relative to expected wages during the previous ten years), and percentage rural.

Data availability severely inhibits following such an approach on the state level. Of the ten variables used in the three studies combined, only three are available annually for states. Nevertheless, such an approach may be used with a subset of the national variables. An illustrative equation of this sort for Wyoming from 1958 to 1975 is shown in table 1–2. Although the signs of the coefficients are consistent with expectations, the significance levels are not reassuring. In fact, when the same equation was estimated for six other states, two to four states had coefficients on real income, expected earnings, and inflation which were opposite in sign to the Wyoming coefficients.

Assume for the sake of argument that theoretically pleasing, time-series equations of this kind can be estimated successfully for every state. The cross-section equation presented previously has important implications for the use of such equations in forecasting population 20 years into the future (as government agencies now do). The coefficients of the time-series equations probably would change with changes in the rural, Spanish, Mormon, and other racial, religious, and ethnic populations. One test of this possibility would be to see whether differences across states in the coefficients of the time-series equations are associated with population composition at one point in time. In other words, does fertility in states with, say, higher rural populations exhibit less sensitivity to changes in real income and expected wages? If so, forecasting fertility accurately may require forecasting such changes in population composition. Generalizing

Table 1–2. Time-Series Results: The General Fertility Rate of Wyoming, 1958–75

Variable	Coefficient	t-Statistic
Female labor force participation rate	−.130	2.61
Real income per capita	.007	.53
Expected earnings	−.035	2.62
Inflation rate	−.002	1.26
Constant	46	.92
R^2 = .92 MAPE = 3.81	DW = 1.23	

the terms used by Alonso (1980), developmental, demographic, and cultural factors may have to be considered as well as cyclical factors affecting the state's economy.

Future Methods. Whether the theoretical frameworks discussed here can be used successfully to forecast fertility remains an empirical question. Two strategies are apparent. Fertility can be forecast with time-series equations such as the Wyoming equation. This strategy probably will be followed in single region economic-demographic models, but its success is doubtful in the multiregional context. The need to find a general theoretical specification which serves all states successfully probably will be insurmountable. Alternatively, national fertility can be forecast with models using the richer data base available on the national level. Then state fertility can be forecast on the basis of forecast national rates and other state and national data, such as relative female labor-force participation rates. This strategy is very similar to one used in top-down or satellite regional econometric models, in which regional output is a function of national output and variables such as relative wages and relative energy costs. (The national output variable captures national trends which also affect the region but are not modeled explicitly on the regional level such as interest rates or export demand.) Those states whose fertility trends are only weakly related to national trends could be treated independently, perhaps using ARIMA or other empirical time-series methods, with appropriate adjustments to reconcile total state fertility and national fertility.

Migration

The Census Method

The Bureau of the Census forecasts inmigration and outmigration for each state on the basis of 1965–70 interstate migration reported in the 1970 *Census of Population* and estimated 1970–75 migration rates derived from both the 1965–70 pattern and estimated 1970–75 net migration by state. Migration of college students and military personnel is modeled separately, but otherwise no distinction is made between labor force and non-labor force migration.

In keeping with its strategy of making "illustrative" projections rather than forecasts, the Census Bureau extrapolates separately the 1967–75 and 1970–75 migration rates. First, outmigration is projected by applying outmigration rates by age, sex,, and race for each state to the relevant population subgroups in the state. Second, the resulting national sum of outmigrants is allocated back to individual states as inmigration on the basis of the states' shares of national interstate migration during the relevant historical period, 1965–75 or 1970–75.

This approach can be considered atheoretical, in that observed rates are simply extended into the future. Changes in the spatial pattern of total net migration over time thus result entirely from changes in population composition, i.e., the number of people in each age, race, and sex cohort in each state. Economic conditions and other factors thought to affect migration decisions are not incorporated into the projection process.

Theoretical Perspectives on Migration

Human Capital. In the human capital approach, migration is seen as an investment to increase the productivity of human resources. The present value of migration from one place to another is the difference in the present value of lifetime earnings at the destination and the origin minus the costs of migration. The conceptual framework can be readily extended to consider all costs and benefits of migration, including psychic costs, such as leaving behind friends (Sjaastad 1962). If discounted benefits exceed discounted costs, "investing" in migration will increase utility.

Neoclassical theories of regional growth have a narrower perspective on migration. Individuals are posited to move in response to wage rate differentials (for example, see Borts and Stein 1964; Ghali et al. 1978; Smith 1974 and 1975). These models, however, assume full employment with wages changing until the labor market clears. In the absence of full employment and such wage flexibility, wages as a measure of the expected earnings at the destination must be multiplied by the probability of gaining employment.

Measuring the probability of obtaining employment is a key problem in migration research. The basic concept is simple. Data are needed on job vacancies (employment opportunities or supply of jobs) and on the number of people seeking employment (employment competition or demand for jobs). Unfortunately, data on job vacancies are generally not available. Also, observed unemployment as a measure of expected employment competition ignores (1) discouraged workers who are not searching actively but may move directly into employment if job opportunities become available, (2) natural increase or aging of the labor force, i.e., the entry of teenagers and the retirement of elderly, and (3) other migrants attracted by the same employment opportunities.

Since the desired measures are not available, various proxies for the probability of gaining employment have been used in the literature. Measures of opportunity include population (Greenwood and Sweetland 1972; Levy and Wadycki 1974; Miller 1973; and Rogers 1967), the employment-to-population ratio (Dahlberg and Holmlund 1978), the growth in employment (Todaro 1969, 1976; Duffy and Greenwood 1980), and the rate of new hirings (Fields, 1976, 1979). The measure of competition for those employment opportunities typically is unemployment, but Blanco (1963) constructs the "prospective change" in the number of unemployed, which adjusts for aging of the labor force and changes in college enrollment and military levels.

Almost all empirical studies have used measures of employment opportunity and competition individually in migration equations. Fields (1976, 1979), Gleave and Cordey-Hayes (1977), Plaut (1981), and Todaro (1969), on the other hand, developed transformed variables to represent the probability of gaining employment. Fields used the ratio of new hiring and unemployment rates, Gleave and Cordey-Hayes and Plaut used the ratio of vacancies to unemployment, and Todaro used the ratio of employment growth to unemployment.

Distance and Previous Migration. Geographical studies of migration have long observed an inverse relationship between migration and distance. Although not always discussed in that context, distance can be incorporated into the human capital approach. It can represent a proxy for transportation costs, psychic costs, and uncertainty (Greenwood 1975a). Psychic costs may result from separation from family and friends; the greater the distance of the move, the lower the frequency of reunion and the higher the psychic cost (Schwartz 1973). Since information declines with distance, uncertainty increases and with it the expected value of the income stream at the destination. Empirical estimates of migration-distance elasticities ranged from $-.50$ to -1.50 in 11 studies with a median value of -1.06 (Shaw 1975, p. 83).

The information and psychic costs arguments also can be used to include variables measuring past migration in a human capital framework. The migrant stock (the number of persons born in state i but living in state j) is a measure of information flow back to i from j; also the presence of friends and relatives from home provides support to new inmigrants and reduces the psychic costs of moving to a new environment (Greenwood 1969).

Demographers have noted that a large proportion of migrants are repeat migrants or return migrants. Thus, high inmigration is likely to be reflected in high outmigration of repeat migrants; ostensibly psychic costs of outmigration are lower for people who recently migrated into an area than for long-time residents. Likewise, previous outmigration may lead to inmigration of return migrants whose psychic costs are lower to return than to move to another destination. Thus, previous inmigration has been used to predict outmigration and vice versa (e.g., Greenwood 1975b).

Socioeconomic Factors. Demographers and economists also have observed differences in migration rates by age, sex, race, education, and labor-force status. For example, young adults in their early 20s have the highest migration rates, with a monotonic decrease beyond that age except for possibly a minor peak at retirement age; the migration rates of children mirror the rates of their parents (Rogers 1979). These observations are consistent with the human capital approach, too, because older people have less time to reap the differential earnings from migration (Lewis 1977) and may have more psychic investment at home. As Lowry (1966, p. 27) notes, younger people are "less encumbered with family and community responsibilities, real estate ownership, and vested interest in job seniority," so their costs in moving are lower. Similarly, recent studies indicate that the probability of interstate migration is lower for families with working wives (Lichter 1980; Long 1974; Sandell 1977).

Empirical studies have found that economic variables such as employment growth, unemployment, and wages are less successful in explaining migration flows of women and nonwhites (e.g., Rogers 1967). Quite possibly, this result stems from an aggregation problem. Aggregate figures may not adequately reflect economic opportunities and wages available to blacks and women, an argument made in the case of nonwhites in the South by Greenwood and Gormely (1971).

The human capital approach suggests that economic conditions at the origin and the destination have similar roles in explaining migration between two places. For example, income levels at each place are involved in calculating the present value of the differential income streams associated with moving and staying. Nevertheless, variables measuring economic conditions at the origin, including income, unemployment, and wages, frequently have been found insignificant in cross-section studies (e.g., Fields 1979; Levy and Wadycki 1974; Lowry 1966; Miller 1973; and Rogers 1967). Furthermore, a positive relationship is often observed between inmigration and unemployment rates at the destination (Greenwood 1975a).

Misspecification often is the problem when end-of-period economic conditions are used in such studies, but DaVanzo (1978) suggests a more general possibility for the unexpected and insignificant findings. Families whose heads are employed may be expected to be insensitive to unemployment at the origin in deciding whether to migrate, but the unemployed may be very responsive. Since the unemployed constitute a relatively small part of the population, the aggregate results frequently indicate insensitivity to unemployment at the origin. As was the case for studies of black and female migration, economic research may be suffering from over-aggregation of basic data.

Alternative Opportunities. Another important concept in modeling migration is alternative opportunities, a type of opportunity cost. The likelihood of selecting a particular destination depends in part on conditions at alternative destinations. Some disagreement exists in the literature on the definition of the appropriate set of alternatives, but various measures have been incorporated successfully into cross-section studies of migration flows. Levy and Wadycki (1974) and Wadycki (1979) use the highest population, lowest unemployment rate, and highest average wage from among all regions that are no further away from the origin region than the destination. They speculate that, since information is likely to be inversely related to distance, a migrant moving 600 miles away also knew of opportunities less than 600 miles away (Levy and Wadycki 1974, p. 206). However, as Feder (1979, 1980) points out, increased distance may reduce the attractiveness of alternatives and limit information about them, but it need not eliminate them from consideration. Therefore, he proposes a measure that weights conditions at all possible destinations inversely to their distance from the origin.

Quality of Life. Finally, several studies of migration have incorporated measures of the quality of life and amenities. Liu (1975) constructed an index of the quality of life for each state from more than 100 variables grouped into nine categories. For example, the "individual status" category included 14 variables, among them the labor-force participation rate, the number of motor vehicles per capita, expenditures on education per capita, and a "quality index of medical service." The "living conditions" category included a crime index, the percentage of families in poverty, recreational acres per capita, telephones per capita, library books per capita, symphony orchestras per capita, motor vehicle deaths per capita, the average number of sunshine days, the average annual humidity, and ten other variables. Each variable in each component was given an equal weight, and the components were weighted equally in constructing the overall index. Liu regressed 1960–70 net migration rates for each state on its 1970 index, but was able to explain only 8 percent of the variation in the rates (albeit 52 percent in the nonwhite rate). Similarly, Cebula and Vedder (1973) and Cebula (1979) found that economic variables are far more important than quality-of-life, environmental, or climatic variables in cross-section regression studies. Also, five measures of climate were rarely significant in 17 cross-section studies of net migration into BEA areas from 1958 to 1975 (Duffy, Greenwood, and McDowell 1979). On the other hand, Alperovitch, Bergsman, and Ehemann (1975), Clark and Ballard (1980), Graves (1980), and Miller (1973) were successful in partially explaining either inmigration or outmigration or both with climate variables in cross-section studies, and Milne (1981) used population density successfully in a time-series analysis.

An alternative to the neoclassical and human capital view of the role of wage differentials in migration has been presented by Graves and Linneman (1979) and Graves (1980). Wage differentials represent compensation for differences in climate and amenities. The demand for climate and amenities, like any other good, is expected to change with relative prices and income. For example, with increasing incomes, the demand for outdoor leisure activities increases and with it the desire to locate in more "appropriate" amenity-rich environments. Migration then takes place as a result of changing demand for location-fixed amenities. Graves argues that

> one would not expect income differentials to lead to migration since those differentials reflect compensation for climate differences, i.e., equilibrium consumption choices.... This theoretical point accounts for the difficulty experienced by some authors... in finding significant income and unemployment coefficients of the correct sign (1980, p. 229).

Although this claim may be overstated, viewing climate and other amenities as highly income-elastic consumption goods ("superior goods") is potentially useful for forecasting migration *within* the human capital framework. In fact, Plaut (1981) finds that net migration into Texas, ostensibly an amenity-rich state, increases with per capita real income in the United States.

In summary, many factors combine to create migration flows. The social science literature has documented the roles of economic conditions, demographic characteristics, distance and previous migration patterns, alternative opportunities, and climate, amenities, and other aspects of the quality of life.

Forecasting Migration

As is the case in forecasting births, the available data severely limit the modeling strategies. In fact, the development of methods for forecasting migration can be viewed as largely an effort to overcome data limitations. Procedures have been developed to create the necessary data for conventional methods to be used, and new methods have been developed that require only the data available. In recognizing data's dominant role, the discussion of methods in this section is organized by data source. Doing so gives it a strong orientation to the U.S. context and ignores the fact that other methods are appropriate for countries with different kinds of migration data—particularly Canada and the Netherlands which have annual data series such as are not available in the United States. Yet, since most countries produce less migration data than the United States, the methods discussed here and in subsequent chapters do have wide applicability internationally.

Four data sources and their related forecasting methods will be discussed in turn. They are (1) the Continuous Work History Sample (CWHS), (2) the annual population estimates (PE), (3) the decennial census, and (4) a relatively new source, data derived from the federal income tax and available from the Internal Revenue Service (IRS). Each data series will be described sufficiently so that readers can draw appropriate analogies to non-U.S. data series.

Continuous Work History Sample (CWHS)

The CWHS is a 1-percent sample of all persons who have a social security account number and have worked during the year in covered jobs. Currently this sample covers over 90 percent of paid workers. Migration data are derived by comparing an individual's address from one time period to another; if the addresses are in different states, the person is counted as an interstate migrant. The CWHS data have been used in several recent studies of migration, among them Ballard and Clark (1981), Clark (1982), Clark and Ballard (1980), McCarthy and Morrison (1977), Plane and Isserman (1983), and Smith and Slater (1981). Since an annual time series of migration flows, by age, sex, and other characteristics is available beginning in 1958 (the year many state economic time series also begin), the CWHS data would seem to be ideally suited for economic-demographic modeling.

Unfortunately the CWHS data suffer from numerous, severe problems that make them very unreliable. The most serious flaws stem from reporting errors and processing errors, but there also are problems stemming from varying coverage over time by demographic class, by industry, and, therefore, by place; definition of location as place of work, not place of residence; and spurious migration caused by changes in employers' accounting practices (see Isserman, Plane, and McMillan [1982] for further details as well as an evaluation of the other data sources). When CWHS migration data are compared to other data, two conclusions are amply supported: the CWHS data greatly overestimate migration, perhaps by 50 to 100 percent depending on the year; and numerous observed state-to-state flows seem highly unlikely. Moreover, examination of the process used to generate CWHS data provides a clear explanation of why the overestimation and spurious migration occurs. Until these problems are corrected, there is little sense in forecasting on the basis of these data.

Population Estimates (PE)

The only other annual migration time series is limited to net migration. Very little age detail is offered and no information is available on race or labor-force status. These data are a by-product of the annual population estimation program at the Bureau of the Census. Net migration is calculated as a residual from the basic equation of demographic change:

net migration = estimated population change − births + deaths.

Since data on births and deaths are registered vital statistics, errors in the population estimates are reflected almost entirely in the net migration data. Given the similar magnitudes of the errors in estimating population change and in the rates of annual net migration (both average between 1 and 2 percent across the states), errors of 50 percent or more in the migration data can be expected (Isserman, Plane, and McMillen 1982).

Despite the errors, PE net migration has been used in at least three economic-demographic modeling efforts. Ledent (1978) forecast net migration into the Tucson SMSA as a function of change in total employment and the lagged regional and national unemployment rates, and Milne (1981) forecast interregional net migration among the nine census regions as a function of relative wages, relative unemployment, and relative population density ("a proxy for crowding problems" related to the quality of life). Plaut (1981 and chapter 5 in this book) has come closest to modeling the human capital theory explicitly. In his model of Texas, expected income is represented by relative wages and the relative vacancy to unemployment ratio using data on employment advertisements in newspapers to measure vacancies. National real per capita income is included as a measure of changing responsiveness to environmental conditions, and lagged population is included as a result of positing a partial adjustment model. Spatial factors and demographic detail, however, are missing from among those factors discussed in the previous section.

These equations do not fit the historical data particularly well. Ledent reports an R^2 of .83, Milne a range from .66 to .90, and Plaut one of .88. The mean absolute percentage error for five years beyond the sample period was 22.5 in Plaut's model. All these statistics are very disappointing for time-series equations. Plaut's theoretical structure is appealing, but when applied to two other states it fared poorly. When the vacancy measure was replaced by an inferior proxy, employment change plus separations (because the vacancy measure was not readily available), the modified equation did far better in Texas than in either Ohio or Pennsylvania (table 1–3).

The implicit net migration modeling approach of Ballard, Gustely, and Wendling (1980) is also worth mentioning. No attempt is made to model migration rates directly. Instead, the population estimates are themselves

Table 1-3. Time Series Results: Net Migration to Texas, Ohio, and Pennsylvania

	Texas	Ohio	Pennsylvania
Relative wages	.19	.39	−.04
	(3.58)[a]	(4.09)	(.58)
Employment opportunity ratio	.005	−.0009	−.001
	(1.25)	(.90)	(.23)
National per capita income	.06	−.07	.003
	(2.99)	(2.89)	(.51)
Lagged population	−.08	.32	−.0008
	(2.25)	(3.27)	(.75)
Constant	.48	−2.90	—[b]
	(1.70)	(3.30)	
$\bar{R}^2$	.74	.50	−.16
MAPE	107.0	392.5	56.7
DW	.85	2.17	1.16

[a]The numbers in parentheses are t-statistics.
[b]This equation was constrained to go through the origin because of an ill conditioned data matrix.

modeled in five age groups. For instance, the population 18–44 is a function of itself lagged, a two-year moving average of the region's share of national employment, relative per capita income, and a time trend. The employment term represents job opportunity, income represents "an inducement to migrate," and the time trend represents "historical changes in environmental attractiveness." Note how similar this population equation is to Plaut's migration rate equation. Here the coefficient of the lagged population term, however, measures natural increase rather than lags in migration.

In dynamic simulations the average mean absolute percentage error in sample from 1963 to 1976 for all 50 states was only 1 percent of total population. Yet, this summary statistic is less impressive than it might seem because the annual rate of population change did not exceed 1 percent for 26 states from 1970 to 1975. In short, Ballard, Gustely, and Wendling have modeled natural increase and migration implicitly by including their determinants as independent variables. The regression coefficients essentially are crude replacements for demographers' painstakingly derived death and migration rates. This approach does not preserve any of the advantages and information of demographic accounts.

Summarizing, the prospects for time-series modeling of migration in the United States are not bright. The absence of a reliable series for in- and outmigration makes impossible multiregional modeling with interesting approaches to alternative opportunities, lagged migration flows, and distance. For instance, with flow data a spatial element could be added to the expected income concept by weighting alternative opportunities by lagged migration flows or distance. The demographers' knowledge of the different propensities associated with age, race, sex, military status, and labor-force status also cannot be included. Perhaps the best that can be done is to model net migration on the basis of expected income with intervening opportunities discounted by distance in a multiregional version of Plaut's model.

Decennial Census

The decennial census provides the most detailed information on interstate migration in the United States. State-to-state flows can be disaggregated by age, sex, race, labor-force status, education, military status, income, and other characteristics. At present, however, only two observations are available since 1958 (the beginning of most economic time series), namely, migration from 1955 to 1960 and 1965 to 1970. Thus, the most recent migration data available in 1984 include moves which occurred 19 years ago (although comparable data on migration between 1975 and 1980 from the 1980 census are expected to be available any moment).

The richest modeling of migration has occurred using the census data on migration with census data on socioeconomic characteristics of the population. Transferring these models to the context of forecasting migration, however, necessitates forecasting all independent variables in the migration equations. This need raises two problems: the difficulty of forecasting some of the independent variables, such as educational achievement and income distribution, and the compatibility of the migration data with economic models that can forecast economic variables related to migration. Since the first problem is similar to that discussed in the fertility section (e.g., with respect to percentage Mormon), only the second will be discussed here.

The most satisfactory way of forecasting employment change, unemployment, wage levels, and other economic conditions related to migration is through the use of regional econometric models. Almost all of these use annual time-series data. A cross-section approach to migration can be consistent with a time-series approach to economic conditions, but an important problem is encountered with the census data. Migration measured in the census is for a five-year period. Since annual migration is considerably more than one-fifth of five-year migration because of repeat migrants and return migrants, a cross-section equation based on five-year migration data can be expected to underestimate annual migration. If the cross-section equation is used to estimate migration over a five-year period in conjunction with an annual econometric model, the possibilities for modeling the annual economic consequences of demographic change are severely curtailed.

In response to the need for annual data by age for modeling and other purposes, several efforts have been made to create such annual time series. All use decennial census data in combination with the annual population estimates referred to above. The basic procedure entails: (1) aging the population of the census year using data on births and deaths, either actual vital statistics or the underlying rates, (2) comparing the total aged population with the independently derived population estimate and deriving total net migration by subtracting the aged population from the estimate, and (3) imposing an age structure on the net migration total to generate migration by age. Such an approach can generate annual time series of population by age, migration by age, and even in- and outmigration by age. Variations within this framework have been developed by Greenberg and Renfro (see chapter 6), Irwin (1980), and Taylor (1982). The resulting data have been used in time-series models, even though they share the weaknesses of other data derived from the population estimates— i.e., measurement error is concentrated into the migration figures.

Internal Revenue Service (IRS)

A new annual migration series has been generated at the Bureau of the Census by matching income tax returns between two periods and comparing the respondents' addresses. Data on annual migration flows currently are available for 1975–76, 1976–77, 1978–79, and 1980–81, but they lack the demographic detail available from the census. Nevertheless, this data series can be used to circumvent the one-year, five-year compatability problem and will be more valuable in the future as more observations are added to the time series.

Age detail can be imposed on the IRS data using the decennial census. Then cohort-specific, one-year migration rates can be calculated. The observed changes in those rates from one time period to another can be modeled as functions of economic conditions. In other words, the demographic rates are forecast to change with changing economic conditions. The advantageous properties of the demographic cohort-component model are retained, but the rates themselves become endogenous variables in an economic-demographic modeling system. This approach will not be discussed further here, since it is described in chapter 10 (because it is used in the ECESIS model) and in Isserman, Plane, Rogerson, and Beaumont (1985).

Future Methods

This review of the literature, data sources, and modeling options suggests that successful demoeconomic forecasting of migration is no easy task. The absence of good time-series data on migration means, quite simply, that the nature of the phenomenon being modeled is still unknown. The pattern over time of even aggregate migration flows remains a puzzle with mostly blank pieces. Nevertheless, more attempts probably will be made to model net migration in regional economic-demographic models (see chapters 5 and 6). More reduced-form population equations like that of Ballard, Gusteley, and Wendling (1980) probably also will be seen. In the multiregional context, the approach used in ECESIS seems a useful strategy given the limited data available presently. One hopeful point for the future of time-series migration modeling in the United States is the IRS migration data. Perhaps in another decade this series will be long enough to permit time-series modeling of migration—although again with little demographic detail.

Conclusion

Although the argument for linking economic and demographic change is strong, perhaps even obvious from a theoretical viewpoint, the best strategy for doing so is far from obvious. True, the theoretical and empirical literatures are extensive on such obvious areas of economic-demographic interaction as fertility and migration. Typically in this literature a theoretical framework is posited, and some empirical work is presented which does not contradict the theory. This empirical work, however, is usually an analysis either (1) of a single place over time or (2) of a cross-section of places at a single time. To be useful in multiregional forecasting, on the other hand, the theory must either (1) explain changes in every region in the model, not just in a single place, or (2) generate cross-section parameters that are constant or at least predictable. Such tests are far more demanding than those to which most social science theories have been subjected.

The need to do well in many regions, to explain behavior, say, in the 50 states, with a single theoretical framework is a major step in distinguishing good theory from the results of ad hoc data experimentation and ex post facto theorizing. Consequently, however, the theoretical cupboard for economic-demographic modeling (and of the relevant disciplines themselves) may be far more bare than is presently apparent.

A major obstacle to economic-demographic modeling on the regional level is data paucity, as should be clear from previous sections. Often only crude proxies can be used in implementing elegant theories, thus further reducing the probability of developing a general theoretical model successful in forecasting. Indeed it often cannot be determined whether the root of failure is poor data or poor theory.

These considerations of theory and data are intended to contribute to a realistic, not pessimistic, assessment of the prospects for multiregional economic-demographic forecasting. Such forecasting is possible, as subsequent chapters demonstrate. The time and resources needed to do so well, however, should not be underestimated. The data and modeling requirements are immense compared to standard demographic projections. The economy of each region must be modeled to forecast the economic conditions that are believed to be determinants of population change and, in turn, are affected by population change.

References

Alonso, W. 1980. Population as a system in regional development. *American Economic Review* 70, 2: 405–509.

Alperovich, G.; Bergman, J.; and Ehemann, C. 1975. An econometric model of employment growth in U.S. metropolitan areas. *Environment and Planning A* 7:833–862.

Anker, R. 1978. An analysis of fertility differentials in developing countries. *Review of Economics and Statistics* 60, 1: 58–69.

Ballard, K.P., and Clark, G.L. 1981. The short-run dynamics of interstate migration. *Regional Studies* 15, 3: 213–228.

Ballard, K.; Gustely, R.; and Wendling, R. 1980. *NRIES: National-Regional Impact Evaluation System*. Washington, D.C.: U.S. Government Printing Office.

Becker, G., and Lewis, H. 1973. On the interaction between the quantity and quality of children. *Journal of Political Economy* 81, 2/2: S278–288.

Blanco, C. 1963. The determinants of interstate population movements. *Journal of Regional Science* 5: 77–84.

Bongaarts, 1978. A framework for analyzing the proximate determinants of fertility. *Population and Development Review* 4, 1: 105–132.

Borts, G., and Stein, J. 1964. *Economic growth in a free market*. New York: Columbia University Press.

Butz, W., and Ward, M. 1979a. The emergence of countercyclical U.S. fertility. *American Economic Review* 69, 3: 318–328.

———. 1979b: Will U.S. fertility remain low?: a new economic interpretation. *Population and Development Review* 5, 4: 663–688.

Cain, G., and Dooley, M. 1976. Estimation of a model of labor supply, fertility, and wages of married women. *Journal of Political Economy* 84, 4, pt. 2: S179–S199.

Cain, G., and Weininger, A. 1973. Economic determinants of fertility: results from cross-sectional aggregate data. *Demography* 10, 2: 205–223.

Cebula, R. 1979. *The determinants of human migration*. Lexington, MA: D.C. Heath and Company.

Cebula, R., and Vedder, R. 1973. Some determinants of interstate migration of blacks, 1965–1970. *Western Economic Journal* 11:500–505.

Clark, G.L. 1982. Dynamics of interstate labor migration. *Annals of the Association of American Geographers* 72, 3: 297–313.

Clark, G., and Ballard, K. 1980. Modeling out-migration from depressed regions: the significance of origin and destination characteristics. *Environment and Planning A* 12: 799–812.

Dahlberg, A., and Holmlund, B. 1978. The interaction of migration, income, and employment in Sweden. *Demography* 15, 3: 259–266.

DaVanzo, J. 1978. Does unemployment affect migration?: evidence from microdata. *Review of Economics and Statistics* 60, 4: 504–514.

Davis, K., and Blake, J. 1956. Social structure and fertility: an analytical framework. *Economic Development and Cultural Change* 4, 4: 211–235.

DeFronzo, J. 1976. Testing the economic theory of fertility with cross-sectional and change data. *Social Biology* 23, 3: 226–234.

DeTray, D. 1973. Child quality and the demand for children. *Journal of Political Economy* 81, 2/2: S70–95.

Duffy, M., and Greenwood, M. 1980. Explorations in migration forecasting: time-series and cross-sectional evidence. Paper presented at the Western Regional Science Association annual meeting, Monterey, California.

Duffy, M., Greenwood, M., McDowell, J. 1979. A cross-sectional model of annual interregional migration and employment growth: intertemporal evidence of structural change, 1958–1975. Paper presented at the North American Regional Science Association annual meeting, Los Angeles, California.

Easterlin, R. 1976. The conflict between aspirations and resources. *Population and Development Review* 2, 3/4: 417–425.

Feder, G. 1979. Alternative opportunities and migration: an exposition. *Annals of Regional Science* 13, 3: 57–67.

———. 1980. Alternative opportunities and migration: evidence from Korea. *Annals of Regional Science* 14, 1: 1–11.

Feeney, G. 1973. Two models for multiregional population dynamics. *Environment and Planning A* 5: 31–43.

Fields, G. 1976. Labor force migration, unemployment and job turnover. *Review of Economics and Statistics* 58, 4: 407–15.

———. 1979. Place-to-place migration: some new evidence. *Review of Economics and Statistics* 61, 1: 21–32.

Gardner, B. 1972. Economic aspects of the fertility of rural-farm and urban women. *Southern Economic Journal* 38: 518–524.

———. 1973. Economics of the size of North Carolina rural families. *Journal of Political Economy* 81, 2/2:S99–S127.

Ghali, M.; Akiyama, M.; and Fujiwara, J. 1978. Factor mobility and regional growth. *Review of Economics and Statistics* 60, 1: 78–84.

Gleave, D., and Cordey-Hayes, M. 1977. Migration dynamics and labour market turnover. *Progress in Planning* 8, 1.

Graves, P. 1980. Migration and climate. *Journal of Regional Science* 20, 2: 227–237.

Graves, P., and Linneman, P. 1979. Household migration theoretical and empirical results. *Journal of Urban Economics* 3:383–404.

Greenwood, M. 1969. An analysis of the determinants of geographic labor mobility in the United States. *Review of Economics and Statistics.* 51, 2: 189–194.

———. 1975a. Research on internal migration in the United States: a survey. *Journal of Economic Literature* 13:397–433.

———. 1975b. A simultaneous-equations model of urban growth and migration. *Journal of the American Statistical Association* 70, 352: 797–810.

Greenwood, M., and Gormely, P. 1971. A comparison of the determinants of white and nonwhite interstate migration. *Demography* 8, 1: 141–55.

Greenwood, M., and Sweetland, D. 1972. The determinants of migration between standard metropolitan statistical areas. *Demography* 9, 4: 665–681.

Gregory, P.; Campbell, J.; and Cheng, B. 1972. A simultaneous equation model of birth rates in the United States. *Review of Economics and Statistics* 49, 4: 374–380.

Heer, D., and Boynton, J. 1970. A multivariate regression analysis of differences in fertility of United States counties. *Social Biology* 17, 3: 180–193.

Irwin, R. 1980. Methodology for experimental estimates of the population of counties, by age and sex: July 1, 1975. *Current Population Reports*, P-23, No. 103, U.S. Bureau of the Census. Washington, D.C.: U.S. Government Printing Office.

Isserman, A.; Plane, D.; and McMillen, D. 1982. Internal migration in the United States: an evaluation of federal data. *Review of Public Data Use* 10: 289–309.

Isserman, A.; Plane, D.; Rogerson, P.; and Beaumont, P. 1985. Forecasting interstate migration with limited data: a demographic-economic approach. *Journal of the American Statistical Association* 80, 390: 277–285.

Joseph, H. 1980. Estimation of fertility using a stock-adjustment model. *Review of Economics and Statistics* 62, 4: 545–554.

Keyfitz, N. 1980. Multistate demography and its data: a comment. *Environment and Planning A* 12, 5: 615–622.

Ledent, J. 1978. Regional multiplier analysis: a demometric approach. *Environment and Planning A* 10: 537–560.

Leibenstein, H. 1975. The economic theory of fertility decline. *Quarterly Journal of Economics* 89, 1: 1–31.

———. 1976. The problem of characterizing aspirations. *Population and Development Review* 2, 3/4: 427–431.

Levy, M., and Wadycki, W. 1974. What is the opportunity cost of moving?: reconsideration of the effects of distance on migration. *Economic Development and Cultural Change* 22: 198–214.

Lewis, W. 1977. The role of age in the decision to migrate. *Annals of Regional Science* 11, 3: 51–60.

Lichter, D. 1980. Household migration and the labor market position of married women. *Social Science Research* 9: 83–97.

Liu, B-C. 1975. Differential net migration rates and the quality of life. *Review of Economics and Statistics* 57, 3: 329–337.

Long, L. 1974. Women's labor force participation and the residential mobility of families. *Social Forces* 52, 3: 342–348.

Long, J., and Wetrogan, S. 1980. The utility of birth expectations in population projections. In *Predicting fertility: demographic studies of birth expectations*, ed. G.E. Hendershot and P.J. Placek. Lexington, MA: D.C. Heath and Company.

Lowry, I. 1966. *Migration and metropolitan growth: two analytical models.* San Francisco: Chandler Publishing Company.

McCarthy, K.F., and Morrison, P.A. 1977. The changing demographic and economic structure of nonmetropolitan areas in the United States. *International Regional Science Review* 2, 2:123–142.

Michael, R. 1973. Education and the derived demand for children. *Journal of Political Economy* 81, 2/2:S128–167.

Miller, E. 1973. Is outmigration affected by economic conditions? *Southern Economic Journal* 39:396–405.

Milne, W. 1981. Migration in an interregional macroeconomic model of the United States: will net outmigration from the Northeast continue? *International Regional Science Review.* 6, 1: 71–83.

O'Connell, M. 1981. Regional fertility patterns in the United States: convergence or divergence? *International Regional Science Review* 6, 1: 1–14.

Phillips, L.; Votey, H.; and Maxwell, D. 1969. A synthesis of the economic and demographic models of fertility: an econometric test. *Review of Economics and Statistics* 51, 3: 298–308.

Plane, D. A., and Isserman, A. M. 1983. U.S. interstate labor force migration: an analysis of trends, net exchanges, and migration subsystems. *Socio-Economic Planning Sciences* 17: 5–6.

Plaut, T. 1981. An econometric model for forecasting regional population growth. *International Regional Science Review* 6, 1: 53–70.

Rees, P., and Wilson, A. 1977. *Spatial population analysis.* London: Arnold Publishing.

Rindfuss, R. 1978. Changing patterns of fertility in the South: a social-demographic examination. *Social Forces* 57, 2: 621–635.

Rogers, A. 1967. A regression analysis of interregional migration in California. *Review of Economics and Statistics* 49, 2: 262–267.

———. 1968. *Matrix analysis of interregional population growth and distribution.* Berkeley: University of California Press.

———. 1975. *Introduction to multiregional mathematical demography.* New York: Wiley.

———. 1979. Migration patterns and population redistribution. *Regional Science and Urban Economics* 9: 275–310.

———. 1980. Introduction to multistate mathematical demography. *Environment and Planning A* 12, 5:489–498.

Rogerson, P. 1979. Prediction: a modified Markov chain approach. *Journal of Regional Science* 19, 4: 469–478.

Sandell, S. 1977. Women and the economics of family migration. *Review of Economics and Statistics* 59, 4: 406–414.

Sanderson, W. 1976. On two schools of the economics of fertility. *Population and Development Review* 2, 3/4: 469–477.

Schultz, T. P. 1973. Explanation of birth rate changes over space and time: a study of Taiwan. *Journal of Political Economy* 81, 2/2: S238–278.

Schultz, T. W. 1973. The value of children: an economic perspective. *Journal of Political Economy* 81, 2/2: S2–13.

Schwartz, A. 1973. Interpreting the effect of distance on migration. *Journal of Political Economy*: 1153–1169.

Shaw, P. 1975. *Migration theory and fact*. Philadelphia: Regional Science Research Institute.

Sjaastad, L. 1962. The costs and returns of human migration. *Journal of Political Economy* 70 (Supplement): 80–93.

Smith, D. 1974. Regional growth: interstate and intersectoral factor reallocations. *Review of Economics and Statistics* 56, 3: 353–359.

———. 1975. Neoclassical growth models and regional growth in the U.S. *Journal of Regional Science* 15, 2: 165–181.

Smith, T., and Slater, P. 1981. A family of spatial interaction models incorporating information flows and choice set constraints. *International Regional Science Review* 6, 1: 15–31.

Taylor, C. 1982. Demographic disaggregation in the construction of regional econometric models: a statistical evaluation. *International Regional Science Review* 71: 25–51.

Todaro, M. 1969. A model of labor migration and urban unemployment in less developed countries. *American Economic Review* 59: 138–148.

———. 1976. Urban job expansion, induced migration and rising unemployment. *Journal of Development Economics* 3: 211–225.

U.S. Bureau of the Census. 1977a. Fertility of American women: June 1976. *Current Population Reports*, Series P-25, No. 784. Washington, D.C.: U.S. Government Printing Office.

———. 1979. Projections of the population of the United States: 1977 to 2050. *Current Population Reports* Series P-25, No. 784. Washington, D.C.: U.S. Government Printing Office.

———. 1979. Illustrative projections of state populations by age, race, and sex: 1975 to 2000. *Current Population Reports*, Series P-25, No. 796. Washington, D.C.: U.S. Government Printing Office.

———. 1980. Geographic mobility: March 1975 to March 1979. *Current Population Reports*, Series P-20, No. 353. Washington, D.C.: U.S. Government Printing Office.

Wachter, M. 1975. A time-series fertility equation: the potential for a baby boom in the 1980's. *International Economic Review* 16, 3: 609–624.

Wadycki, W. 1979. Alternative opportunities and United States interstate migraion: an improved econometric specification. *Annals of Regional Science* 13, 3: 35–41.

Waite, L., and Wetrogan, S. 1979. Changes in childbearing plans of American wives: 1971–1974. *Social Science Research* 8:327–347.

Westoff, C., and Ryder, L. 1977. The predictive validity of reproductive intentions. *Demography* 14: 431–453.

Willekens, F. 1980. Regional demographic modeling. In *Modeling the multiregional economic system*, ed. F.G. Adams and N.J. Glickman, pp. 179–191. Lexington, MA: D.C. Heath.

Willis, R. 1973. A new approach to the economic theory of fertility behavior. *Journal of Political Economy* 81, 2/2: 514–69.

2 FORECASTING REGIONAL BIRTHS: AN ECONOMIC-DEMOGRAPHIC APPROACH

Dennis Ahlburg

Introduction

> *That all data refer to the past and all use of data the future implies a line between past and future drawn at "now." Without continuities that make possible extrapolation across that line statistical data would be useless, indeed the very possibility of purposeful behavior would be in doubt (Keyfitz 1977).*

The mechanism by which economic, demographic, and social variables affect total national births is known with greater certainty than is the distribution of these births across regions. Indeed, the U.S. Bureau of the Census predicts convergence of regional fertility rates, whereas the MIT-Harvard Joint Center predicts a further widening of regional differences (Jackson et al. 1981). Consequently, a two-step forecasting procedure is presented here. An economic-demographic model produces forecasts of total live births and other demographic variables, and then the regional shares of national total live births are forecast. Since the mechanism by which total live births are distributed across regions is not known, a parsimonious estimation approach is adopted which uses historical data on birth shares. An alternative approach would be to estimate a separate economic-demographic model for each region, but before attempting to do so, the simpler and less costly approach developed here should be explored. Although concentrating on regional births, the approach taken in this chapter could also be used to estimate marriages and divorces by region and births, marriages, and divorces by state.

In the next section a national economic-demographic forecasting model for the United States is described and simulated forecasts for 1977–81 are discussed. A forecast of total births for the USA for the 1980s is also presented and compared with projections produced by the U.S. Bureau of the Census. The estimating equations for regional birth shares and their forecasting accuracy for 1977–79 are discussed in the third section. Forecasts of regional total live births are presented in the fourth section, and the sources of forecast error are investigated. Finally, forecasts of regional births for 1982–90 are compared to Census Bureau projections.

A Structural Model of U.S. Total Live Births

The Model

The economic-demographic forecasting model seeks to integrate the main elements of the two major schools of economic demography (the neo-classical microeconomic approach of the Chicago-Columbia school and the relative income approach of Easterlin) with the rich demographic and sociological literature on fertility. Fertility, however, cannot be studied in isolation. Fertility decisions are linked to decisions on labor-force participation, marriage, and divorce. Consequently, the model is specified as a system of structural equations in which interrelationships among these demographic decisions are explicitly considered. Economic impacts are incorporated by embedding the model in the Wharton Annual Industry and Forecasting model of the U.S. economy. Only the birth rate equation will be discussed here, but a discussion of the other equations of the model is found in Ahlburg (1979, 1981).

Child-bearing and -rearing is time intensive. With increasing real wages for women and with strict substitution between market work and non-market work, the consumption of time-intensive commodities is reduced, and more time is allocated to market work and less to non-market work, including child-bearing and -rearing (Gronau 1977). As a consequence, the birth rate will be inversely related to the female labor-force participation rate.

The same relationship is hypothesized from role compatibility theory: in developed societies, mother and worker roles are incompatible, so one or the other role may be assumed at each point in time. If a woman does occupy both roles, she will have few children as a consequence (Smith-Lovin and Tickamayer 1978; Stycos and Weller 1967). An increasing participation rate also may signify a stronger attachment of women to career goals rather than maternal goals (Westoff 1978).

The birth rate is also hypothesized to be a positive function of relative income, i.e., actual income relative to income aspirations. In Easterlin's theory, individuals formulate their income aspirations (or expected standard of living) on the basis of the income received by their fathers during their adolescences (Easterlin 1973, 1980). Relative income is thus a cross-cohort income measure. Since the data needed to construct such a measure of relative income are available only since 1947, Wachter's temporal formulation of relative income is adopted (Wachter 1975). Relative income is defined as actual income relative to expected income, where expected income is based on past income. As income rises relative to some weighted average of past income, a couple makes a decision to conceive in the current period, which leads to a birth in the next period (thus, the one-year lag on relative income). Couples decide to conceive because compared to the past, they are in a better position to finance the birth and its ancillary demands.

Since the majority of births occur within wedlock, the birth rate is expected to be a positive function of the total stock of marriages and the net additions to this stock (marriages) and a negative function of reductions in the stock (divorces). Marriage may be interpreted as a derived demand for children. That is, children are the prime objective, but because of societal customs marriage precedes the birth of children. An increase in the marriage rate signals an increase in the demand for children which, with an appropriate lag, should be observed as an increase in the birth rate.

An increasing divorce rate shifts women from a group with a high risk of conception to one with a low risk. In addition, divorce rates may affect child-bearing within existing marriages. A high divorce rate may be interpreted as a signal of lower probability of marital success and thus decreases the accumulation of marital-specific capital such as children (Michael 1978).

A rise in the median age at marriage will tend to decrease the birth rate since it decreases the length of the child-bearing period (Rindfuss and Bumpass 1976). In addition later marriage encourages secondary socialization into extrafamilial roles by increasing the probability of educational attainment, work before marriage, and financial independence (Smith-

Lovin and Tickameyer 1978). These roles consume time and resources and thereby constrain fertility (Pratt and Whelpton 1958).

These theoretical expectations are largely consistent with the empirical findings reported in table 2-1. The birth rate is negatively related to the female participation rate and the median age at marriage and positively related to the marriage rate, the total stock of marriages, and relative income. The divorce rate has no statistically significant effect on the birth rate. The independent variables are lagged one year to reflect the assumed gestation period between the decision to have a child and its ultimate arrival. Alternative lag structures were investigated by estimating Almon lags of various degrees and lengths, but none was consistently superior to the simple one-year lag. The construction of the relative income variable, however, does introduce a longer lag structure.

One of the most widely accepted findings in the economics of fertility is the positive relationship between income and fertility in developed countries (Becker 1960). When incorporated into this study, absolute real income was positively signed but not statistically significant, possibly because of the inclusion of relative income.

The birth rate used in this study, births per person over 16 years of age, is open to the criticism that it may reflect changes in the age-distribution of the population rather than changes in fertility. However, when the

Table 2-1. The Birth Rate Equation, 1921-76[a]

Variable	Coefficient[b]
Female labor force participation rate	−0.560
	(6.361)
Relative income lagged	12.879
	(3.534)
Marriage rate lagged	0.600
	(5.834)
Median age at marriage lagged	−3.284
	(2.332)
Total stock of marriages lagged	0.233
	(4.152)
Constant	17.704
	(0.395)
DW = 2.065	

[a]The birth and marriage rates are defined as rates per 100,000 people over 16 years of age. The equation is estimated by two-stage least squares.

[b]The values in parentheses are t-values.

percentage of women 15–44 was added as an independent variable, it had the correct sign but was not statistically significant.

Birth rates reflect decisions on both completed family size and the timing of births. It is extremely difficult to unravel the timing component from the completed family size component, but an attempt was made to do so by including a series on expected number of births as a proxy for completed family size and assuming the other independent variables determine timing of births. The expectations variable was positive and significant but substantially reduced the forecasting accuracy of the model. An investigation of the birth expectations series, which is used by the U.S. Bureau of the Census in formulating population projections, revealed that it lags rather than leads fertility, so it was excluded from the forecasting model.

The Forecast Accuracy of the Model. Two descriptive statistics were employed to investigate the accuracy of the forecasts and to compare them with the accuracy of U.S. Bureau of the Census projections. The statistics are the mean absolute percentage error (MAPE) and root mean square percentage error (RMSPE). They are unit free and nonparametric, and are widely accepted as being important and valid under different axioms (Dhrymes 1975). The Census Bureau projections analyzed are the Series D projection of total live births for the period 1971 to 1976 (U.S. Bureau of the Census 1970) and the Series II projections thereafter (U.S. Bureau of the Census 1977). On their dates of publication, these series were thought to represent the most likely path of future fertility.

Table 2–2 shows that the structural economic-demographic model

Table 2-2. Accuracy Statistics for the Total Live Birth Forecasts

	Mean Absolute Percentage Error	*Root Mean Square Percentage Error*
Four Period Forecast, 1977 to 1980		
Structural model	3.7	4.6
Bureau of the Census, Series II	4.9	5.1
Six Period Forecast, 1971 to 1976		
Structural model	5.6	7.5
Bureau of the Census, Series D	14.8	16.4

presented here is superior in forecast accuracy to the approach of the U.S. Bureau of the Census. Beginning with the 1977–80 period, the forecasts are identical for 1977, but from 1978 to 1980 the structural model became increasingly more accurate than the Bureau's Series II projections. The model's percentage errors are relatively small and are particularly impressive considering that the forecast period follows the 1976 turning point in the total birth series. The structural model was estimated again using data from 1921 to 1970 and then used to forecast total births over the period 1971 to 1976. It clearly outperforms the Series D forecasts.

The Forecasts. Table 2–3 presents the forecasts of total live births which are used to generate forecasts of regional live births and the Census Bureau total live birth projections. The forecasts shown in table 2–3 are generated purely by the model, with no forecaster intervention through constant adjustments or any other means. Forecast error for 1977 through 1979 could have been reduced by a constant adjustment of 180,000 births (the

Table 2-3. Forecasts Compared to Census Bureau Projections of Total Live Births (in Thousands)

Year	Census Bureau Total Live Births[a]			Economic-Demographic Model	
	Series I	Series II	Series III	Total Live Births	General Fertility Rate
1977	3,725	3,277	2,961	3,087	65.6
1978	3,995	3,412	2,944	3,172	66.0
1979	4,230	3,575	3,052	3,379	66.2
1980	4,438	3,733	3,223	3,571	68.8
1981	4,606	3,839	3,351	3,674	69.8
1982	4,741	3,904	3,402	3,721	69.8
1983	4,849	3,951	3,410	3,767	69.9
1984	4,937	3,985	3,408	3,826	70.2
1985	5,006	4,007	3,397	3,883	70.5
1986	5,055	4,018	3,378	3,942	70.8
1987	5,086	4,019	3,353	3,998	71.4
1988	5,097	4,009	3,322	4,054	72.2
1989	5,089	3,987	3,286	4,093	72.8
1990	5,063	3,956	3,244	4,129	73.2

[a]Series I, II, and III assume total fertility rates (average number of lifetime births per woman) of 2.7, 2.1, and 1.7, respectively.

1971–76 mean absolute error), but this would have made the comparisons with the census projections suspect.

A consistent increase in total births is forecast through the 1980s, generated by rising relative income and marital stock and a declining median age at marriage. The forecast of rising births reflects an underlying rise in the general fertility rate, not just a rise in the number of women of child-bearing age. The model forecast lies between the Census Series II and III projections through 1987 and between Series I and II from 1988 until 1990. Yet, the three Census series project declines from 1987 or 1988 onward, whereas the structural model predicts a steady increase in total live births.

Modeling the Regional Shares

The Trends

The regions used in this analysis are shown in the map in figure 2–1, and their shares of total births for the period 1948 to 1979 in figure 2–2. During the 1950s the shares of the New England, Mountain, West South Central, and South Atlantic regions were relatively stable. The shares of the West North Central, Mid-Atlantic, and East South Central regions decreased, while the Pacific share increased. The East North Central share fluctuated somewhat but on balance was the same at the opening and close of the decade. Generally these trends continued in the 1960s. In the 1970s the significant developments were the declines of the East North Central and Atlantic regions and the strong gains of the Pacific, West South Central, and Mountain regions. For a more detailed account of these trends and a discussion of their possible underlying causes, see Jackson et al. (1981, ch. 3).

The Search for the Best Line

Much research has been directed toward finding the curves which best fit historical patterns of population change. These curves then have been used to predict the future. This approach, which implies total dependence upon information embedded in the historical data, may be appropriate when the processes generating the data are unknown or incompletely understood (Ascher 1978). Then "the existing trend is probably a more reliable indicator of future patterns than are the potentially false signals indicated by the forecasters' incomplete understanding" (Keyfitz 1977, p. 203).

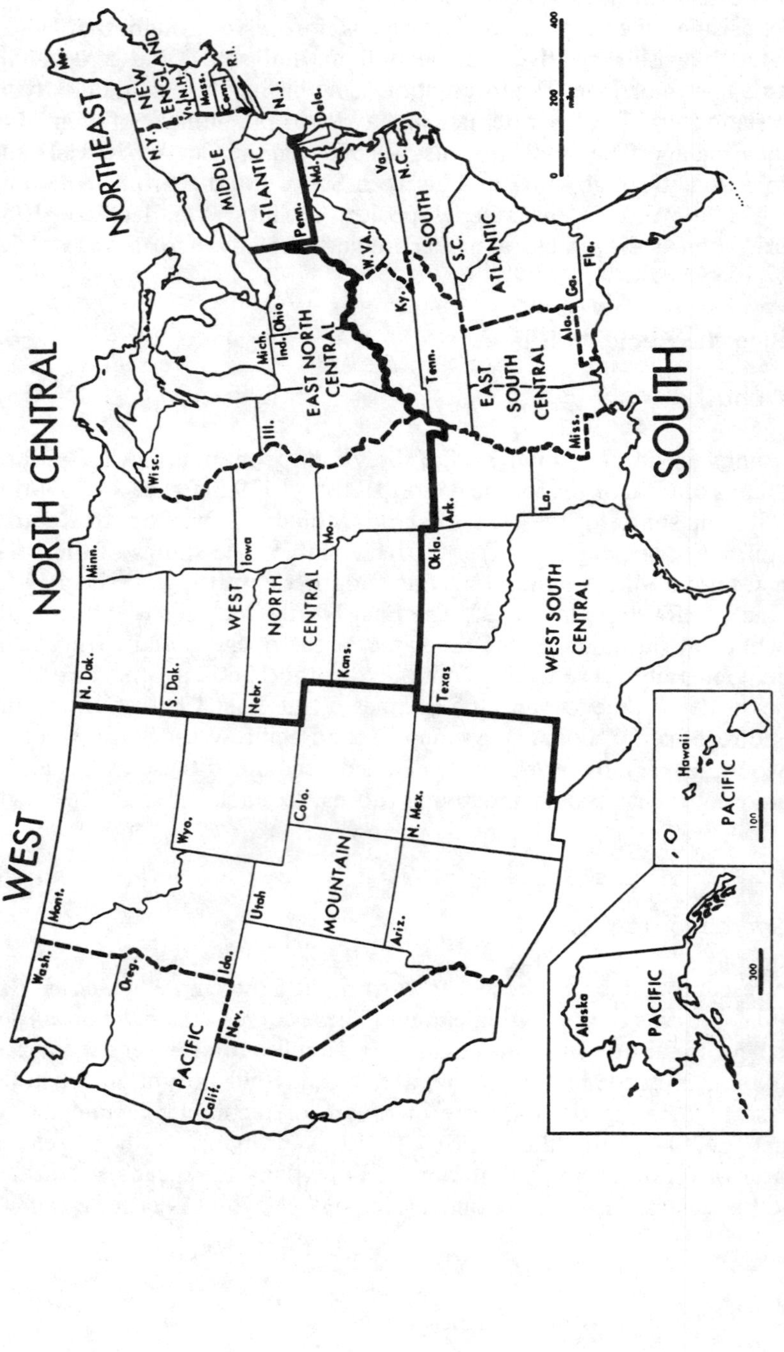

Figure 2-1. Map showing the regions and divisions of the United States

FORECASTING REGIONAL BIRTHS

Given the present uncertainty concerning future regional growth paths, an atheoretic approach is used here to determine birth shares. In essence, the best-fitting line is sought for each region. Such a search generally reduces to a choice between a mechanistic (mathematical) or empirical model. Since the past performance of mechanistic models has been relatively poor (Ascher 1978) and since the national component of this method to forecasting regional births is regression-based, the empirical approach is pursued here.

No single functional form can adequately describe the historical pattern of regional birth shares for all regions, as may be seen from figure 2–2. Table 2–4 reports the results of fitting first and second degree polynomials to the regional birth shares for the period 1948 to 1979. First degree polynomials fit the historical patterns for the New England, East North Central, South Atlantic, West South Central, and Pacific regions better than do second degree polynomials, but the latter fit the Mid-Atlantic, West

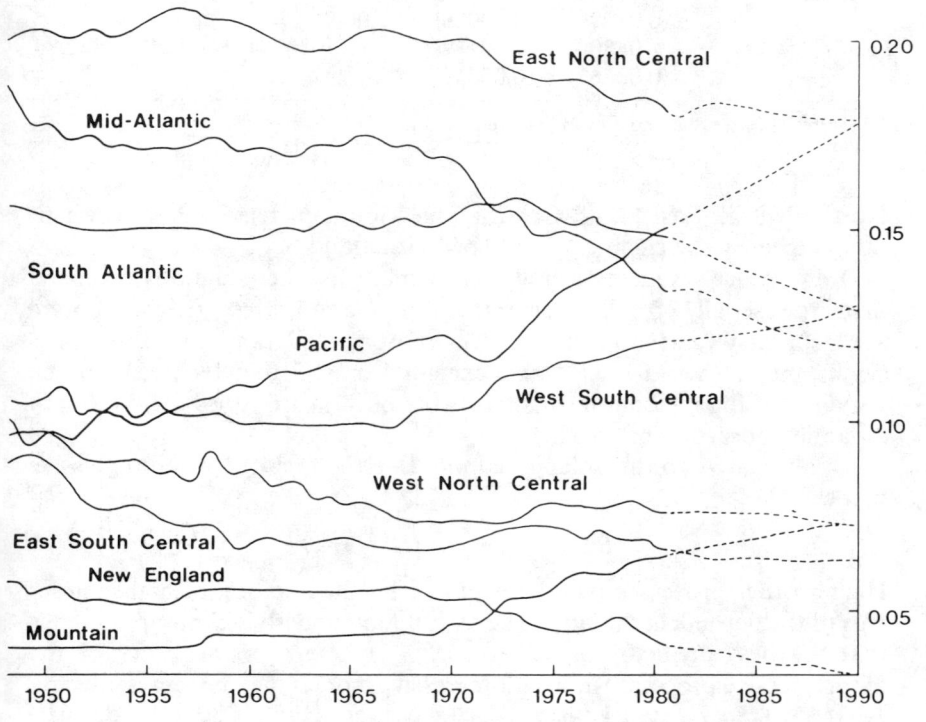

Figure 2-2. Regional shares of total live births

Table 2-4. Time Trend Models of Regional Birth Shares 1948-79[a]

Region	Constant	Time	Time^2	$\bar{R}^2$	DW	F
New England	0.06979 (0.01388)	−0.00069 (0.00038)		0.93	1.63	170.23
Mid-Atlantic	0.15575 (0.00448)	+0.00281 (0.00053)	−0.00010 (0.00002)	0.97	1.81	485.61
East North Central	0.21737 (0.00528)	−0.00089 (0.00022)		0.90	1.39	284.56
West North Central	0.10154 (0.00296)	−0.00166 (0.00040)	0.00003 (0.00001)	0.88	1.90	113.62
South Atlantic	0.14911 (0.00303)	+0.00015 (0.00013)		0.65	1.50	55.81
East South Central	0.08243 (0.00569)	−0.00123 (0.00078)	+0.00002 (0.00001)	0.92	1.85	168.38
West South Central	0.06413 (0.01751)	+0.00158 (0.00055)		0.91	2.15	313.53
Mountain	0.06396 (0.01099)	−0.00210 (0.00086)	+0.00006 (0.00002)	0.99	1.22	1136.95
Pacific	0.08806 (0.00267)	+0.00172 (0.00013)		0.98	1.59	872.76

[a]Figures shown in parentheses are standard errors.

North Central, East South Central, and Mountain regions best. (Best fit was judged by the significance of coefficients and $\bar{R}^2$.)

Ordinary least-squares estimation of many of the equations exhibited first-order serially correlated errors, so the equations presented incorporate a Cochrane-Orcutt adjustment. All but one equation are statistically significant at the 0.01 level and explain from 85 to 99 percent of the variance of the regional birth shares; the birth share series for the South Atlantic appears to be trendless.

An alternative to the polynomial model is the first-order autoregressive model:

$$BS_t^i = a_1 + a_2 BS_{t-1}^i + \varepsilon_t.$$

Higher order processes may be explored by the addition of higher order lags of the dependent variable. The assumption underlying this approach is that the best predictor of BS_t^i is BS_{t-k}^i, where k is the order of the autoregressive process. These autoregressive models may be represented by ARIMA (p,o,o) models (see McCleary and Hay 1980, pp. 53–61). McDonald (1981) has shown their usefulness for demographic forecasting, but ARIMA models of birth shares are not explored in this study because of the short time series available.

The estimated autoregressive equations are shown in table 2–5. In general, the first-order autoregressive process adequately describes the historical data, although second-order processes for the East North Central, West North Central, and Mountain regions cannot be rejected. The processes for the East North Central, West North Central, South Atlantic, and East South Central regions are stationary, but those for the other regions are not.

The explanatory power of the autoregressive equations is as high as that of the time-trend equations, but the presence of a lagged dependent variable implies that the coefficients are biased. They are, however, consistent, since a Cochrane-Orcutt adjustment has been used on the equations that exhibited first-order serial correlation. Logarithmic autoregressive models were also estimated but, in general, they were inferior to the other models.

It may be argued that the autoregressive model is theoretically naive in that, at a minimum, theory suggests that the regional distribution of births is a function of the spatial distribution of potential mothers. However, annual data on the age distribution of women are not available until 1958, and then only for age group 18–44 years. The birth share was regressed on lagged marriage shares, but forecasts based on these models were less accurate than the autoregressive birth-share models. The relative failure of the marriage-share variables probably reflects the mobility of the underlying population, particularly those 20–34 years of age. Although explicitly atheoretic, these autoregressive models are an example of the time-series approach to demographic forecasting advocated by McDonald (1981).

Fundamental Structural Change?

One of the major problems to be faced when searching for a relationship between past and future values of a series is temporal instability in the relationship. Changes in the structure of the relationship often adversely affect the accuracy of forecasts. If the historical series exhibits homogeneity, then a long experience base may be used. If, however, the historical series exhibits sudden or sharp changes, a short base is usually preferable, based on the assumption that the future is more likely to be similar to the recent past.

Several writers have argued that demographic relationships underwent fundamental structural change in the 1970s. Brown (1981) stated that

Table 2-5. Autoregressive Models of Regional Birth Shares, 1948-79

Region	Constant	Birth Share Lagged One Period	Birth Share Lagged Two Periods	$\bar{R}^2$	DW	F
New England	-0.00132 (0.00289)	1.01690 (0.05376)		0.92	1.67	357.7
Mid-Atlantic	-0.00187 (0.00690)	1.00150 (0.04857)		0.93	1.36	425.17
East North Central	0.01565 (0.01890)	0.91905 (0.09124)		0.90	2.09	262.09
East North Central	0.00982 (0.01429)	1.30960 (0.17938)	-0.36035 (0.19941)	0.90	2.09	126.36
West North Central	0.82445 (0.06057)	0.01410 (0.00514)		0.86	2.45	185.26
West North Central	0.01032 (0.00525)	0.55737 (0.16852)	0.31051 (0.14964)	0.88	1.98	102.65
South Atlantic	0.07016 (0.12445)	0.52938 (0.16020)		0.65	2.02	55.89
East South Central	0.01001 (0.00326)	0.85154 (0.04579)		0.92	1.98	345.83
West South Central	-0.00299 (0.00684)	1.03210 (0.06416)		0.90	1.99	258.83
Mountain	-0.00225 (0.00181)	1.06490 (0.03865)		0.99	2.23	2106.59
Mountain	-0.00126 (0.00133)	1.50110 (0.17501)	-0.464.63 (0.19202)	0.99	2.26	1015.68
Pacific	-0.00151 (0.00429)	1.02690 (0.03766)		0.97	1.84	1096.09

traditional models can no longer be relied on exclusively to explain the post-1970 population distribution because of an increasing "nonmaterialistic" element in locational decisions. Burghardt and Geraci (1980, p. 343) reported that poor Census Bureau population estimates for the South can be traced to "basic changes in the structural relationship between southern populations and symptomatic variables." Heaton and Fuguitt (1980, p. 509) even have characterized the post-1970 period as "a new epoch in which traditional patterns (of centralization) are obsolete."

Figure 2–2 suggests that the regional distribution of total live births also has undergone fundamental change since 1970. Thus, perhaps a short experience base, i.e., the 1970s, should be used when trying to predict future regional birth shares rather than the longer period examined in tables 2–4 and 2–5. This decision need not and should not be based on inferences drawn from figure 2–2 because the Chow (1960) test enables testing for structural change in the regional shares of total live births. Indeed, Chow tests reveal that a fundamental shift occurred in three regions in the 1970s. The shift was most pronounced in the West South Central and South Atlantic regions and only somewhat less so in the Mid-Atlantic region.

For those regions that exhibited structural change, the equations of tables 2–4 and 2–5 were re-estimated over the period of 1970–79. Overall, the models fit the shorter period less well than the entire period, the coefficients are generally different, and, in the case of the linear model for the South Atlantic region, of opposite sign, and the autoregressive models for the Mid-Atlantic and West South Central regions are now stationary. These changes in coefficients probably reflect both the structural change and also imprecision arising from the smaller number of degrees of freedom.

The Best Model

To choose the best model, the equations were re-estimated using data from 1948 to 1976 and from 1970 to 1976. The model with the smallest forecast error for the period 1977 to 1979 was judged to be the single best model.

The error statistics examined were the mean absolute error (MAE), the Theil statistic, and Theil's decomposition of forecast error. The Theil statistic, U, compares the actual forecast to a forecast of no-change. If U is less than one, then the model is more accurate than a no-change forecast (Bliemel 1973).

All models were more accurate than an assumption of constant birth

Table 2-6. Accuracy Statistics for Best Equation Forecasts of Regional Birth Shares for 1977-79 Using 1948-76 Data

Region	Best-Equation	MAE^a	U^b	UM^c	UR^d	UD^e	Direction of Error
New England	First-order Autoregressive	0.0007	0.010	0.680	0.320	0.000	−
Mid-Atlantic	First-order Autoregressive	0.0008	0.006	0.862	0.035	0.103	+
East North Central	Second-order Autoregressive	0.0012	0.003	0.184	0.520	0.296	+
West North Central	Second-order Autoregressive	0.0008	0.006	0.731	0.257	0.012	−
South Atlantic	First-order Autoregressive	0.0010	0.003	0.148	0.065	0.787	+
East South Central	First-order Autoregressive	0.0016	0.012	0.080	0.315	0.605	+
West South Central	First-order Autoregressive	0.0012	0.005	0.976	0.000	0.024	−
Mountain	Second-order Autoregressive	0.0015	0.013	0.928	0.026	0.046	+
Pacific	First-order Autoregressive	0.0009	0.004	0.307	0.118	0.575	−

[a] Mean Absolute Error.
[b] Theil statistic for No-Change Comparison.
[c] Proportion of forecast error due to incorrect mean.
[d] Proportion of forecast error due to incorrect regression slope.
[e] Proportion of forecast error due to random disturbance.

shares over the period 1977–79. The most accurate forecasts using the longer data series were generated by first-order autoregressive equations for six regions and second-order equations for the remaining three (see table 2–6). Thus, in no instances was a polynomial equation most accurate. In general most of the forecast error came from a systematic tendency to under- or overpredict the mean of the actual regional birth share. For all regions except the West South Central and East North Central, the model estimated over the full post-war period gave the most accurate forecasts using either accuracy statistic.

The shares of all regions should sum to unity. This constraint must be imposed by choosing one region's share to equal one minus the sum of the other eight regional shares. The residual region chosen was the South Atlantic since it was the least satisfactorily modeled region. The specification used in the empirical work does not ensure that the individual share forecasts will lie between zero and one, but since no forecast exceeded these bounds, it was not necessary to employ a specification, such as the logistic, which would guarantee it.

The forecasts for 1977–79 were mechanistic, but those for 1980–81 referred to in the next section have been adjusted by the MAE of the 1977–79 forecasts. This constant adjustment improved their accuracy.

Forecasts of Regional Total Live Births

Simulated Forecasts, 1977–81

In the previous sections the forecasting models for national total live births and regional shares were developed. In this section these forecasts will be combined to present three sets of forecasts of regional total live births. The first set is actual birth share multiplied by forecast national births; the second is forecast birth share multiplied by actual national births; and the third set, the full forecast, is forecast birth share multiplied by forecast national births. These forecasts are compared to the actual regional births to identify the main source of error in the forecasting method proposed in this chapter.

In comparing the Mean Absolute Percentage Errors (MAPE's) for the three sets of forecasts for the period 1977–79, the most significant source of forecast error was the forecast of national total live births (table 2–7). It led to a mean absolute percentage forecast error of about 5 percent. The model, in common with many structural models, did not predict accurately

Table 2-7. MAPE Statistics for Ex-post Forecasts of Regional Total Live Births, 1977-79

Region	1977-79			1980-81		
	Set 1[a]	Set 2[b]	Set 3[c]	Set 1[a]	Set 2[b]	Set 3[c]
New England	5.10	1.66	6.68	0.77	2.05	1.54
Mid-Atlantic	5.10	5.48	4.60	0.75	1.28	1.04
East North Central	5.12	5.26	5.56	0.77	2.84	2.66
West North Central	5.15	0.90	5.81	0.74	1.82	2.23
South Atlantic	5.12	0.90	5.26	0.75	2.72	2.72
East South Central	5.12	3.51	7.17	0.74	2.29	3.05
West South Central	5.10	0.38	5.26	0.77	1.21	0.99
Mountain	5.10	2.20	3.20	0.78	1.27	1.29
Pacific	5.12	0.72	4.44	0.76	0.63	0.14

[a] Actual share times forecast total births, so error is exclusively caused by total births.
[b] Forecast share times actual total births, so error is exclusively caused by shares.
[c] Forecast share times forecast total births.

the turning point which occurred in 1976, so births in 1977 and 1978 were underpredicted. For the Mid-Atlantic, South Atlantic, Mountain, and Pacific regions birth shares were overpredicted, offsetting somewhat the underprediction in national births. For the other regions, birth shares were underpredicted, reinforcing the error from the national birth forecasts. The largest birth share errors were for those regions whose shares have decreased significantly over the 1970s, namely, the Mid-Atlantic and East North Central.

The model forecast national total live births for 1980-81 very accurately (table 2-7). The MAPE's for set 1 forecasts are less than 1 percent. The MAPE's for all regions for the full forecasts are less than 3.1 percent, representing very accurate forecasts of total live births. For all regions except the Pacific, most of the forecast error came from the forecast of the birth share. For the East and West North Central the birth share was overestimated, while for the South Atlantic, the residual region, it was underestimated. For the other six regions there was no systematic tendency to over- or underestimate the regional birth share.

The 1980s

Forecasts of regional birth shares are shown in figure 2-2 and forecasts of total births are presented in table 2-8. Over the 1980s the New England,

Table 2-8. Total Live Births by Region, 1982-90

	1982	1983	1984	1985	1986	1987	1988	1989	1990
New England	164,453	164,240	164,513	164,655	164,758	164,709	164,170	163,304	161,842
Mid-Atlantic	500,428	500,253	501,956	502,897	503,735	504,520	504,672	502,061	499,976
East North Central	686,088	691,991	700,137	707,940	716,187	723,998	731,673	736,711	740,675
West North Central	299,512	302,487	306,836	133,058	315,327	319,423	323,477	326,199	328,638
South Atlantic	542,843	535,285	535,624	535,518	539,998	538,101	535,479	518,153	523,922
East South Central	245,191	248,243	252,126	255,915	259,751	263,454	267,132	269,718	272,076
West South Central	458,384	468,233	479,766	490,859	502,159	513,315	524,535	534,115	539,198
Mountain	244,819	256,530	265,516	274,943	284,189	294,237	307,262	316,376	328,638
Pacific	582,282	599,700	619,410	639,592	660,610	682,021	704,109	723,614	743,565

Mid-Atlantic, and South Atlantic regions will suffer significant declines in their shares of total live births. In contrast, the West South Central, Mountain, and Pacific regions will gain significantly. Of the remaining regions, the East North Central, and West North Central shares will decline slightly, and the East South Central share will remain constant.

The share forecasts predict the developments of the 1970s to continue into the 1980s, with the exception of New England and the East North Central. The New England share fluctuated in the 1970s but is predicted to decline in the 1980s, while the East North Central share, which declined through the 1970s, is predicted to stabilize in the 1980s.

The regions with large declines in birth shares will also experience stagnation in the number of total live births. In contrast, the regions whose shares will increase will also experience significant percentage increases in births. The Mountain, Pacific, and West South Central regions will be large gainers, and the relative losers will be the Atlantic regions and New England. Even though the East and West North Central shares will decline slightly, they will still experience sizeable increases in total births, as will the East South Central region, although its share of births will remain constant.

The ranking of regions by percentage increase in total live births is quite similar to the rankings of regions by rate of natural increase by the U.S. Bureau of the Census (1979) and the MIT-Harvard Joint Center study (Jackson et al. 1981, p. 62). The ranking by percentage change in births tends to be somewhat closer to the Joint Center ranking than the Census Bureau ranking. The major difference is the ranking of the East North Central region, which is ranked higher by the Census Bureau than by the others.

There are large differences, however, between the regional birth forecasts produced here and the Census Bureau projections. The forecasts are 19 to 32 percent higher than the Census projections for the Mountain, Pacific, and West South Central regions between 1985 and 1990. The forecasts for the New England and Mid-Atlantic regions, on the other hand, are 25 and 17 percent lower, respectively. The forecasts and projections would be much closer if the census projections were to be revised in recognition of their underestimation from 1975 to 1980 for the Mountain, Pacific, and West South Central regions and their overestimation for the New England and the Mid-Atlantic regions.

Possible Revisions of the Model Forecasts

Three factors may lead to a revision of the model forecasts. In the post-war era, regional fertility rates have converged in the upswing and diverged in the downswing. Since 1973 the fertility rates of the western regions have "shown an early propensity to level out and increase while other regions continued their decline until later in the decade" (Jackson et al. 1981, p. 75). If these developments portend a new upswing in fertility, then the rate of increase in births forecast for the non-western regions is probably too low. The second qualification relates to regional differences in the timing of childbirth. The East South Central, West South Central, and South Atlantic regions exhibit higher-than-average fertility during the early part of the reproductive ages and lower-than-average in the later part. The East North Central, New England, and Mid-Atlantic regions have the opposite pattern. Since the bulge of the baby-boom generation (born 1957–62) is now in the early part of the child-bearing years, observed fertility in the 1970s in the former regions may tend to lead to an overstatement of long-run fertility and to an understatement in the latter regions. This effect for the latter regions has probably been reinforced by the 1970s recession (Jackson et al. 1981, p. 77), although migration from these regions will offset this potential source of error.

The third factor deals with the autoregressive birth-share models for the Pacific and Mountain regions. Both imply explosive growth of the birth shares of these regions. Thus, the long-run share forecast is probably less accurate than the short-run. These equations should be re-estimated as new data become available.

References

Ahlburg, D.A. 1979. Alternative approaches to forecasting U.S. fertility. Ph.D. dissertation, University of Pennsylvania.
———. 1981. An economic-demographic forecasting model of U.S. births, marriage, divorce and female labor force participation. Minneapolis: University of Minnesota Industrial Relations Center Working Paper 81-07.
Ascher, W. 1978. *Forecasting: an appraisal for policy makers and planners*. Baltimore: Johns Hopkins University Press.
Becker, G.S. 1960. An economic analysis of fertility. In *Demographic and economic change in developed countries*, a report of the National Bureau of Economic Research. Princeton, NJ: Princeton University Press.
Bliemel, F. 1973. Theil's forecast accuracy coefficient: a clarification. *Journal of Marketing Research* 10, 4: 444–6.
Brown, D.L. 1981. Spatial aspects of post-1970 work force migration in the United States. *Growth and Change* 12, 1: 9–20.
Burghardt, J.A., and Geraci, V.J. 1980. State and local annual population

estimation methods employed by the Bureau of the Census. *Review of Public Data Use* 8, 3: 339–54.

Chow, G.C. 1960. Tests of equality between sets of coefficients in two linear regressions. *Econometrica* 28:P 591–605.

Dhrymes, P. 1975. Criteria for evaluation of econometric models. In *The Brookings model: perspectives and recent developments*, ed. L.R. Klein and G. Fromm, pp. 477–520. New York: North Holland.

Easterlin, R.A. 1973. Relative economic status and the American fertility swing. In *Family economic behavior: problems and prospects*, ed. E.B. Sheldon, pp. 170–223. Philadelphia: J.B. Lippincott.

―――. 1980. *Birth and fortune: the impact of numbers on personal welfare*. New York: Basic Books.

Gronau, R. 1977. Leisure, home production and work: the theory of the allocation of time revisited. *Journal of Political Economy* 85, 6: 1099–1124.

Heaton, T.B., and Fuguitt, G.V. 1980. Dimensions of population redistribution in the United States since 1950. *Social Science Quarterly* 61, 3–4: 508–523.

Jackson, G.; Masnick, G.; Bolton, R.; Bartlett, S.; and Pitkin, J. 1981. *Regional diversity: growth in the United States, 1960–1990*. Boston: Auburn House.

Keyfitz, N. 1977. *Applied mathematical demography*. New York: John Wiley and Sons.

McCleary, R., and Hay, R.A. 1980. *Applied time series analysis for the social sciences*. Beverly Hills: Sage Publications.

McDonald, J. 1981. Modeling demographic relationships: An analysis of forecast functions for Australian births. *Journal of American Statistical Association* 76, 376: 782–801.

Michael, R.T. 1978. The rise in divorce rates, 1960–1974: age specific components. *Demography* 15, 2: 177–182.

Pratt, L., and Whelpton, P.K. 1958. Extrafamilial participation of wives in relation to interest in and liking for children, fertility planning and actual and desired family size. In *Social and psychological factors affecting fertility*, ed. P.K. Whelpton and C.V. Kiser. New York: Milbank Memorial Fund.

Rindfuss, R., and Bumpass, L. 1976. How old is too old?: age and the sociology of fertility. *Family Planning Perspectives* 8, 5:226–230.

Smith-Lovin, L., and Tickameyer, A.R. 1978. Nonrecursive models of labor force participation, fertility behavior and sex role attitudes. *American Sociological Review* 43, 4: 541–557.

Stycos, J.M., and Weller, R.H. 1967. Female working roles and fertility. *Demography* 4, 1: 210–17.

U.S. Bureau of the Census. 1970. Projections of the population of the U.S. by age and sex: 1970 to 2020. *Current Population Reports*, Series P-25, No. 448. Washington, D.C.: U.S. Government Printing Office.

―――. 1977. Projections of the population of the U.S.: 1977 to 2050. *Current Population Reports*, Series P-25, No. 704. Washington, D.C.: U.S. Government Printing Office.

———. 1979. Illustrative projections of state populations by age, race, and sex: 1975–2000. *Current Population Reports*, Series P-25, No. 796. Washington, D.C.: U.S. Government Printing Office.

Wachter, M.L. 1975. A time series fertility equation: the potential for a baby boom in the 1980's. *International Economic Review* 16, 3: 609–624.

Westoff, C.F. 1978. Marriage and fertility in developed countries. *Scientific American* 239: 51–7.

3 FORECASTING INTERREGIONAL MIGRATION: AN ECONOMIC-DEMOGRAPHIC APPROACH

Jacques Ledent

Introduction

A novel migration model based on a demographic-economic approach is proposed in this chapter and then demonstrated with an application to interprovincial migration data for Canada. The first section reviews briefly how past multiregional forecasting efforts undertaken in North America have handled migration. Two approaches are examined: the traditional demographic approach used by U.S. and Canadian census bureaus, and the experimental demographic-economic approach which appeared recently. For the latter approach, the nature of the migration data accessible severely restricts the choice among modeling strategies. If time-series data on interregional migration can be obtained from a primary source, three options are available: net migration, gross inmigration and outmigration, or place-to-place migration flows can be modeled. Among these options, the one that emphasizes regional gross outflows and inflows appears to have received the least satisfactory treatment to date. Thus the rest of this chapter is devoted to improving the use of this option.

The second section proposes a rather appropriate specification that was suggested by ongoing efforts to formulate a mathematical framework for a general theory of movement (Alonso 1978; Fisch 1981). A method is set forth that allows for the calibration of the ensuing model as well as its use as a forecasting tool. Then some preliminary results obtained by applying the method to annual data on Canada's interprovincial migration over the 20-year period of 1961–81 are reported in the next section. Finally, possible extensions of the migration model developed in the chapter are outlined in the concluding section. Although these extensions still focus on gross migration flows, their calibration requires a time-series of the entire matrix of interregional streams which is commonly provided by a primary source of time-series information on migration.

Forecasting Migration in a Multiregional System: The North American Experience

In preparing their official subnational population forecasts, the North American census bureaus continue to rely on a traditional demographic approach. The recent evolution of this approach suggests important implications that are relevant to specification of the migration component in the alternative demographic-economic approach presented later.

The Traditional Demographic Approach

In forecasting multiregional population change, the U.S. Bureau of the Census and Statistics Canada have, until now, used a cohort-component model which treats each component (fertility, mortality, and migration) separately. In the case of the migration component, they simply determine the evolution of each region's net migration level on the basis of exogenously assumed evolutions of the gross out- and inflows. For example, the method used by Statistics Canada to develop its first generation of population projections for Canada and its provinces (Statistics Canada 1974) resorted to rough assumptions about the total exits from and total entries into each province, which reflected typical situations actually observed in the past and expected to be repeated in the future. Unfortunately, the method disregards the spatial dimension of the migration phenomenon. It overlooks the fact that, unlike fertility and mortality, migration is a demographic phenomenon that does not occur in only one place. It involves both the origin and destination, so that the assumptions that can be made about the evolution of the gross outflows and inflows may not be compatible with the past evolution of the place-to-place flows (interregional streams).

This drawback was avoided by the U.S. Bureau of the Census (1967) which proposed a two-step treatment of the migration component and accounted for spatial interdependence. First, outmigration for each region was projected on the basis of cohort-specific rates. Second, the pool of migrants obtained by cumulating each region's outmigrants was allocated back to the individual regions using cohort-specific inmigration shares. This method was later adopted by Statistics Canada (1979) which, for its second generation of multiregional demographic projections, used projected values of the cohort-specific outmigration rates and inmigration shares assumed to reflect typical situations of the past.

This two-step treatment of migration considers spatial interdependence only partially so that a given surplus of outmigrants has the same redistributive consequences regardless of its region of origin. Such a defect, however, is not present in the more sophisticated cohort-component model developed by Rogers (1975). This model—which also avoids the drawback of independence among the three demographic components—explicitly accounts for interregional streams introduced through destination-specific outmigration rates. Recently, it was applied to interregional migration data for Canada (Termote 1980) and for the United States (Long and Frey 1982) and to prepare population forecasts at a subregional level (Bureau de la Statistique du Québec 1981). Moreover, Statistics Canada and the U.S. Bureau of the Census currently are exploring the feasibility of adopting Rogers's model for preparation of their next subnational population projections.

In summary, the demographic approach to multiregional population forecasting displays a definite tendency to shift its focus from gross regional outflows and inflows to interregional streams. This shift reflects a growing desire among model builders to consider explicitly spatial interdependence, which has theoretical and empirical advantages.

The Demographic-Economic Approach Based on Time-series Data

A particularly striking feature of the demographic approach to multiregional population forecasting used by the U.S. and Canadian census bureaus is the use of a migration input (numbers, rates, or proportions) that reflects situations having prevailed at one point or another in the past. The statistically minded model-builder may be tempted to substitute for such an input one that is based on the estimation of statistical relationships expressing the impact of changes in regional economic conditions on interregional migration.

The implementation of the ensuing demographic-economic approach to migration forecasting strongly depends, however, on the type of data available. Thus, in the United States where there is no primary source providing reliable time-series data on migration (see Isserman, Plane, and McMillen 1982), researchers have turned to constructing models emphasizing interregional streams and based on cross-sectional data from the decennial census or alternative sources (Isserman et al. 1985 and chapter 9).

By contrast, in Canada where there exist two alternative sources of time-series data on migration (Statistics Canada 1977; Norris 1983), models have been developed that rely on a replication of the past evolution of migration patterns. Focusing on provincial net migration flows, Foot and Milne (1985) built an economic-demographic model which allows for an implicit but straightforward formulation of interregional interaction and accessibility. The explanatory variables of each provincial net flow are the population level, the wage rate, the unemployment rate in the province concerned, and their counterparts in the rest of the nation obtained as weighted averages of these factors in the other provinces. With regard to an earlier version of this model developed in a U.S. context (Milne 1981), two major improvements have been introduced. First, the weights that, in each regional net migration equation, allow for measurement of the counterparts to the region's economic factors are not determined through a search procedure anymore. Rather, they are specified as functions of the distance to the province of reference. In this way, despite the focus on net migration flows, spatial interdependency is introduced in a rather explicit manner, thus enabling one to measure the consequences of exogenous changes in the economic conditions of one or several provinces on each province's net migration flow. Second, consistency of the projected net flows, which in Milne's early model was artificially obtained by dropping one of the net migration equations (and thus deriving the corresponding net flow as a residual), is now ensured by a simultaneous estimation of the various provincial equations performed under the restriction that the sum of the dependent variables be equal to zero.

Foot and Milne have exploited only partially the potential offered by Canadian primary sources of time-series migration data. Such sources make it possible to adopt models based on alternative choices of the dependent variable in the migration equations. For example, it would be rather straightforward to extend their model to the joint consideration of gross outmigration and inmigration flows. Each net flow equation would then be replaced by two gross flow equations where the independent variables would be set in a symmetric fashion and the estimation would be conducted as before (under the built-in constraint ensuring proper closure of the multiregional population system) but with twice as many equations.

Since the entire matrix of interregional streams is available annually, however, an alternative route requiring even easier implementation would be to focus on interregional streams: that is, to have a separate equation for each stream where the independent variables would be economic factors relating to the origin and destination regions. Such a route has, in fact, been followed in two past modeling efforts: one undertaken in connection with the CANDIDE project developed in the early 1970s (Canadian Department of Regional Economic Expansion 1975) and another recently developed at the Conference Board of Canada (Jeacock 1982). In these efforts, interprovincial migration streams were modeled to respond to changes in per capita income and unemployment rates (in both cases) as well as some additional variables (in the second case).

Both of these modeling efforts have proven unsuccessful, however, and have fallen short of reproducing adequately past variations in the provinces' population changes, and particularly, parts of such changes due to migration. Several reasons appear to account for such an unfortunate result. First, despite the relatively high level of spatial aggregation, the migration streams between certain provinces are of small magnitude so that their annual variations are often affected by random variations that cannot be the basis of a statistical analysis. Second, short-distance migration is often triggered by factors that are not economic in nature, thus making it difficult to substantiate the impact of economic factors on migration streams between adjacent provinces, especially within the Atlantic region. Third, the coefficients of the independent variables often have the wrong sign and, more important, are quite unstable. Such an unfortunate feature prevents the use of the estimated equations to assess the impact of a change in a region's economic conditions on the migration streams that originate or end there. In addition to all this, the performance of the modeling option focusing on interregional streams is doomed to diminish with the number of regions considered, so that its use may not be advisable for more than a few regions of roughly equivalent importance.

In summary, migration modeling from time-series data, as demonstrated by the Canadian experience, has not yet developed satisfactorily. The current situation is, in fact, akin to the one that prevailed a few years ago in the United States in the modeling of the same phenomenon from cross-sectional data. Interestingly, the parallel just drawn between the two branches of migration modeling according to the type of the data available (time-series or cross-sectional) suggests that a step forward for the time-series case could perhaps be made by adopting a modeling strategy similar to the one set forth by the Urban Institute (Alperovich, Bergsman, and Ehemann 1977) in the cross-sectional case. The feasibility of such a strategy, which explicitly considers the spatial dimension but involves a calibration stage carried out at the level of the regional gross outflows and inflows, is investigated in the remainder of this chapter.

A Demographic-Economic Model of Migration Applicable to Time-Series Data: Generalities

Duplicating the theoretical substratum of the Urban Institute's model, a migration model is specified consisting of a set of mutually consistent equations concerning interregional streams as well as regional gross flows.

Specification

Each interregional stream M_{ij} is assumed to be proportional to : (1) a global measure v_i of the unfavorable properties of region i; (2) a global measure w_j of the attractive properties of region j; and (3) a relational term t_{ij} reflecting the difficulty of moving between regions i and j. Thus

$$M_{ij} = k \, v_i \, w_j \, t_{ij}, \qquad (3.1)$$

where k is a factor to be discussed later on. Equation 3.1 makes the implicit assumption that a change in the economic conditions of the origin i has an identical impact on all migration streams originating in region i; similarly a change at the destination j has an identical impact on all streams terminating in region j. This homogeneity assumption contrasts sharply with the presence of differing impacts in the models noted above (Canadian Department of Regional Economic Expansion 1975; Jeacock 1982), but precisely this assumption will yield empirical coefficients that are generally of the right sign as well as stable (unlike the coefficients of these models).

Two equations for the total flows out of and into each region can be derived from equation 3.1 by summing over all possible destinations

$$M_{i.} = \sum_{j \neq i} M_{ij} \qquad (3.2)$$

and origins

$$M_j = \sum_{i \neq j} M_{ij}, \quad (3.3)$$

respectively. Substitution yields

$$M_{i.} = k\, v_i\, D_i \quad (3.4)$$

where

$$D_i = \sum_{j \neq i} w_j\, t_{ij} \quad (3.5)$$

and

$$M_{.j} = k\, w_j\, C_j \quad (3.6)$$

where

$$C_j = \sum_{i \neq j} v_i\, t_{ij}. \quad (3.7)$$

Equations 3.4 and 3.6 readily demonstrate an interesting particularity of this model. In contrast to gross migration flow equations in some migration studies (Termote and Fréchette 1979), the regional outflows and inflows are not affected only by economic factors relating to the regions of reference (denoted by v_i and w_j). They also depend on the economic factors prevailing in the other regions (summarized in the weighted sums D_i and C_j). This feature follows from the joint consideration of equations 3.1 through 3.3 which allows each regional flow equation to pick up the impact of economic conditions at alternative regions of destination in the outflow case and alternative regions of origin in the inflow case. The migration model just formulated is ambiguous under certain aspects. Multiplying each composite variable v_i by a common factor $\frac{1}{\Delta}$ yields

$$v'_i = \frac{1}{\Delta} v_i$$

and multiplying each composite variable w_j by a common factor $\frac{1}{\phi}$ yields

$$w'_j = \frac{1}{\phi} w_j.$$

This multiplication leaves the structure of the model unchanged as

$$M_{ij} = k' v'_i w'_j t_{ij},$$
$$M_{i.} = k' v'_i D'_i, \quad \text{where } D'_i = \sum_{j \neq i} w'_j t_{ij}, \text{ and}$$

$$M_{.j} = k' w'_j C'_j, \quad \text{where } C'_j = \sum_{i \neq j} v'_i t_{ij}, \text{ and}$$

$$k' = k \Delta \phi.$$

It thus follows that the composite variables representing the unfavorable and attractive characteristics of each region do not really intervene through some absolute values v_i and w_j, respectively. Rather, they play their role through some relative values $\bar{v}_i$ and $\bar{w}_j$

$$\bar{v}_i = \frac{v_i}{v_r} \text{ and } \bar{w}_j = \frac{w_j}{w_r},$$

where r is an arbitrary region of the system. Therefore, $\bar{v}_i$ and $\bar{w}_j$ are substituted for v_i and w_j in equation 3.1, and $\bar{v}_i$ and $\bar{w}_j$ also appear in equations 3.4 through 3.7 instead of v_i and w_j.

The composite variables $\bar{v}_i$ and $\bar{w}_j$ from equations 3.4 and 3.5 can be written as

$$\bar{v}_i = \frac{M_{i.}}{kD_i} \qquad (3.8)$$

and

$$\bar{w}_j = \frac{M_{.j}}{kC_j}. \qquad (3.9)$$

If the internal structure of $\bar{v}_i$ and $\bar{w}_j$ is known, it suffices to run, for each region, two regressions: one explaining the variations of $\bar{v}_i$ in terms of the unfavorable characteristics of region i and another explaining the variations of $\bar{w}_j$ in terms of the attractive characteristics of region j.

The feasibility of such a procedure rests upon the prior determination of the multiplicative factor k and of the weighted sums D_i and C_j. Combining 3.1, 3.4, and 3.6 results in

$$M_{ij} = \frac{M_{i.}M_{.j}}{kD_iC_j} t_{ij}, \qquad (3.10)$$

an equation showing that the model is a doubly constrained spatial interaction model with the matrix of interregional stream M_{ij} biproportional to the matrix of relational terms t_{ij} (see Bacharach 1970). Moreover, if a_i and b_j are the balancing factors of this spatial interaction model,

$$a_i = \left[\sum_{j \neq i} M_{.j} b_j t_{ij} \right]^{-1} \qquad (3.11)$$

and

$$b_j = \left[\sum_{i \neq j} M_{i.} a_i t_{ij} \right]^{-1}. \qquad (3.12)$$

FORECASTING INTERREGIONAL MIGRATION

The weighted sums D_i and C_j are equal to the reciprocals of those balancing factors, up to a multiplicative factor (common to all sums in each series):

$$D_i = \mu \frac{1}{a_i} \qquad (3.13)$$

and

$$C_j = \gamma \frac{1}{b_j}, \qquad (3.14)$$

where μ and γ are such that

$$\mu\gamma = \frac{1}{k}. \qquad (3.15)$$

Thus, if the matrix of relational terms t_{ij} would be known, the system defined by equations (3.11) and (3.12) could be solved iteratively to yield the values of a_i and b_j and, hence, the values of D_i and C_j. This system has a unique solution that is determined up to a common multiplicative factor (λ for the balancing factors a_i associated with the origin regions and $1/\lambda$ for the balancing factors b_j associated with the destination regions). Nevertheless, the ratios a_m/a_n and b_m/b_n as well as the products $a_m b_n$ ($m, n = 1, \ldots, R$ where R is the number of regions in the system) are unequivocably determined.

Drawing the factor k from equation (3.8),

$$k = \frac{M_{i.}}{\bar{v}_i D_i}$$

and thus

$$\frac{M_{i.}}{\bar{v}_i D_i} = \frac{M_{r.}}{\bar{v}_r D_r}.$$

Since r is such that $\bar{v}_r = 1$,

$$\bar{v}_i = \frac{M_{i.}}{M_{r.}} \frac{D_r}{D_i}$$

and, after substitution of equation 3.13,

$$\bar{v}_i = \frac{M_{i.}}{M_{r.}} \frac{a_i}{a_r}. \qquad (3.16)$$

Similarly,

$$\bar{w}_j = \frac{M_{.j}}{M_{.r}} \frac{b_j}{b_r}. \qquad (3.17)$$

In summary, finding the solution to a spatial interaction model—the one consisting of finding the matrix of interregional streams with row and column totals equal to the observed outflows and inflows, respectively, that is biproportional to the matrix of relational terms t_{ij}—allows one to ascertain the values of $\bar{v}_i$ and $\bar{w}_j$ necessary for calibrating our migration model.

Solving the spatial interaction model also determines the value of the multiplicative factor k as well as the values of the weighted sums D_i and C_j. The values of k, D_r, and C_r can be obtained as the solutions of a three-equation system in these three variables. In particular

$$k = M_r M_{.r} a_r b_r.$$

Then use of the expressions for D_r and C_r leads to the following (which D_r and C_r also verify):

$$D_i = \frac{1}{M_{.r} b_r a_i} \text{ and } C_j = \frac{1}{M_r a_r b_j}.$$

Thus the revised model (with $\bar{v}_i$ and $\bar{w}_j$ substituted for v_i and w_j) does not suffer from any ambiguity.

Discussion

This model is similar to the one underlying Alonso's (1978) general theory of movement. The similarity is no coincidence, as this chapter originally had the objective of demonstrating the feasibility of using the Alonso model as a tool for preparing multiregional population forecasts. Although Alonso's model is indeed suitable for such a purpose, its implementation proved harder than originally anticipated (see Ledent 1982). This unfortunate result led to the adoption of a simpler migration model that, in fact, is a special case of the Alonso model. The analytical framework proposed by Alonso involves "systemic" variables which, as a result of a similar derivation, play the same role as the weighted sums D_i and C_j. However, these variables also appear in the interregional stream equation with exponents of $(\alpha_i - 1)$ and $(\beta_j - 1)$, respectively. In other words, the migration model specified above corresponds to the subcase of the Alonso model where $\alpha_i = 1$ (for all i's) and $\beta_j = 1$ (for all j's), i.e., to the situation in which interregional streams depend on the composite variables relating to the origin and destination regions but not on the systemic variables. Consequently, borrowing from the ideas developed by Alonso, the weighted sum D_i can be viewed as the pull-in exerted by the alternative destinations on the origin i and the weighted sum C_j as the push-out exerted by the alternative origins on the destination j.

To be exact, the equivalence just noted between the Alonso model and this model should be qualified because this model includes, in the stream and flow equations 3.1, 3.4, and 3.6, a multiplicative factor k, which does not appear in the Alonso model. The importance of introducing such a factor, which Anselin and Isard (1979) and Anselin (1982) have advocated in the case of Alonso's general model, has been shown above in conjunction with the consideration of relative rather than absolute values for the two composite variables specific to each region.

Implementation

Recall that the migration data consists of, for each region, two time-series, one for total outmigration ($M_{i.}$) and one for total inmigration ($M_{.j}$). The implementation of the migration model proposed above involves two successive stages: (1) calibration of the model; that is, empirical estimation of the relationships linking the composite variables $\bar{v}_i$ and $\bar{w}_j$ to their constitutive components; and (2) use of the model as a forecasting tool, that is, derivation of the forecasts of the regional outflows and inflows and interregional streams.

Calibration. If the matrix of relational terms t_{ij} known, equations 3.11 and 3.12 allow one to determine the values of the balancing factors a_i and b_j and lead, by way of equations 3.16 and 3.17, to the values of $\bar{v}_i$ and $\bar{w}_j$. In some instances, however, the system of regions may not be closed in the sense that it does not exhaust the whole territory within which internal migration is considered. This situation occurs, for example, if one considers the system of metropolitan areas within a country. Fortunately, as suggested by Porell and Hua (1981) and Porell (1982), the balancing factors a_i and b_j can be obtained by performing a fixed coefficients regression:

$$\ln \frac{M_{ij}}{t_{ij}M_i M_j} = z_0 + \sum_{m \neq s_1} x_m D_m + \sum_{n \neq s_2} y_n D'_n \quad (3.18)$$

where D_m is a dummy variable (= 1 if $m = i$; 0 otherwise), D'_n is a dummy variable (= 1 if $n = j$; 0 otherwise), z_o, x_m, and y_n are the coefficients to be determined, and s_1 and s_2 are two regions whose selection is needed to avoid overdetermination of the system (s_1 and s_2 may, in fact, be taken as identical). Then, since the balancing factors are defined up to a multiplicative factor, a_{s_1} can be set equal to one, thus obtaining b_{s_2} equal to e^{z_0} and more generally

$$a_i = e^{x_i}$$

and

$$b_j = e^{z_0 + y_j}.$$

Having determined the balancing factors a_i and b_j by either one of the two methods described and, from there, derived the values of the composite variables $\bar{v}_i$ and $\bar{w}_j$, the calibration stage goes on with performing the regressions reflecting the variations of the latter variables in terms of their constitutive elements.

Recalling for this purpose that these elements are, respectively, the unfavorable and attractive characteristics of each region, we can then write

$$\bar{v}_i = c_{vi} \left(\prod_k \bar{X}_{ki}^{r_{ki}} \right) \quad (3.19)$$

and

$$\bar{w}_j = c_{wj} \left(\prod_l \bar{Y}_{lj}^{s_{lj}} \right) \quad (3.20)$$

where $\bar{X}_{ki}$ is the value of the kth unfavorable characteristic of region i, r_{ki} is the elasticity or movement response of region i to changes in the value to the kth characteristic, Y_{lj} is the value of the lth attractive characteristic of region j, s_{lj} is the elasticity or movement response of region j to changes in the value of the lth characteristic, and c_{vi} and c_{wj} are constants.

A question of interest here is the measurement of the X- and Y-elements entering the definitions of the composite variables $\bar{v}_i$ and $\bar{w}_j$. Since the variables reflect a region's repulsive and attractive powers relative to such powers in the other regions (and especially in the arbitrarily defined region r), then constitutive elements should be gauged in a relative fashion, i.e.,

$$\bar{X}_{ki} = \frac{X_{ki}}{X_{kr}} \text{ and } \bar{Y}_{lj} = \frac{Y_{lj}}{Y_{lr}}$$

where X_{ki} (Y_{lj}) is the actual value of the kth favorable (lth) attractive characteristic of region i (j). With such a measurement of the various regional characteristics, $\bar{X}_{kr} = 1$ and $\bar{Y}_{lr} = 1$ so that, in accordance with prior restraints, we have $\bar{v}_r = 1$ and $\bar{w}_r = 1$.

Given definitions 3.19 and 3.20 of the composite variables $\bar{v}_i$ and $\bar{w}_j$, respectively, the values of the various constants $v_{oi} = e^{r_{oi}}$ and $w_{oi} = e^{s_{oj}}$ and of the various elasticities r_{ki} and s_{lj} (i and $j \neq r$) can be found by performing the following two regressions in double logarithmic form:

$$\ln \bar{v}_i = r_{oi} + \sum_k r_{ki} \ln \bar{X}_{ki} \tag{3.21}$$

and

$$\ln \bar{w}_j = s_{oj} + \sum_l s_{lj} \ln \bar{Y}_{lj}. \tag{3.22}$$

Since at a macroscopic level, the migration process should be handled in probabilistic terms to reflect adequately the decision to migrate, it appears necessary to include in the composite variable $\bar{v}_i$ a term $\bar{P}_i = P_i/P_r$, controlling for the level of the origin population. As a result, the set of equations associated with outmigration is to be replaced by another based on

$$\ln \frac{\bar{v}_i}{\bar{P}_i} = r_{oi} + \sum_k r_{ki} \ln \bar{X}_{ki}. \tag{3.21'}$$

Usage as a Forecasting Tool. In the case of an exhaustive territorial partition, the use of this migration model for forecasting purposes is rather straightforward. The presence of a multiplicative factor in the interregional stream equation 3.1 raises, however, a difficulty. Knowledge of the future values of the composite variables $\bar{v}_i$ and $\bar{w}_j$ yields forecasted values of the interregional streams M_{ij}, up to a constant factor k which, moreover, varies from each forecasting interval to the next.

This finding actually means that the migration model does not focus on the values of the regional flows and interregional streams ($M_{i.}, M_{.j}, M_{ij}$) but rather on their relative values ($M_{i.}/M_{..}, M_{.j}/M_{..}, M_{ij}/M_{..}$ where $M_{..} = \sum_{i \neq j} M_{ij}$

is the total number of movements in the system). Analytically, this can be seen from the following equation readily derived from equation 3.1:

$$\frac{M_{ij}}{M_{..}} = k'\bar{v}_i\bar{w}_j t_{ij} \qquad (3.23)$$

where

$$k' = \frac{1}{\sum_{m \neq n} \bar{v}_m \bar{w}_n t_{mn}}.$$

It thus follows that, to use this model as a forecasting tool, the evolution of the total number of movements $M_{..}$ or, better, the overall propensity to migrate $m_{..} = M_{..}/P = M_{..}/\sum_k P_k$ should be determined beforehand.

Briefly, implementation of the forecasting ability of the model involves in each forecasting interval the following steps:

1. Determination of the values of each region's unfavorable and attractive characteristics either exogenously or from an economic model

2. Derivation of the beginning-of-the-interval population levels P_i (except for the first interval) from an appended components-of-change model of multiregional growth. If the migration flows are in terms of migrations rather than surviving migrants, they can be obtained from:

$$P_i(t) = P_i(t-1) + N_i(t-1) + M_{.i}(t-1) - M_{i.}(t-1) + EXT_i(t-1)$$

$$(3.24)$$

where $N_i(t-1)$ and $EXT_i(t-1)$ are region i's natural increase and external migration balance, respectively, between times $t-1$ and t.

3. Derivation of the forecasted values of the composite values $\bar{v}_i$ and $\bar{w}_j$ from equations 3.21' and 3.22, respectively, and of the total number of migrations $M_{..}$.

4. Derivation of the forecasted values of the interregional streams M_{ij} from equation 3.23.

An Application to Interprovincial Migration in Canada: 1961–81

The method now will be illustrated with an application to interprovincial migration in Canada. The migration data used for this purpose are annual data (between June 1 of two consecutive years) on the gross flows entering and leaving each province for a 20-year period (1961–62 to 1980–81). These data were drawn from Statistics Canada (1977).

Calibration

The calibration of the model starts with the determination of the matrix of relational terms t_{ij}. For this purpose, a doubly constrained spatial interaction model is fit to an interregional stream matrix on the basis of the power function

$$t_{ij} = d_{ij}^{-h}$$

where d_{ij} is the road distance between provinces i and j. Thanks to the abundance of migration data from the family allowance source, this interregional stream matrix is chosen as the matrix obtained by cumulating all of the annual stream matrices over the 20-year period at hand. Alternative but less adequate choices would be to pick either one of these annual matrices or any or a combination of the five-year interregional stream matrices over the same 20-year period provided by the quinquennial census. Use of the automatic Newton-Raphson method (see Ledent 1980, p. 349) leads to a value of h equal to $-.8782$.

From the ensuing values of the relational terms t_{ij}, the balancing factors a_i and b_j and the composite variables $\bar{v}_i$ and $\bar{w}_j$ are estimated for each of the 20 annual periods. First, the values of the balancing factors are derived by applying the first of the two methods noted above: namely, that relying on equations 3.11 and 3.12. Then, having retained the largest Canadian province, Ontario, as the reference region (region where the composite variables are chosen equal to 1), the composite variables of the other provinces are derived by applying 3.16 and 3.17.

Next is the empirical estimation of the regression equations showing the variations of the composite variables $\bar{v}_i$ and $\bar{w}_j$ in terms of their constitutive elements. Following the human capital approach to migration, these composite variables are assumed to reflect expected income in the regions of origin and destination, respectively. Because of stringent resource constraints, they are made dependent on only a few socioeconomic factors. Both $\bar{v}_i$ and $\bar{w}_j$ are, in all provinces, hypothesized to be functions of two factors: (1) a labor income proxy (in real terms) obtained by dividing the province's average annual wage in current dollars by the consumer price index in the province's main city and (2) an employment opportunity proxy taken as the province's unemployment rate. In the case of the origin variable $\bar{v}_i$, a third factor is added to account for the alleged impact of welfare benefits on retaining potential outmigrants. This factor is a nonlabor income proxy measured by the ratio of the total benefits from unemployment insurance to total labor income. All of these factors plus the population level are measured in relative terms using Ontario values as numeraires. Finally, to account for the exceptional situation created by intermittent political unrest in Quebec, a dummy variable equal to one in 1969–70, 1970–71, 1977–78, and to zero otherwise, is included in all equations.

Results obtained by applying an ordinary least-squares estimation technique to equations 3.21' and 3.22 are shown in table 3–1. The labor income proxy performs well in both origin and destination equations. The coefficient of this variable picks up the expected negative sign in eight out of the nine origin equations (the only exception being Alberta) and the expected positive sign in seven out of the nine destination equations (the exceptions being Quebec and Manitoba). When having the right sign, the coefficient is significant, at the 5 percent level of confidence, seven out of eight times for the origin equations but only two out of seven times for the destination equations.

By contrast, the performance of the proxy for employment opportunity is less adequate in both origin and destination equations. The coefficient of this variable still has the expected positive sign in six out of the nine origin equations (exceptions being for Newfoundland, Saskatchewan, and Alberta) and the expected negative sign in eight out of the nine destination equations (the exception being Quebec). However, when having the right sign, the coefficient is significant, at the 5 percent level of confidence, in only three instances: once in the case of the origin equations and twice in the case of the destination equations.

As might be expected from the above results, the labor income proxy has generally a larger impact than the unemployment rate on migration flows out of and into each province (compare the absolute values of the corresponding t-statistics). British Columbia is an exception.

The performance of the nonlabor income proxy in the origin equations is even less impressive since the coefficient of this variable has a positive sign in seven instances (only two being significant) and a negative sign in two instances (one being significant). Welfare benefits may or may not have a retention effect on potential outmigrants.

Finally, the dummy variable reflecting political unrest in Quebec performs quite successfully. Recall that regional outflows and inflows were deflated by the corresponding flows for Ontario. Therefore, since political unrest in Quebec means less outmigration and more inmigration for Ontario, the coefficient of the dummy variable should be positive in the origin equations and negative in the destination equations. In fact, it has the expected sign in all equations but one: the origin equation for British Columbia. Moreover, it is significant at 5 percent or better in four of the origin equations and eight of the destination equations.

Simulated Forecasts

Next, simulated forecasts over the 20-year observation period are carried out on the basis of the procedure described in the second section, using the equations just estimated.

No effort is made to model the natural increase and external migration components in the population change equation 3.24, because the purpose here is to evaluate the performance of the migration model. The natural increase rate and the external migration balance equal their observed values. Also, instead of determining endogenously the total number of interprovincial migrants $M..$, this number is set equal to its observed value, a choice to be discussed later.

The results of this forecasting exercise are very encouraging. They are at least as good as the results of a similar exercise based on a time-series model focusing on interregional streams (Jeacock 1982). The loss of information involved in shifting from interregional streams to regional outflows and inflows does not appear, at first glance, to result in a worse modeling performance. (This assertion should, however, be reexamined in the light of a more meaningful comparison based on the use of the same explanatory variables in both models.)

Outflows are forecast more accurately than inflows (compare the first two columns in table 3-2). The mean average percentage error (MAPE) on outflows for all the provinces is 5.9 percent, whereas the corresponding MAPE on inflows is 7.8 percent. Also, the range across provinces of the error made on outflows is smaller (3.0 to 7.6 percent) than the error in inflows (4.3 to 12.4 percent). The better accuracy obtained with outflows reflects for a large part the lesser performance (in terms of explanatory power) of the destination equations vis-a-vis the origin equations: the destination equations include three independent variables as against five in the origin equations (if one includes the population term accounted for in the dependent variable). Additional insights into the forecasting ability of the model can be obtained by comparing, in each province, the forecast population level with the actual level. As can be seen from the last column of table 3-2, the relatively low error levels pertaining to the provincial migration flows result in accurately predicted population levels. The

Table 3-1. Impact of the Constitutive Socioeconomic Factors on the Provincial Composite Variables[a]

Province	Intercept	Labor Income	Unemployment Rate	Non-labor Income Ratio	Dummy Variable
1. Origin composite variable $\bar{v}_i$					
Newfoundland	0.354	−1.848	−0.053	−0.017	0.228
	(1.65)	(3.22)	(0.56)	(0.14)	(2.98)
Prince Edward Island	−0.386	−0.815	0.157	0.136	0.089
	(1.87)	(3.58)	(1.02)	(1.30)	(1.38)
Nova Scotia	−0.335	−1.956	0.127	0.280	0.071
	(3.30)	(10.49)	(0.88)	(2.21)	(1.98)
New Brunswick	−0.148	−1.864	0.122	0.084	0.131
	(0.62)	(4.41)	(0.66)	(0.41)	(2.07)
Quebec	−1.437	−2.084	0.128	0.164	0.225
	(6.04)	(1.63)	(0.69)	(0.56)	(3.48)
Ontario	—	—	—	—	—
Manitoba	0.120	−4.325	0.246	−0.337	0.029
	(1.03)	(4.34)	(1.27)	(2.28)	(0.63)
Saskatchewan	−0.550	−1.891	−0.167	−0.327	0.179
	(3.84)	(4.84)	(0.99)	(1.49)	(2.46)
Alberta	0.845	0.847	−0.105	0.372	0.065
	(8.21)	(1.77)	(0.84)	(3.77)	(1.64)
British Columbia	0.122	−1.890	0.971	0.162	−0.038

2. Destination composite variable $\bar{w}_j$

Newfoundland	−1.242 (0.547)	1.885 (2.29)	−0.484 (3.57)	—	−0.378 (3.34)
Prince Edward Island	−3.225 (16.42)	0.381 (1.09)	−0.509 (2.25)	—	−0.258 (2.54)
Nova Scotia	−1.594 (15.20)	0.115 (0.33)	−0.326 (1.81)	—	−0.235 (3.29)
New Brunswick	−1.986 (23.28)	0.412 (1.16)	−0.068 (0.48)	—	−0.190 (2.45)
Quebec	−2.216 (17.33)	−4.315 (4.21)	0.525 (1.78)	—	−0.367 (3.69)
Ontario	—	—	—	—	—
Manitoba	−1.673 (10.76)	−0.945 (0.84)	−0.212 (0.72)	—	−0.178 (2.42)
Saskatchewan	−1.853 (10.80)	0.272 (0.90)	−0.272 (1.38)	—	−0.200 (2.15)
Alberta	−0.026 (0.151)	3.841 (4.65)	−0.242 (0.97)	—	−0.181 (2.18)
British Columbia	−0.079 (0.90)	0.784 (0.50)	−0.245 (0.81)	—	−0.068 (0.68)

[a]The figures in parentheses are the t-statistics corresponding to each independent variable.

Table 3-2. Gross Migration Flows and Population Levels: Mean Average Percentage Error on Forecasted Values over the Sample Period

Province	Outflow	Inflow	End-of-the-Year Population
Newfoundland	7.5	12.4	1.05
Prince Edward Island	7.2	9.1	0.47
Nova Scotia	3.6	4.3	0.21
New Brunswick	6.2	6.4	0.64
Quebec	6.3	8.9	0.18
Ontario	3.0	4.3	0.15
Manitoba	5.0	5.7	0.50
Saskatchewan	7.6	9.0	1.35
Alberta	4.6	6.1	0.59
British Columbia	7.5	11.5	1.00
Average	5.9	7.8	0.61

population MAPE ranges from 0.15 percent (Quebec) to 1.35 percent (Saskatchewan) for an average value of 0.61 percent across provinces.

Finally, an interesting feature of the above simulation exercise worth mentioning here is its relatively even performance (beyond short-term variations) over the whole simulation period. Table 3-3, which displays the year-to-year variations, for both migration flows and population levels, of the mean average percentage error does not show any progressive deterioration in model performance over the years.

Discussion

Since the composite variables $\bar{v}_i$ and $\bar{w}_j$ were taken equal to one for Ontario, one must ask whether this particular choice has much impact on the performance of the model. To answer this question, another province, Quebec (the second most populous), was substituted for Ontario and the method applied again. The empirical results are broadly similar to those obtained earlier, but overall they are slightly worse: there are a few more coefficients among the 36 pertaining to the two main explanatory factors (labor income and unemployment) that have the wrong sign and the population MAPE is comparatively higher over the whole period. Repeating the experiment by substituting one of the eight remaining provinces

Table 3-3. Gross Migration Flows and Population Levels: Mean Average Percentage Error Across Provinces, Year to Year

Year	Outflows	Inflows	End-of-the-Year Populations
1961–62	9.0	15.5	0.44
1962–63	6.8	10.0	0.72
1963–64	4.1	5.9	0.83
1964–65	5.1	6.3	0.84
1965–66	4.9	7.0	0.77
1966–67	5.4	9.6	0.73
1967–68	5.6	5.2	0.79
1968–69	6.8	5.4	0.70
1969–70	5.8	6.0	0.75
1970–71	3.8	5.0	0.64
1971–72	3.5	8.3	0.62
1972–73	6.1	9.0	0.58
1973–74	7.1	9.6	0.67
1974–75	7.9	8.3	0.54
1975–76	5.4	7.2	0.51
1976–77	3.4	5.3	0.58
1977–78	7.3	8.1	0.53
1978–79	4.7	6.0	0.37
1979–80	7.7	9.1	0.35
1980–81	6.8	8.7	0.32
Average	5.9	7.8	0.61

brings out, in each case, similar conclusions so that the best performance is obtained when the values of the socioeconomic variables in Ontario are chosen as numeraires. This finding, after all, is not surprising. Given that it has the largest provincial population and plays the leading role in the Canadian economy, Ontario is characterized by socioeconomic factors that are relatively less affected by random fluctuations and are the closest to reflecting national economic conditions.

Annual interprovincial migration was set equal to its observed value to stress the small impact the endogenous determination of $M_{..}$, given the normal variation of this variable, has on forecasting accuracy. Over the sample period, the interprovincial migration propensity oscillated around its average value, between 16 and 20 per 1,000. These variations could certainly reflect changes in some relevant socioeconomic factors for the country. Yet, assuming that over the sample period this propensity remained constant to its average observed value results in forecasts very similar to those obtained when $M..$ is set equal to its observed value. The population MAPE, for example, never differs by more than a few hundredths of a percentage point from the corresponding MAPE observed previously. Thus, ensuring that the region whose economic factors are chosen as numeraires is identified optimally is much more important than refining the determination of the future values of the overall migration totals.

Perhaps the element deserving the most attention in view of a more accurate demonstration of the model is the assumed constancy of the matrix of relational terms. Given likely variations over time in the deterring effect of distance on migration, more flexibility is needed in the treatment of this matrix. This flexibility can only come from having available several observations of the interregional stream matrix (census observations, for example). Other elements worth considering in improving the method are (1) substitution of the alternative method described by Porrell and Hua (1981) for the spatial interaction method used for assessing the matrix of relational terms, (2) consideration of additional socioeconomic factors affecting the composite variables $\bar{v}_i$ and $\bar{w}_j$, and (3) substitution of a more efficient technique for the ordinary least-squares technique used to estimate 3.21' and 3.22. A particularly attractive technique for the latter is the seemingly unrelated regression technique (Zellner 1962) which makes use of the possible correlation of error terms across the regional equations.

Conclusions and Extensions

The matrix of relational terms was kept constant because it was hypothesized that this matrix was derived from just one cross-sectional observation of the matrix of interregional streams. However, sources of migration data such as Canada's family allowance and taxation sources allow a time-series observation of the interregional stream matrix which might be used to perform an annual assessment of the matrix of relational terms. Specifically, the spatial interaction procedure used in the third section to derive the value of the parameter h appearing in the expression of t_{ij} as a negative power function of d_{ij} could be applied, in each time period, to derive simultaneously the values of h and of the balancing factors a_i and b_j. (Application of the spatial interaction procedure to the interregional stream matrix drawn annually from the family allowance results in a parameter h which, after oscillating between 0.89 and 0.95 during the first 14 years of the 20-year observation period, decreases monotonically to reach 0.66 in the 1980–81 period.) From there, the rest of the method developed above would remain in force, except that it would be necessary to project beforehand the evolution of the distance parameter h and thus of the matrix of relational terms.

If the extension just outlined would introduce some flexibility in assessing the ease of moving between regions, it would not, however, remove the above-mentioned difficulty associated with such an assessment. One possibility of doing away with such a difficulty would be to use the following dynamic version of equation 3.1:

$$M_{ij}(t) = kR\bar{v}_i(t)R\bar{w}_j(t)t_{ij}(t) \qquad (3.1')$$

where

$$R\bar{v}_i(t) = \frac{\bar{v}_i(t)}{\bar{v}_i(t-1)}$$

$$R\bar{w}_j(t) = \frac{\bar{w}_j(t)}{\bar{w}_j(t-1)}$$

$$t_{ij}(t) = \frac{M_{ij}(t-1)M_{..}(t-1)}{M_{i.}(t-1)M_{.j}(t-1)}. \qquad (3.25)$$

As indicated by the similarity of equation 3.1' to equation 3.1, this extension of our migration model should be implemented in much the same way as the original model. In particular, model calibration should begin with the determination of the series relating to the composite variables, here $R\bar{v}_i(t)$ and $R\bar{w}_j(t)$ from the time-series on outflows ($M_{i.}$) and inflows ($M_{.j}$), respectively. This determination should take advantage of a newly derived matrix of relational terms (see equation 3.25) which does not require any prior estimation of the impact of distance from cross-sectional data. In each time period, the matrix of relational terms readily follows from the observation of the interregional stream matrix in the previous period.

References

Alonso, W. 1978. A theory of movements. In *Human settlements: international perspective on structure, change, and public policy*, ed. N. Hansen. Cambridge, MA: Ballinger.
Alperovich, G.; Bergsman, J.; and Ehemann, C. 1977. An econometric model of migration between US metropolitan areas. *Urban Studies* 14:135–145.

Anselin, L. 1982. Implicit functional relationships between systemic effects in a general model of movement. *Regional Science and Urban Economics* 12:365–380.

Anselin, L., and Isard, W. 1979. On Alonso's general theory of movement. *Man, Environment, Space and Time* 1, 1:52–63.

Bacharach, 1970. *Biproportional matrices and input-output change.* London: Cambridge University Press.

Bureau de la Statistique du Québec. 1981. Perspectives démographiques pour le Québec et ses régions administratives, 1976–2001: Analyse des principaux résultats (version préliminaire). BSQ, Québec.

Canadian Department of Regional Economic Expansion. 1975. Overview of Candid-R. WP#1, CDREE, Ottawa.

Fisch, O. 1981. Contributions to the general theory of movement. *Regional Sciences and Urban Economics* 11:157–173.

Foot, D.K., and Milne, W.J. 1985. Net migration modelling in an extended, multiregional gravity model. *Journal of Regional Science* 25, 1:119–133.

Isserman, A.M.; Plane, D.A.; and McMillen, D.B. 1982. Internal migration in the United States: an evaluation of federal data. *Review of Public Data Use* 10:285–311.

Isserman, A.; Plane, D.A.; Rogerson, P.; and Beaumont, P. 1985. Forecasting interstate migration with limited data: a demographic economic approach. *Journal of the American Statistical Association* (80, 390:277–285).

Jeacock, R.L. 1982. A provincial population forecasting model emphasizing interprovincial migration. A Technical Paper from the Conference Board of Canada, Ottawa.

Ledent, J. 1980. Calibrating Alonso's general theory of movement: the case of interprovincial migration flows in Canada. *Sistemi Urbani* 2/3:327–358.

———. 1982. Forecasting with Alonso's theory of movement: the case of interprovincial migration streams in Canada. *Proceedings of the 13th Annual Pittsburgh Conference on Modeling and Simulation*, Instrument Society of America, Research Triangle, North Carolina.

Long, L., and Frey, W. 1982. *Migration and settlement: 14. United States.* RR 82-15. International Institute for Applied Systems Analysis, Laxenburg, Austria.

Milne, W.J. 1981. Migration in an interregional macroeconomic model of the United States—will net outmigration from the Northeast continue? *International Regional Science Review* 6, 1:71–84.

Norris, D. 1983. New sources of Canadian small area migration data. *Review of Public Data Use* 11, 1:11–25.

Porell, F.W. 1982. Intermetropolitan migration and quality of life. *Journal of Regional Science* 22, 2:137–158.

Porell, F.W., and Hua, C.-I. 1981. An econometric procedure for estimation of a generalized systemic gravity model under incomplete information about the system. *Regional Science and Urban Economics* 11, 4:585–606.

Rogers, A. 1975. *Introduction to multiregional mathematical demography.* New York: John Wiley.
Statistics Canada. 1974. *Population projections for Canada and the provinces 1972–2000.* Catalogue 91-514 (occasional). Information Canada, Ottawa.
_____. 1977. *International and interprovincial migration in Canada.* Catalogue 91-208 (annual). Information Canada, Ottawa.
_____. 1979. *Population projections for Canada and the provinces, 1976–2001,* Catalogue 91-514 (occasional). Information Canada, Ottawa.
Termote, M. 1980. *Migration and settlement: 6. Canada.* RR 80-29, International Institute for Applied Systems Analysis, Laxenburg, Austria.
Termote, M., and Fréchette, R. 1979. *Les variations du courant migratoire interprovincial.* Institut national de la recherche scientifique, I.N.R.S.-Urbanisation, Montreal, Québec.
U.S. Bureau of the Census. 1967. Revised projections of the population of states: 1970 to 1985. *Current Population Reports,* Series P-25, No. 375. Washington, D.C.: U.S. Government Printing Office.
Zellner, A. 1962. An efficient method of estimating seemingly unrelated regressions and tests for aggregation bias. *Journal of the American Statistical Association* 57:348–368.

II REGIONAL ECONOMIC-DEMOGRAPHIC MODELING

4 ECONOMIC-DEMOGRAPHIC INTERACTIONS IN THE GROWTH OF TEXAS
Thomas Plaut

Introduction

Two forces—the continuing shift of jobs and people from the North and East to the South and West, and the rapid increase in energy prices—have combined to make Texas a major focus of economic and population growth within the United States. During the 1970s, Texas gained 2.2 million jobs and 3 million new people, more jobs and people than any other state except California. Texas employment grew at twice the national rate and its population at two-and-a-half times the national rate over this period.

The key linkage between regional economic growth and population growth is population migration. As a regional economy expands, "people follow jobs" when people migrate into the region to take advantage of new employment opportunities, and "jobs follow people" when the growth of markets and increasing consumer demands attract new industry to the region and spur the growth of trade, services, and other regionally oriented activity. Therefore, any attempt to model and forecast the growth of the Texas economy must pay serious attention to the causes and consequences of population migration.

This chapter describes population determination and economic-demographic interactions in a recently developed long-run forecasting and policy analysis model for the state of Texas. The primary focus of the Texas Economic-Demographic Forecasting Model (TEDFM) is on capturing the strong interrelationship of the state's economic and population growth through the migration linkage.

The chapter is organized by first outlining, in the following section, the overall structure of TEDFM. The third section describes the determination of population, and the fourth describes demographic-economic interactions in the model. Forecasting tests are presented in the fifth section, followed by forecasts of Texas economic and population growth in the sixth section. The final section summarizes the major results of the chapter and discusses implications for future work.

Overall Structure of the Model

The Texas Economic-Demographic Forecasting Model is made up of approximately 300 simultaneous equations and identities and includes about 300 endogenous variables and 100 exogenous variables. The structure of the equations is derived from economic theory and practical considerations; they are estimated on annual time-series data for the period 1960–78.

The main idea behind the model is that the relative attractiveness of Texas to people and business determines its long-run growth. The relative attractiveness of Texas to people (in terms of wages, the availability of jobs, and environmental conditions in the state compared to the rest of the country) determines population migration, which is combined with births and deaths to give the state's population and its potential labor force. The relative attractiveness of Texas to business (as measured by access to markets and the costs of doing business) determines investment in the state, which then gives the state's capital stock and its capacity to produce.

This supply-side approach to modeling the Texas economy is quite different from the typical demand-oriented regional econometric model that concentrates on relationships between national demands and regional production.[1] A supply-side model is superior to the demand-oriented approach for modeling the long-run growth of a fast-growing, industrializing economy like Texas'. However, since this model does not concentrate on modeling short-term economic fluctuations in the Texas economy over the business cycle, it may be less useful for short-run forecasting (i.e., up to two years) than demand-oriented models.

Submodels and Industrial/Demographic Detail

The Texas model is made up of four interacting submodels (see figure 4–1). The demographic submodel determines population migration, births, deaths, and population for 32 age-sex groups and 6 broad age groups. The manufacturing submodel determines manufacturing investment and manufacturing activity (i.e., capital stock, manhours, and output) for 10 industries. The production submodel gives gross product for 11 economic sectors and 3 mining industries. The labor-market submodel gives employment and wages for 10 manufacturing industries, 3 mining industries, and 10 nonagricultural economic sectors; in addition, it determines personal income by source. The industrial and demographic details maintained in TEDFM are listed in table 4–1.

Causal Process in the Model

The causal process can be outlined as follows. First, the relative attractiveness of Texas determines population migration on one hand, and manufacturing investment on the other. The model focuses on manufacturing investment (which is only part of total investment in Texas) because manufacturing is highly mobile across regions and because of the availability of good capital expenditures data from the Census of Manufacturers and the Annual Survey of Manufactures.

Second, population migration is combined with births and deaths to give the state's population and its age-sex structure.

Third, manufacturing investment is summed to give productive capacity (i.e., capital stock) by industry. The capital stock in each industry, along with national demands for Texas production, then determines manhours and output through a production-function framework.

Fourth, nonmanufacturing production by major economic sector is determined. Agricultural and mining production are linked to Texas' resource base and to national and world demands. Output in construction, service-producing sectors, and state and local government are tied to the overall level of Texas activity as measured by gross product, personal income, and/or population. Federal civilian and military activity in Texas is given by federal policy and thus is exogenous to the model.

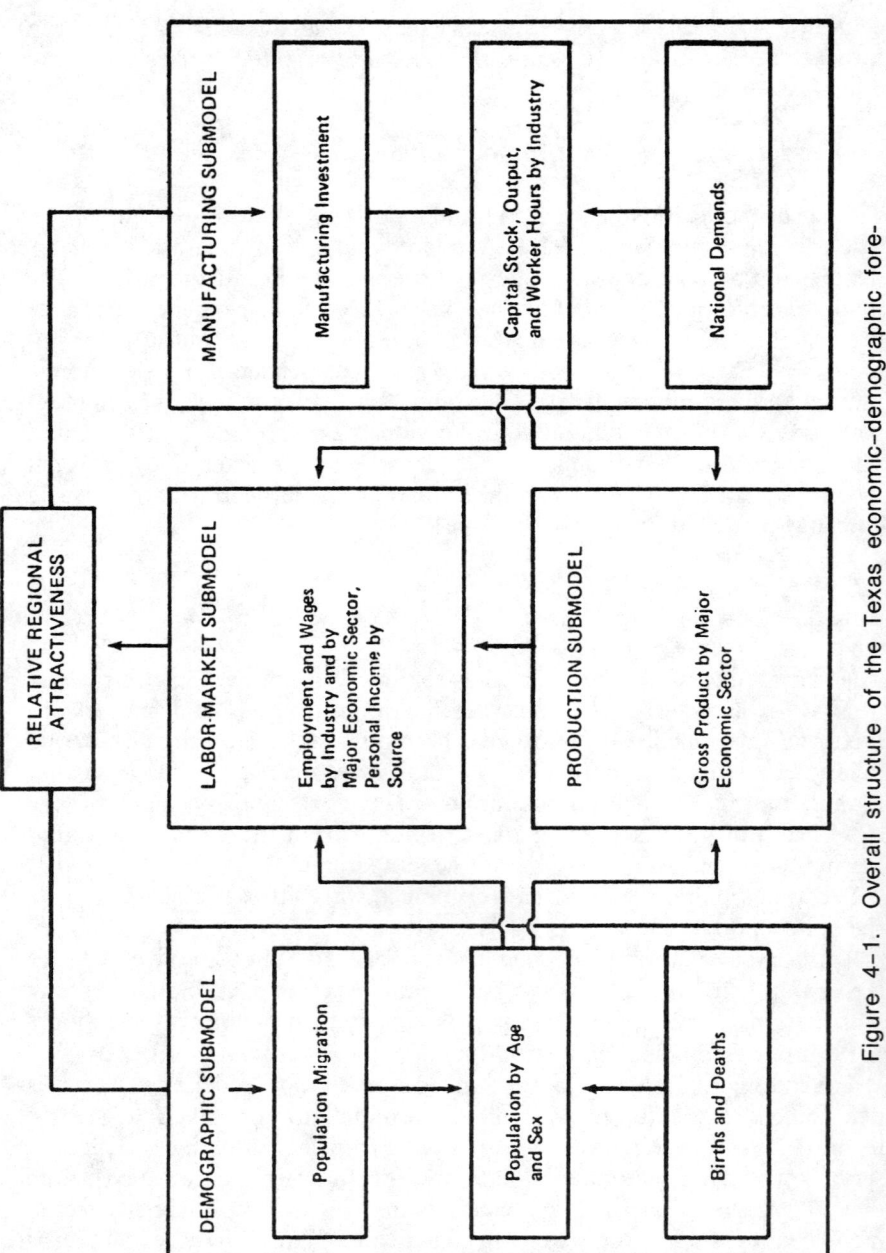

Figure 4-1. Overall structure of the Texas economic-demographic forecasting model

Table 4-1. Industrial and Demographic Detail Maintained in the Texas Economic-Demographic Forecasting Model

Industrial Detail

Major Economic Sectors
Agriculture
Mining
Construction
Nondurable manufacturing
Durable manufacturing
Transportation and public utilities
Wholesale and retail trade
Finance, insurance, and real estate
Services
Federal government (civilian and military)
State and local government

Mining Industries
Oil and gas fields
Oil and gas services
Other mining

Manufacturing Industries
Food and kindred products
Paper and pulp products
Petroleum and chemicals
Other nondurables
Primary metals
Fabricated metals
Nonelectrical machinery
Electronics
Transportation equipment
Other durables

Demographic Detail

32 Age-Sex Groups
Males 0-4, 5-9,..., 75 and over
Females 0-4, 5-9,..., 75 and over

Broad Age Groups
Age 0-4   Age 45-64
Age 5-17   Age 65 and over
Age 18-44   Age 16 and over

Fifth, the supply of and the demand for labor interact in the labor-market submodel to give employment and income by industry and sector. The supply of labor is mainly a function of Texas' population and its age structure, and the demand for labor is determined mainly by the level of production. Two variables link the supply of and the demand for labor— namely, the wage rate and the level of job availability.

Finally, many of the variables determined in the labor-market submodel feed back into the state's relative attractiveness vector. These variables include the state's wage rate and job availability, which determine population migration, and Texas personal income, which determines manufacturing investment (because of the growth in markets).

Population Determination

The demographic submodel produces estimates of the population for 32 age-sex groups (males and females aged 0–4, 5–9, ..., 75+) through a cohort birth-aging-migration routine. The 32 age-sex population estimates are then combined into population estimates for 6 broad age groups (0–4, 5–17, 18–44, 45–64, 65+, and 16+), which are used extensively throughout the rest of the model.

For each age-sex group, the population in the current year (POP) is equal to the survived population from the previous year ($SPOP$) plus net migration (NM)

$$POP_{i,j,t} = SPOP_{i,j,t} + NM_{i,j,t} \qquad (4.1)$$

where $i = 1, 2$ for males and females, and $j = 1, \ldots, 16$ for the 16 age groups. In the case of the youngest age groups (males and females 0–4), live births are also added.[2]

The survived population is determined by applying Texas-specific one-year survival rates to the previous year's population by age and sex.[3,4] Because the survival rates are Texas-specific, they implicitly include the effect of the state's large Mexican-American population in the aging-death process.

Birth and Net Migration Equations

The major stochastic equations in the demographic submodel determine Texas births and total net civilian migration into the state. In the birth equation, the Texas birth rate is related to the U.S. birth rate and a

Table 4-2. Birth Rate Equation[a]

U.S. birth rate	1.044
	(28.62)
Net migration–current	3.758
	(2.61)
Lagged one year	3.856
	(5.15)
Lagged two years	2.680
	(3.27)
Lagged three years	.968
	(1.78)
Lagged four years	−.541
	(0.75)
Lagged five years	−1.110
	(1.34)
Constant	.070
	(.93)
$\bar{R}^2$	.99
DW	1.20

[a]The birth rate used here is the number of total births in year t divided by the total population in year $t-1$. The figures in parentheses are t-values of the regression coefficients.

polynomial-distributed lag on past Texas net migration rates (table 4–2). The Texas birth rate closely follows the U.S. birth rate because of similar fertility trends. No attempt is made to model Texas fertility directly because fertility is an extremely complex and not well-understood process. Two recent fertility models, Butz and Ward (1979) and Easterlin, Wachter, and Wachter (1978), for example, have predicted directly opposite shifts in national fertility trends over the next 10 to 20 years. The Texas birth equation, however, allows one to simulate the effects of alternative projections of the U.S. birth rate (which are based on alternative fertility scenarios) on Texas population growth and on the overall state economy.

A third-degree Almon lag on past-net migration rates captures the effect of young inmigrating couples increasing the Texas birth rate (Alonso 1980). A five-year lag was found to work best.

The Texas net migration equation is based on the hypothesis that migrants respond to labor-market and environmental conditions in the state relative to the country. The response, however, is expected to occur with a lag because of the monetary and psychic costs of moving.

Labor-market conditions in Texas relative to the country are summarized by the ratio of "expected incomes." Expected income, as proposed by Todaro (1969, 1976), is a function of two separate variables—the real wage rate and the probability of finding employment. The real wage rate is measured by the money wage rate deflated by the consumer price index. The probability of finding employment is measured by the Conference Board's index of help-wanted advertising divided by an index of the number of unemployed. This measure is a proxy for vacancies-over-unemployment.

The vacancy-to-unemployment ratio is a superior measure of job availability than the often-used unemployment rate because an excess demand for labor will be translated largely into job vacancies once the unemployment rate is pushed down to frictional levels. This consideration is especially important in low-unemployment, fast-growing regions like Texas. For Texas, job vancancies are proxied by a weighted average of the help-wanted index for Dallas, Houston, and San Antonio. For the United States, a weighted average of the index for 51 cities is used. More information on the Conference Board's help-wanted index can be found in Preston (1977).

In contrast to labor-market conditions, environmental conditions in Texas relative to the United States change relatively slowly, over time, or not at all, so any constant relative attractiveness of Texas should be captured in the constant term of the migration equation. Even though environmental conditions change slowly over time, however, people may become increasingly responsive to these conditions in deciding where to move because of rising incomes, increasing leisure time, and the increasing desire to live in amenity-rich areas (Chalmers and Greenwood 1977; Graves 1980; Porell 1982). This effect is captured by including U.S. real per capita income in the migration equation.

The estimated equation for net civilian migration into Texas is shown in table 4-3.

The use of the lagged civilian population of Texas captures a particular lagged-adjustment process. See Plaut (1981) for more details on the specification of the migration model and the dynamics of the adjustment process.[5]

Total net migration is obtained by adding net civilian migration and net military growth.

Migration by Age and Sex

Once total net migration into Texas is determined, it needs to be broken into migration by age and sex in order to determine the age-sex composition of

Table 4-3. Texas Net Migration Equation[a]

Relative real wage rate	.076
	(1.05)
Relative vacancy-to-unemployment ratio	.027
	(3.16)
U.S. real per capita income	.020
	(1.15)
Lagged civilian population	−.092
	(2.33)
Constant	.706
	(2.27)
$\bar{R}^2$	.81
DW	2.03

[a]The dependant variable is the logarithm of one plus the net civilian migration rate. The figures in parentheses are t-values of the regression coefficients.

the population (equation 4.1). One way to do this would be to attempt to apply fixed age-sex migration proportions to total net migration. However, a simple comparison of the Texas age-sex migration proportions for the 1950s (Bowles and Tarver 1965) to those for the 1960s (Bowles, Beale, and Lee 1975) indicates that the proportions are extremely unstable from one period to the next. Even when the age-sex distributions of in- and outmigrants are very close to each other and very stable over time (and both of these conditions appear to be true based on an examination of census migration data), small changes in the level of inmigration and/or outmigration can lead to large changes in the age-sex composition of net migration. Thus, in order to obtain more accurate estimates of net migration by age and sex, estimated net migration is broken into inmigration and outmigration and the age-sex compositions of the inflows and outflows are computed separately.

The theoretical construct underlying the disaggregation of net migration into inmigration and outmigration is the Lowry (1966) push-pull theory of migration, which holds that outmigration is determined mainly by the demographic composition of the population, whereas inmigration is determined mainly by economic opportunities in the region. Most migration research since Lowry has found that this conclusion may be too restrictive and that after controlling for the population's propensity to migrate, outmigration is also related to regional economic conditions (Miller 1973). Still, the push of the demographic composition of the population, especially a high concentration of relatively young and highly mobile persons, appears to predominate in determining regional outmigration, and the pull of economic opportunities predominates in determining inmigration (Greenwood 1973, 1975; Fields 1979).

Texas Test. A small test of the validity of the Lowry push-pull theory of migration for Texas can be made by comparing Census of Population state migration data for 1955–60 to those for 1965–70. From 1955–60 to 1965–70, net migration into Texas increased from −28,100 to 138,800. From one period to the next, inmigration into the state increased from 682,400 to 915,200 (8.5 percent to 9.4 percent), while outmigration increased from 710,500 to 776,400 (8.9 percent to 8.0 percent). A comparison of the inmigration and outmigration rates for the two periods thus indicates that the increase in net inmigration into the state is accomplished by both an increase in the inmigration rate and a decline in the outmigration rate. However, 79 percent of the decline in the Texas outmigration rate from 1955–60 to 1965–70 can be predicted by applying Texas age-sex specific outmigration rates to the state's 1965 population by age and sex.

Texas' population in 1965 was relatively older than in 1955, and this appears to be responsible for most of the decline in the outmigration rate from one period to the next. On the other hand, economic growth in the state was much stronger during 1965–70 than 1955–60 (the differential between Texas and U.S. employment growth increased from 3.5 percent to 7.7 percent), which probably is the cause of most of the increase in inmigration. In this limited test, the Lowry push-pull theory of migration appears to be strongly verified.

Calculations. Specifically, Texas net migration is disaggregated into inmigration and outmigration by age and sex through the following set of calculations.

Outmigration by age and sex (*OM*) is determined by applying fixed one-year outmigration rates (*omr*) to the previous-year's population by age and sex:

$$OM_{i,j,t} = omr_{i,j} \cdot POP_{i,j,t-1} \qquad (4.2)$$

Outmigration rates are obtained from the 1965–70 Texas migration data in the 1970 Census of Population.

Inmigration by age and sex (*IM*) is determined by (1) adding up outmigration by age and sex to get total outmigration, (2) adding total net migration to outmigration to obtain total inmigration, and (3) applying fixed inmigration probabilities (*imp*) to total inmigration and the proportion of the U.S. population in each age-sex group:

$$IM_{i,j,t} = \left(NM_t + \sum_{i=1}^{2} \sum_{j=1}^{16} OM_{i,j,t} \right) \cdot imp_{ij} \cdot \left[\frac{POPUS_{i,j,t}}{POPUS_t} \right] \quad (4.3)$$

The inmigration probabilities are also obtained from the 1965–70 Texas migration data in the 1970 Census of Population and represent the proportion of inmigrants in each age-sex group relative to the proportion of the U.S. population. The use of these inmigration probabilities rather than fixed inmigration proportions allows the age-sex composition of inmigration to shift as the demographic composition of the U.S. population changes.

Demographic-Economic Linkages

Other population linkages in the Texas model can be grouped into those that affect labor demand and those that affect labor supply. Labor demand, as measured by jobs or desired employment, and labor supply, measured by the labor force, then interact in the labor-market submodel to determine the Texas vacancy-to-unemployment ratio, which feeds back to affect net migration into the state.

Demand-Side Linkages

Texas' total population and its school-age population indirectly affect labor demand through a number of linkages. Dividends, interest, and rents and transfer payments are determined on a per capita basis because these income sources flow directly to people. Total state personal income is then determined by adding dividends, interest, and rents and transfer payments to wages and salaries and other sources of nonwage income.

Personal income is a key measure of the size of the Texas market and the demand for regionally produced goods and services throughout the model. Texas personal income affects manufacturing investment in the state as firms expand to serve fast-growing markets. The sum of investment flows over time then determines the manufacturing capital stock by industry. Industry output, manhours, and jobs are related to the capital stock and to national demands for Texas output through a production-function framework.

Texas personal income also affects the output of five regionally oriented sectors: construction; transportation and public utilities; finance, insurance, and real estate; trade; and services. The level of output in these sectors is then the major determinant of the demand for labor.

State education expenditures and local education expenditures depend in part on the size of the school-age population (5–17). Similarly, the total population is a major determinant of state expenditures in areas other than education and local noneducation expenditures. Total state and local government expenditures determine state and local government output, which is the major determinant of this sector's demand for labor.

Supply-Side Linkages

In contrast to labor demand, the linkages between Texas population and labor supply are direct. The Texas labor force participaton rate (LFP), which is defined as the labor force divided by the civilian population 16 and over, is related to: (1) the real wage rate; (2) the vacancy-to-unemployment ratio; (3) a time trend capturing the increasing participation of women in the labor force; and (4) the proportion of the civilian population in prime working ages. The results are shown in table 4-4. The logistic dependent variable, $\log[LFP/(0.75 - LFP)]$, captures the acceleration in the Texas

Table 4-4. Labor Force Participation Rate Equation[a]

Real wage rate	.543
	(.52)
Vacancy-to-unemployment ratio	.112
	(1.74)
Time trend	.026
	(3.72)
Proportion of civilian population in prime working ages	8.278
	(1.69)
Constant	−2.079
	(.24)
$\bar{R}^2$	.88
DW	1.23

[a]The dependent variable is described in the text. All variables are transformed into logarithms. The figures in parentheses are t-values of the regression coefficients.

labor-force participation rate in the 1970s, which is due mainly to the increasing participation of women in the labor force. The rate of increase in the labor-force participation rate, however, is expected to slow in the future and level out at 75 percent as the participation rate of women approaches that of men.

Labor Market Interactions

The key linkage between the demand for labor and labor supply is the Texas vacancy-to-unemployment ratio. It is determined by: (1) the ratio of Texas jobs to the labor force; (2) U.S. vendor performance, which acts as a leading indicator of business cycle conditions;[6] and (3) the lagged Texas vacancy-to-unemployment ratio. One would also expect that the Texas wage rate is related to the demand and supply for labor because wage rates are bid up in a tight labor market, but a significant relationship could not be found. The actual equation used is shown in table 4-5.

The growth rate in the Texas (money) wage rate relative to that of the United States is related to the growth rate in Texas productivity (current dollar output per employee) relative to U.S. productivity and the growth rate in the Texas consumer price index relative to the U.S. index.[7] When the Texas vacancy-to-unemployment ratio relative to the U.S. ratio was added to this equation to measure the excess demand for labor in Texas relative to the U.S. demand, its coefficient was small and insignificant—probably because many of the symptoms of a tight labor market are picked up by the productivity growth and price growth variables. A fast-growing economy

Table 4-5. Vacancy-to-Unemployment Ratio Equation[a]

Ratio of jobs to the labor force	2.594
	(2.48)
U.S. vendor performance	.696
	(3.84)
Lagged ratio	.559
	(4.11)
Constant	−2.251
	(2.78)
$\bar{R}^2$	.90
DW	1.30

[a] All variables are expressed in logarithms.

typically experiences not only a tight labor market but also rapid productivity growth and rapid growth in consumer prices.

Forecasting Accuracy

The major test of the forecasting accuracy of the model is a dynamic in-sample simulation of the model from 1961 to 1978. Out-of-sample tests of the model are not possible because accurate measures of many of the endogenous variables, such as manufacturing investment and gross product, are available only through 1978 or 1979. However, since the model has proved to be very stable in various forecasting applications, it is probably a useful forecasting tool.

The mean absolute percentage errors (MAPE) in model predictions of aggregate Texas variables such as gross product, personal income, nonagricultural employment, and population in the in-sample simulation are all around 1 percent. The MAPE for Texas gross product is 1.14 percent, and the MAPE for population is 1.02 percent. These error statistics compare favorably to the forecast errors from other regional econometric models and are well below the 3 percent level that Glickman (1977, p. 68) suggests is acceptable for regional models.

Population by Age

Errors in predicting population in the six broad age groups are shown in table 4-6. As expected, the errors in forecasting population by age are larger than those in forecasting total population. (Many of the errors in forecasting population by age cancel out when the estimates are summed to calculate total population and the population over 16.) The errors stem from two sources: the first is errors in predicting Texas' total births and net migration, the major inputs into the cohort-component, demographic model from the stochastic equations; the second is errors in the cohort-component, demographic model in producing the age-group estimates.

When exact figures for births and net migration are fed into the cohort-component, demographic model, the errors in predicted population by age are similar to those in the fully dynamic simulation: the mean absolute percentage error for the population 0 to 4 is 3.33 percent; for the population 5 to 17 it is 2.83 percent; for 18 to 44, 1.67 percent; for 45 to 64, 1.72 percent; and for the population over 65 it is 1.70 percent. Thus,

Table 4-6. Mean Absolute Percentage Errors in Forecasting Population by Age and the Components of Change, Dynamic In-Sample Simulation for 1961-78

Variable	MAPE (%)
Population 0–4	3.36
Population 5–17	3.29
Population 18–44	1.78
Population 45–64	1.71
Population 65+	1.68
Population 16+	0.93
Births	2.31
Deaths	3.09
Net migration	90.90

most of the error in forecasting population by age appears to be caused by the second source, the cohort-component, demographic model.

Why the cohort-component, demographic model does not reproduce the Census Bureau estimates of population by broad age group more closely is difficult to determine. Part of the difference between the two sets of population figures probably results from the estimation of migration by age. The model breaks total net migration into migration by age essentially by using 1965–70 inmigration and outmigration data. If the model misallocates migration by age, it may consistently underestimate or overestimate the population in some age groups, but generally this does not seem to be a problem (see table 4–7).

A tendency does exist for the model to overpredict the population 0 to 4 and underpredict the population 65 and over with increasing bias during the 1970s. The model may allocate too much migration to the youngest age groups and too little migration to the older groups. Until migration information from the 1980 *Census of Population* becomes available, however, it is not possible to integrate more accurate estimates of migration, by age, into the model.

Population Components of Change

Table 4–6 shows the errors in predicting the components of population change—births, deaths, and net migration. The forecast errors in predicting births and deaths are relatively small, but the error in predicting net

Table 4-7. Percentage Error of Predicted Population by Age, In-Sample Simulation, 1961-78

Year	Population Age Groups				
	0-4	5-17	18-44	45-64	65+
1961	−0.5	−0.0	0.8	0.3	−0.4
1962	−1.9	−1.2	−0.2	0.2	−0.3
1963	−2.1	−1.6	0.9	0.5	0.2
1964	−2.6	−2.4	2.3	0.8	0.7
1965	−2.7	−1.8	1.4	1.0	1.7
1966	−1.8	−2.4	1.0	0.8	1.3
1967	−0.7	−3.9	−0.6	0.3	1.2
1968	−1.3	−6.2	−1.4	−1.4	−0.1
1969	−0.7	−7.7	−0.1	−2.7	−0.7
1970	3.1	−7.7	0.7	−3.3	−0.6
1971	3.2	−6.2	0.9	−3.0	−1.3
1972	3.2	−5.2	1.1	−2.9	−1.7
1973	2.5	−4.3	2.4	−2.8	−2.1
1974	3.6	−3.0	3.8	−2.5	−2.4
1975	5.9	−1.9	3.9	−2.3	−3.1
1976	8.7	−1.7	3.9	−2.3	−3.5
1977	8.9	−1.2	3.8	−1.9	−4.2
1978	7.3	−0.9	2.9	−1.7	−4.9

migration is large, around 90 percent. This large error is due to two factors: net migration is extremely volatile from year to year and thus is difficult to track, and net migration is measured with large error because much of the error in the Census Bureau's annual population estimates is transferred into the estimates of net migration by year (Isserman, Plane, and McMillen 1982; Plaut 1979, pp. 6-8).

Even though net migration is forecast with a large error, the overall trends in net migration into Texas from 1961 to 1978 are captured in the simulation (figure 4-2). The main trend is the movement from small net outmigration during 1961 to 1967 to large net inmigration during 1968-78. The model does miss the shift from net outmigration to net inmigration by two years (1970 instead of 1968), however, and overpredicts net migration into the state for the next five years to compensate.

The trend in the overall population growth of the state is captured quite well (see table 4-8). The error in predicting total population is small, despite the error in net migration.

ECONOMIC-DEMOGRAPHIC INTERACTIONS IN TEXAS' GROWTH

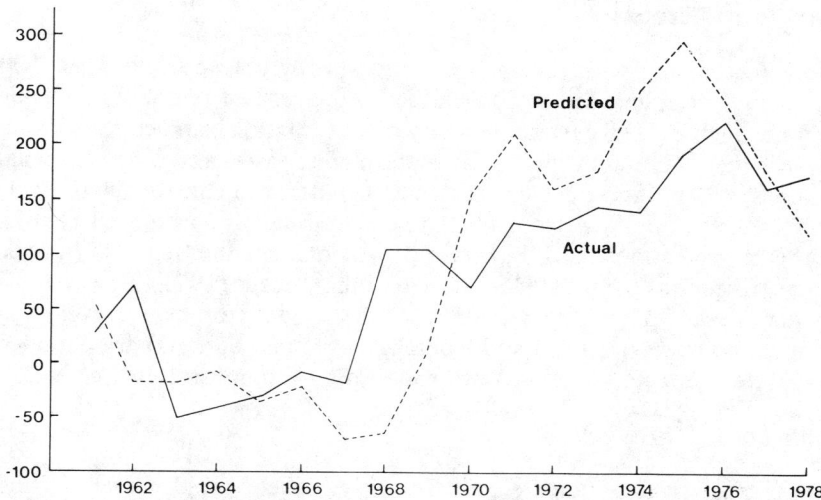

Figure 4-2. Actual (solid line) and predicted (dashed line) net migration into Texas, 1961-78

Table 4-8. Actual Versus Predicted Values for Total Population (Thousands), 1961-78

	Actual	*Predicted*	*% Error*
1961	9820	9842	0.2
1962	10053	9992	-0.6
1963	10159	10134	-0.2
1964	10270	10277	0.1
1965	10378	10380	0.0
1966	10492	10486	-0.1
1967	10599	10532	-0.6
1968	10819	10573	-2.3
1969	11045	10689	-3.2
1970	11244	10962	-2.5
1971	11510	11304	-1.8
1972	11759	11590	-1.4
1973	12019	11879	-1.2
1974	12268	12246	-0.2
1975	12568	12669	0.8
1976	12903	13046	1.1
1977	13192	13356	1.2
1978	13498	13606	0.8

Long-Term Forecasts

Before forecasting with the model, forecasts for the approximately 100 exogenous variables need to be obtained. Forecasts of national economic variables such as (1) wages, availability of jobs, markets, and costs of doing business; (2) manufacturing investment, interest rates, and other financial variables; (3) inflation and prices; and (4) demand and business cycle conditions are obtained from the Data Resources, Incorporated (1982), long-term projections. U.S. birthrate projections are the Series II (middle range) projections from the U.S. Bureau of the Census (1977). Forecasts of the few Texas exogenous variables in the model (for example, energy production and agricultural and federal government outputs) are obtained from state agency sources and or produced by judgmental projections.

Major Forecast Results

The forecast results indicate that Texas' relatively rapid economic and population growth will continue over the next 20 years, with the state's real gross product reaching $235.5 billion (in 1972 $) and its population reaching 22.3 million in the year 2000 (table 4–9).

Texas will continue to grow much faster than the nation, but its rate of economic growth over the next 20 years is expected to be somewhat slower than the extremely high growth rates established in the 1970s. Texas' real gross product is forecast to grow 4.5 percent per year from 1980 to 2000, a significant reduction from the 5.6 percent annual growth rate experienced during the 1970s.

Texas' population, on the other hand, is forecast to grow at about the same rate over the next two decades (2.3 percent per year) as during the 1970s (2.4 percent per year).

Three factors contribute to the slowdown in Texas economic growth over the 20 years: (1) the current national recession and the expectation of generally slow national economic and population growth over the next two decades; (2) the increased importance of cyclically sensitive manufacturing industries in Texas and a projected slowdown in the rate of manufacturing expansion in the state: and (3) the expectation of generally flat (real) world oil prices over the first half of the 1980s and a moderate rate of growth in oil prices thereafter.

Population Growth

Net migration into Texas is expected to remain high throughout the forecast period. Migration into the state, however, will decline from 1981 to

Table 4-9. Texas and U.S. Gross Product and Population, 1960–2000

	Historical			Forecast		Average Annual Growth Rate (%)			
Variable	1960	1970	1980	1990	2000	1960–70	1970–80	1980–90	1990–2000
Gross product (billions of 72$)									
Texas	36.8	57.5	99.2	153.8	235.5	4.6	5.6	4.5	4.4
United States	737.2	1085.6	1480.9	1947.9	2459.0	4.0	3.2	2.8	2.4
Texas/U.S.	0.050	0.053	0.067	0.079	0.096	1.2	1.8	1.6	1.8
Population (millions)									
Texas	9.6	11.2	14.2	17.8	22.3	1.6	2.4	2.3	2.3
United States	180.7	204.9	226.5	247.8	264.7	1.3	1.0	0.9	0.7
Texas/U.S.	0.053	0.055	0.063	0.072	0.086	1.2	2.4	2.6	3.6

Source: Texas Economic-Demographic Forecasting Model and Data Resources, Incorporated (1982).

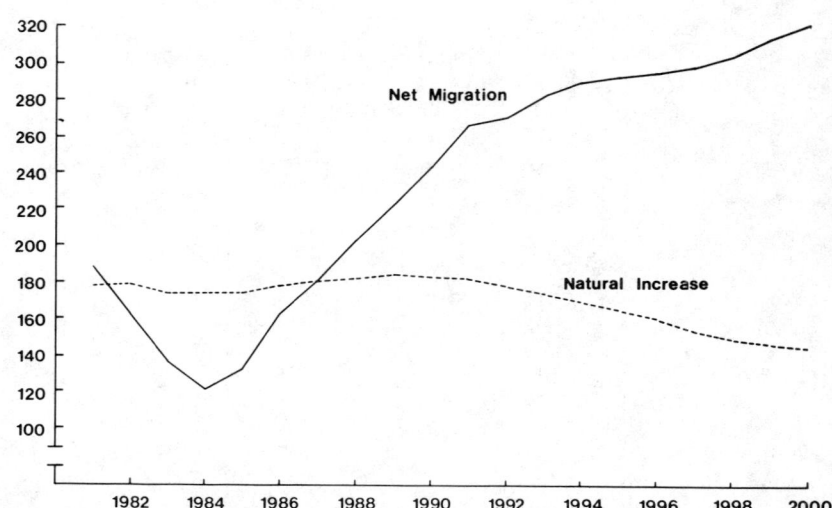

Figure 4-3. Forecasted net migration and natural increase in Texas, 1981-2001

1984, and then begin increasing (figure 4-3). The slowdown in migration into Texas during the first half of the 1980s is due to relatively slow state economic growth (due mainly to flat oil prices) and the national recovery from recession. As the economic growth of Texas relative to the United States increases in the mid-1980s, migration into Texas begins increasing.

Natural increase (births minus deaths) in Texas is forecast to remain fairly constant during the 1980s and then begin declining in the 1990s as the birth rate declines and women of child-bearing age grow older.

Most of Texas' population growth over the next 20 years will be caused by migration from other states. During the 1980s, 49 percent of Texas population growth will be due to migration (the rest will be due to natural increase), but during the 1990s 64 percent will be due to migration.

The population forecast of 22.3 million for the year 2000 falls roughly in the middle of projections made by others. The U.S. Bureau of the Census (1979) projects a 2000 population of 17.4 million, and the U.S. Bureau of Economic Analysis (1981), 18.8 million. The Texas Department of Water Resources (1981) predicts 21.2 million; the Texas 2000 Project (Young 1982) suggests 22.0 million; and the Texas Department of Health (McClellan 1982) projects 26.8 million.

The high inmigration of young adults into Texas will increase the proportion of the state's population in the prime working ages of 18 to 64. This proportion is projected to increase from 60.1 percent in 1980 to 62.4

percent in the year 2000. The declining birth rate will lead to a decreasing proportion of Texas' population who are children (0 to 17 years old): from 30.3 percent in 1980 to 26.5 percent in 2000. Finally, because Texas already has a relatively young population and because retirement migration into the state is relatively unimportant, the proportion of Texas' population over 65 is expected to decrease slightly from 9.6 percent in 1980 to 9.2 percent in 2000. (In contrast, the proportion of the U.S. population over 65 is projected to increase from 11.3 percent to 12.2 percent over the next 20 years [U.S. Bureau of the Census 1977]).

Conclusion

The Texas model fairly accurately quantifies the strong interaction of economic and demographic variables in the growth of Texas. It is a useful tool for forecasting future state economic and population growth, but there are at least two parts of the model that can be improved and strengthened.

First, more research needs to be devoted to identifying the sources of inaccuracy in the cohort-component, demographic model estimates of population by age and sex. The most likely source of error is in the misallocation of migration by age. When the migration data from the 1980 Census of Population become available, major shifts in migration by age from 1965–70 to 1975–80 will become apparent. This new information will be valuable in recalibrating the model.

Second, the demand linkages between population and economic activity in the model probably need to be strengthened. Currently the dominant regional demand variable is personal income, but perhaps population, population in certain age groups, and/or labor force could also be included in the equations for regionally oriented output. Future work will be focused on identifying these linkages.

Notes

1. For a review of regional econometric models, see Olson, Plaut, and Holt (1980).
2. Total births are broken into births by sex by using the fixed proportions of 51.2 percent male and 48.8 percent female.
3. Texas survival rates for 1960 and 1970 are taken from the Texas life tables published by the National Center for Health Statistics (1965, 1975). Survival rates for 1961 to 1969 were developed through a linear interpolation of the 1960 and 1970 rates. Texas survival rates for 1971 to 2000 were developed by using the ratio of Texas to U.S. survival rates in 1970 and projected U.S. rates for 1980, 1990, and 2000 from the U.S. Bureau of the Census (1977).

4. After surviving the five-year age-sex groups one year, it is necessary to reallocate the resulting groups (i.e., males 1–5, males 6– 10, etc.) back to the standard groups (males 0–4, males 5–9, etc.). This is done by using fixed single-year, age-sex proportions from the 1970 Texas life table.

5. The migration equation reported here is a bit different from the one reported in Plaut (1981). The difference between the two equations is due to two differences in the net migration data. First, the equation in this chapter is estimated on July-to-July net migration data, while the equation in the earlier one was estimated on smoothed January-to-January data. Second, and more important, the migration equation in this chapter is estimated on revised migration data for the 1970s. The revised migration data were developed from revised Texas population estimates that are consistent with the 1980 census population count and are much higher than the earlier migration estimates.

6. The vendor performance variable measures the percentage of Chicago-area purchasing agents experiencing slower deliveries. When this measure falls, deliveries are faster because new orders and business activity, in general, are down.

7. The Texas wage rate is related to the U.S. wage rate because the threat of migration and interregional information flows tend to keep the state wage rate competitive with the national rate. See Adams, Brooking, and Glickman (1975), Glickman (1977, p. 88), and Milne, Glickman, and Adams (1981) for similar specifications of the regional-national linkage.

References

Adams, F. G.; Brooking, C. G.; and Glickman, N. J. 1975. On the specification and simulation of a regional econometric model: a model of Mississippi. *Review of Economics and Statistics* 57: 286–98.

Alonso, W. 1980. Population as a system in regional development. *American Economic Review, Papers and Proceedings* 70: 405–9.

Bowles, G. K.; Beale, C. L.; and Lee, E. S. 1975. *Net migration of the population, 1960–1970, by age, sex, and color.* Part 5—West South Central States. Washington, D.C.: Economic Research Service, U.S. Department of Agriculture.

Bowles, G. K., and Tarver, J. D. 1965. *Net migration of the population, 1950–60, by age, sex, and color.* Volume I, Part 5—West South Central States. Washington, D.C.: Economic Research Service, U.S. Department of Agriculture.

Butz, W. P., and Ward, M. P. 1979. The emergence of countercyclical U.S. fertility. *American Economic Review* 69: 318–28.

Chalmers, J. A., and Greenwood, M. J. 1977. Thoughts on the rural to urban migration turnaround. *International Regional Science Review* 2: 167–70.

Data Resources, Incorporated. 1982. *U.S. long-term review.* Spring.

Easterlin, R. A.; Wachter, M. L.; and Wachter, S. M. 1978. Demographic influences on economic stability: the United States experience. *Population and Development Review* 4: 1–22.

Fields, G. S. 1979. Place-to-place migration: some new evidence. *Review of Economics and Statistics* 61: 21–32.

Glickman, N. J. 1977. *Econometric analysis of regional systems.* New York: Academic Press.

Graves, P. E. 1980. Migration and climate. *Journal of Regional Science* 20: 227–37.

Greenwood, M. J. 1973. Urban economic growth and migration: their interaction. *Environment and Planning A* 5: 91–112.

_____. 1975. A simultaneous-equation model of urban growth and migration. *Journal of the American Statistical Association* 70: 797–810.

Isserman, A. M.; Plane, D. A.; and McMillen, D. B. 1982. Internal Migration in the United States: an evaluation of federal data. *Review of Public Data Use* 10: 285–311.

Lowry, I. S. 1966. *Migration and metropolitan growth: two analytical models.* San Francisco: Chandler Publishing Company.

McClellan, L. 1982. *Personal communication.*

Miller, E. 1973. Is out-migration affected by economic conditions? *Southern Economic Journal* 39: 396–405.

Milne, W. J.; Glickman, N. J.; and Adams, F. G. 1981. A framework for analyzing regional growth and decline: a multiregion econometric model of the United States. *Journal of Regional Science* 20: 173–89.

National Center for Health Statistics. 1965. *State life tables: 1959–61.* Volume II, Numbers 27–51. Washington, D.C.: U.S. Government Printing Office.

_____. 1975. *State life tables: 1969–71.* Volume II, Numbers 27–51. Washington, D.C.: U.S. Government Printing Office.

Olson, J. A.; Plaut, T. R.; and Holt, C. C. 1980. *Survey of regional and energy models.* Austin, TX: Bureau of Business Research, University of Texas.

Plaut, T. R. 1979. Net migration into Texas and its regions: trends and patterns. Research Reports 79-1. Austin, TX: Bureau of Business Research, University of Texas.

_____. 1981. An econometric model for forecasting regional population growth. *International Regional Science Review* 6: 53–70.

Porell, F. W. 1982. Intermetropolitan migration and quality of life. *Journal of Regional Science* 22: 137–158.

Preston, N. L. 1977. *The help-wanted index: technical description and behavioral trends.* New York: Conference Board, Research Report 716.

Texas Department of Water Resources. 1981. *Population projections.* Austin, TX. Mimeo.

Todaro, M. P. 1969. A model of labor migration and urban unemployment in less developed countries. *American Economic Review* 59: 138–48.

_____. 1976. Urban job expansion, induced migration and rising unemployment. *Journal of Development Economics* 3:211–25.

U.S. Bureau of the Census. 1977. Projections of the population of the United States: 1977 to 2050. *Current Population Reports*, Series P-25, No. 704. Washington, D.C.: U.S. Government Printing Office.

_____. 1979. Illustrative projections of state populations by age, race, and sex:

1975 to 2000. *Current Population Reports*, Series P-25, No. 796. Washington, D.C.: U.S. Government Printing Office.

U.S. Bureau of Economic Analysis. 1981. Memorandum to regional projection users. Washington, D.C. Mimeo.

Young, 1982. The future of Texas' population: one scenario. In *Texas past and future: a survey*, pp. 1–19. Austin, TX.: Office of the Governor, Texas 2000 Project.

5 AN ECONOMETRIC-DEMOGRAPHIC MODEL OF NEW YORK STATE

Carol Greenberg and Charles Renfro

The New York State Econometric-Demographic Model (NYEDM) is an initial attempt to integrate the explanation of population change into an econometric model and to specify at least some of the economic implications of this change, taking into account the effects of both the composition and size of the population at each point in time. The specific approach involves linking a demographic cohort survival model to an econometric model of net migration and fully integrating the population and economic sectors into a simultaneous system. The structure of the system not only addresses the issue of whether people follow jobs or jobs people but also measures the impact of changes in the level and composition of population on economic activity by sector.

The chapter has four sections. The first presents a general description of the structure of the model, with an emphasis on the role of population as a determinant of economic activity. The second section discusses the characteristics of the population sector. The third section reviews the in-sample performance of the model and provides some impact simulation results. The final section presents conclusions and indicates directions for further research.

Overview of the Model

The Regional Economics Department of Chase Econometrics has developed 50 quarterly state econometric models. They are part of a set that includes each state, the District of Columbia, and 111 metropolitan areas. All are used to produce regular forecasts and analyses. Each year, for each area, four ten-quarter forecasts are made and two ten-year forecasts. The state models are mutually independent satellite models to the Chase Econometrics quarterly econometric model of the United States. The term "satellite model" refers to a model that takes as given the behavior of a dominating economy, such as that of the United States, and consequently incorporates selected variables referring to this economy in an exogenous explanatory role. As a basis for generating predictions, regional satellite models normally use forecasts of national economic variables provided by a national econometric model.

NYDEM is an enhanced version of the New York state model. Endogenous population and revenue sectors have been added and "other" nonmanufacturing employment has been disaggregated into three subcategories: finance and insurance; construction and real estate; and transportation, communication, public utilities, and mining. Various equations have been estimated or re-estimated in order to integrate better the economic and demographic components of the new models.

Reduced to its bare essentials, the central core of the New York model can be thought of as consisting of four groups of equations, those explaining: (1) employment by industry group, (2) wages by industry group, (3) wage and salary income originating as the product of employment and wages, and (4) nonwage personal income items. Employment and wages are generally explained at the division level. The sum of employment by industry group provides the total employment identity. The sum of wage and nonwage personal income items provides the statement of the personal income identity.

Some idea of the range of equations appearing in the New York State econometric model is provided by figure 5–1. Employment and wages depend upon the level of economic activity, as expressed by indices of production, capacity utilization, and similar variables. However, particularly in the case of manufacturing, employment also depends upon relative business costs. The product side definition includes such demand components as retail sales, new automobile registrations, and housing starts. Financial variables are included in the form of time, thrift, and demand deposits, commercial and business loans, real estate loans, and loans to individuals. The tax sector incorporates an explanation of state

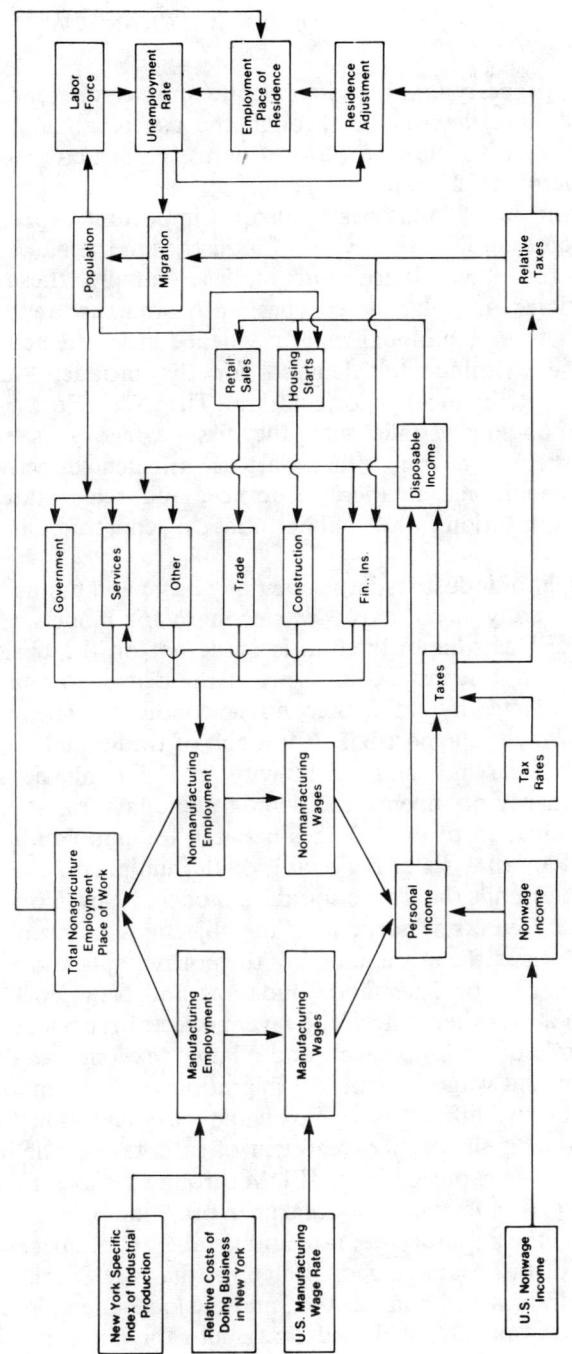

Figure 5-1. Major linkages in the New York economic-demographic model

sales taxes, property taxes, and corporate and personal income taxes, with the last of these determined through the use of an income-distribution matrix in order to allow for the progressive structure of New York's marginal personal tax rates.

The treatment of industries is also an important aspect of the model. There are conceptually two types of industries in the New York model, as well as in the other Chase state models. Initially, these industries are best considered as polar stereotypes: those that are regarded as selling their products in a national market—hence little affected by the degree of domestic (within-state) demand for the product—and those that are fundamentally local in orientation. The New York industry sector that most obviously falls into the first category is manufacturing: however, there are four other sectors affected directly by national economic conditions: finance, insurance, and real estate; communications, transportation, and public utilities; construction; and government.

Such a split of industries into essentially basic and nonbasic categories is a feature of many, if not most, state econometric models. However, in the case of NYEDM, this distinction is made not on the basis of where the product is sold, but instead in terms of the degree to which a particular industry is affected by national economic conditions. The model, therefore, does not follow the export-base approach of traditional regional analysis. Nevertheless, the modeling of activity in the nonbasic sectors, which focuses primarily on income and demographic factors, offers broad scope for an examination of the linkages between the population and economic sectors and an analysis of regional growth multipliers.

NYEDM extends the Chase standard model of New York by including a relatively detailed tax sector. One of the objectives in introducing a revenue sector is to permit the examination of the policy implications of various tax changes on both local demand conditions and New York's relative cost position vis-a-vis other states. The revenue sector represents an attempt to define the role of both tax levels and relative tax loads as determinants of employment and wage growth, net migration, and commuting patterns.

A particularly difficult issue involving the integration of taxes into a regional model is the proper treatment of sales taxes. The impact of sales taxes on prices is captured by NYEDM through the interaction of the sales tax, retail sales, and the local consumer price index. Sales tax revenue is explained by the statutory tax rate and taxable retail sales, which in turn is a function of disposable personal income, the New York consumer price index for durables and nondurables, and the local unemployment rate. The effective sales tax rate then feeds back into the consumer price index to complete the loop. This method insures a simultaneous relationship between tax revenues and local demand.

Another notable feature of the tax sector is the addition of an income-distribution matrix to permit the calculation of New York state personal income tax revenue, given specific marginal tax schedule assumptions. This matrix provides the framework for detailed analysis of the fiscal policy implications of various configurations of income distribution and population growth. For example, since the number of tax returns in each income bracket is linearly related to total population growth in the model, for any given income distribution and level of personal income, the lower the average per capita income, the lower tax liability will be. However, the assumption of a fixed-income distribution can be relaxed in any subsequent use of the model, thus broadening the scope for an examination of the revenue and general economic effects of differential population growth across income classes.

The full integration of the population and economic models in NYDEM involves a respecification of the labor-force sector of the core model. The total number of persons unemployed is calculated as the product of population and the ratio of total unemployed to population; the stochastic equation for this ratio is shown in table 5–1. The labor force is explained as the sum of the unemployed and total resident employment. From both table 5–1 and figure 5–1, it should be evident that this explanation of the civilian labor force and unemployment forms an important connection between the population and econometric models.

In the original design of the model, the labor force was to be explained by a participation rate equation, with the total unemployed then obtained as the differences between the labor force and (residence adjusted) total

Table 5–1. Equation for the Number of Unemployed[a]

Proportion of population in labor force age	17.91
	(29.27)
Employment to population ratio	−7.15
	(14.99)
Payroll to residential employment ratio	−5.22
	(2.87)
Constant	−0.81
	(3.02)
R^2	.95

[a]The dependent variable is the proportion of the population that is unemployed. Figures in parentheses are t-values of the regression coefficients.

employment. However, this participation-rate formulation resulted in sample-period simulations in which the unemployment rate was found to be much too low in many periods and even negative in some periods. The problem with this type of specification is well known: the subtraction of one large magnitude variable from another during simulations can be expected to result in a set of much smaller (residual) values that exhibit a much lower-signal-to-noise ratio than either of the large magnitude variables.

A particularly significant aspect of the combined system is the degree to which population and its components have been integrated into explanation of economic behavior. Population enters explicitly into three employment equations: government, services, and the aggregate category of transportation, communications, public utilities, and mining ("Other"). These equations are among those that play a particularly important role in the integration of the demographic and econometric portions of the model, and they are shown in table 5–2.

In both the government and services employment equations, population appears in a cohort-share variable. A large component of government employment is education-related, so government employment can be expected to be positively related to the relative growth of the school-aged population. Similarly, growth in demand for health services, which comprised 24 percent of services employment in 1980, can be expected to be positively related to the relative growth in the population 65 and over. The population scale effect is accounted for in both equations by stating them in per capita form.

Population plays a slightly different role in the third equation. Essentially, it modifies the relationship between Other Employment in New York and the roughly analogous national employment category. Holding both productivity and population shares constant, Other Employment in New York grows more slowly than it does nationwide, as indicated by the cumulated estimated elasticity of 0.37. The decline in New York's Other Employment from 508,600 in 1970 to 438,200 in 1980 can be attributed, in part, to the decline in the state's population share during the decade from nearly 9 percent of the United States to less than 7.8 percent.

There are only three nonmanufacturing sectors that population does not affect directly: finance and insurance, wholesale and retail trade, and construction and real estate. The first two sectors serve a large export market. The third sector is local in focus, but here there is a secondary link. Although population does not enter directly as a determinant of construction and real estate employment, it does so indirectly through the housing sector, as indicated in figure 5–1. The change in New York's ratio of employment to the population aged 18 to 64 relative to the United States

Table 5-2. Key Nonmanufacturing Equations

1. *Service Employment Per Capita*	
Per capita real personal income	0.56
	(8.23)[a]
Unemployment rate	−0.038
	(4.97)
Per capita finance and insurance employment	0.11
	(2.38)
Elderly proportion of the population	1.32
	(20.23)
Constant	2.59
	(24.92)
R^2	.99
2. *Government Employment Per Capita*	
School-age proportion of population	0.25
	(2.09)
Real per capita grants-in-aid	0.18
	(7.51)
Real per capita non-transfer personal income	0.80
	(6.71)
Constant	2.16
	(6.87)
R^2	.95
3. *Other Employment* *(Transportation, Communications, Public Utilities, and Mining)*	
Labor productivity (nonmanufacturing) lagged	0.37
	(4.45)
New York share of national population	0.41
	(1.95)
Constant	8.72
	(39.27)
R^2	.91

[a]The figures in parentheses are t-values of the regression coefficients.

enters the housing starts equation as a measure of home-buying potential. In turn, housing starts directly affect construction and real estate employment.

Population's effect on the New York economy is pervasive in NYDEM, through both the unemployment rate and the effect of nonmanufacturing employment on income. As figure 5-1 illustrates, the high degree of simultaneity within the New York model assures that population changes affect almost every sector.

The Population Sector

A Model of Net Migration

Modeling the three components of population change—births, deaths, and net migration—combines econometric and demographic features. The demographer's perspective is taken in the calculation of deaths through the application of a cohort-component survival technique. Births, in contrast, are first estimated at the national level by modeling the U.S. total fertility rate, which is then related to New York via demographic assumptions. Migration is modeled at a strictly local level. Net migration is determined stochastically and serves as the link through which the level of economic activity determined within the core of the model affects population growth. The primary difficulty involved in building a model of this type is the reconciliation of fundamental differences between economic and demographic data. This problem has been exacerbated by the lack of detailed demographic data at the state level for intercensal years. This data-availability problem is especially severe in the case of migration data.

Migration is the only component of population change estimated annually by the Census Bureau which is not measured explicitly (Isserman, Plane, and McMillen 1982). Rather, total net migration is derived as the residual of the difference between population in two consecutive periods, net of natural increase. Because births and deaths data represent full coverage and are relatively accurate in contrast to total population estimates, which are derived by averaging three indirect methods, the errors present in these post-censal estimates tend to be forced into the migration component. As a result, these errors may bias the estimated relationship between net migration and economic phenomena. Because the data series used will have such an important effect on any model of net migration, it is important to begin with a consideration of data construction. Consequently, the next section of this chapter describes our treatment of this problem and its implications for modeling the components of population change. The following sections describe the theory and methodology involved in modeling net migration, births, and deaths.

Data Construction

In spite of the limitations of Census Bureau data, it is possible to construct migration series based on an annual cohort-survival model. Such a series was constructed here by surviving the population year by year and comparing the results with the Census Bureau's intercensal estimates for the period from 1970 to 1979. As a first step, the April 1970 population was aged one-quarter by single year of age and sex to conform to the July 1 estimates. A quarterly survival rate was calculated from annual data (National Center for Health Statistics, 1975). Unfortunately, the most recent state survival rate available corresponds to an average of the period from 1969 to 1971. A state-specific series was created by allowing the national rates to determine the growth trend while maintaining the 1970 state-to-U.S. differential. The estimated total deaths were then adjusted to conform to actual deaths for each year of the simulation. Since the distribution of births by age of mother will not affect population totals, total births, adjusted for infant mortality, were added to the survived base-year population to complete the natural increase calculation. By aggregating the "survived" population by age and sex and comparing it to the Census Bureau's intercensual estimates, an approximation of annual net migration was obtained for the following age groups: 0–17, 18–44, 45–64, and 65 and older.[1]

There are several problems with this procedure. One is that it will provide estimates of net migration only, not gross flows. This may be a shortcoming to the extent that inmigration and outmigration are determined by different factors or by common factors to varying degrees. However, since only net flows are required in order to define changes in the population, this limitation is not overly restrictive. A more serious problem results from the recent revisions of Census Bureau post-censal estimates based on the 1980 census. These new intercensal estimates tend to compound the uncertainty introduced by the 1970 population undercount.[2] They cannot be used directly in conjunction with the 1970 actual count for New York without resulting in massive negative net migration between 1970 and 1971. Although several estimates of population undercount for 1970 are available for states (U.S. Bureau of the Census 1979), they are not used by the Census Bureau for either intercensal estimates or state projections because they lack sufficient age detail and otherwise fall short of census data quality standards. In the case of New York, for example, the estimates of undercount range from a high of 2.6 percent to a low of 1.6 percent. The methodological problems associated with the estimates, given the political implications of the undercount, appear to have caused the Census Bureau to refrain from using them.

Another data problem arises from the discrepancy between Census Bureau estimates of the population for 1980 and the actual census count. Although the Census Bureau has revised its 1971–79 estimates of total population to be consistent with the 1980 census, individual age groups have not been revised. Moreover, this revision still ignores the 1970 undercount by essentially interpolating between the 1970 and 1980 census figures. Nevertheless, the 1970 census figures are used here as the starting point for the survival model in order to maintain conformity with the published census data wherever possible and to avoid the necessity of creating alternative intercensal estimates.

Theory and Equation Estimation

The primary purpose in modeling net migration by age group is to be able to differentiate between working-age migrants and other movers. The movement of 18–64 year olds is most significant to New York in terms of both volume and impact on the state's economy. Presumably for this group, the migration decision is determined by expectations of job availability. For modeling purposes, this group is split into two subgroups, based on the hypothesis that economic factors affect the younger cohort to a greater extent than the older group; Becker, as noted in Greenwood (1975), has found that the probability of migration by a labor-force member is likely to decrease as his age increases. The shorter expected remaining working life over which older migrants can realize the benefits of migrating lowers, for them, the rate of return to migration. Gallaway also proposes that job security and family ties are likely to be more important for older persons than for younger ones, further discouraging migration (Greenwood 1975).

The relative attractiveness of a place is also likely to be judged differently by the two groups. In particular, housing costs will probably be more important to the younger group for two reasons. First, this group is likely to include a high percentage of renters interested in purchasing their first house or condominium. Second, since the historical earning period for members of this group is shorter than that of the 45- to 64-year-old group, and wealth accumulation consequently less, price sensitivity is likely to be greater. Furthermore, a member of the older group is more likely to own a house already, in which case a rise in relative house prices in a locality would increase assets, rather than necessarily serve as an incentive for

Table 5-3. Net Migration Equations

	Population Age Group		
	0–17	18–44	45–64
Relative unemployment rate	—	−70.80 (6.52)[a]	−37.29 (4.89)
Relative consumer price index	—	−313.93 (2.63)	—
Relative durable and nondurable price index	—	—	−99.10 (2.31)
Net migrants aged 45–64	0.97 (6.13)	—	—
Time trend	−1.08 (4.52)	—	—
Constant	10.21 (4.13)	387.52 (3.24)	133.52 (2.73)
$\bar{R}^2$	.87	.91	.81

[a]The figures in parentheses are t-values of the regression coefficients.

outmigration; alternatively, a member of this group may rent a dwelling by choice. As a worker approaches retirement, however, concern about general living costs can be expected to increase.

The estimation results support both sets of hypotheses. As table 5–3 indicates, the elasticity on the relative unemployment rate is higher for the 18- to 44-year-olds than for the 45- to 64-year-olds. Also, the younger group reacts negatively to a widening gap between the New York and U.S. total CPI (including house prices), whereas the older group is significantly influenced only by the relative cost of durables and nondurables.[3] The lower R^2 on the 45–64 equation also supports the argument that noneconomic factors are likely to play a role in the middle-aged person's decision to migrate.

Although the elderly share certain characteristics with the 45- to 64-year-old group, their incomes are less affected by cyclical economic conditions than are those of this younger group. Historically, migration of those 65 and older has been quite stable, ranging from −17,600 to −25,700 except in 1975, when outmigration was severely curtailed, apparently by the recession. None of the standard economic indicators explain more than 30 percent of the variation in net migration. For this reason, we have assumed the level of outmigration by the elderly to remain constant at 20,000 per year.

In contrast to the independent movement of the elderly, youth generally follow their parents. Migration of 45- to 64-year-olds is used as a proxy for the parent group.[4] However, this series is a significant indicator only in conjunction with a negative time trend, DUMPOP. This trend variable can be interpreted as reflecting declining fertility rates during the 1970s, which would tend to reduce the ratio of youth-to-young-adult migration over the decade. It also corrects for biases introduced by differential undercount by age reflected in the migration estimates.

A Model of Natural Increase

Population is forecast quarterly by single year of age and sex by simulating the cohort-survival model. New York survival ratios are assumed to change at the national rate based upon Census Bureau projections. Given the small variation between New York and U.S. survival rates in 1970 and the expected convergence of rates over time, it is reasonable to assume the constancy of the ratio of state-to-national survival rates for the forecast period.

New York's projected total fertility rate is linked to the national total fertility rate, which is forecast based upon an econometric equation incorporating elements of the theories of Richard Easterlin (1969). The total fertility rate adjusts gradually toward a desired number of children, is negatively related to relative generation size (indicative of labor market pressure), and is positively related to the lagged unemployment rate (a cyclical indicator of job-market opportunities).

Historically, these variables explain over 97 percent of the variation in the total fertility rate, but tend to overpredict fertility in the forecast period relative to demographic projections. Further research should involve the examination of increased wage detail by demographic groups and explore the limitations of the further expansion of the female labor-force participation rate. As table 5-4 indicates, our total fertility forecast is both lower and more cyclic than the Census Bureau's "middle" projection series (U.S. Bureau of the Census 1982).

In forecasting New York fertility rates, we assume that the relationship between New York and U.S. fertility by age group will remain constant. State age-group fertility rates are constrained to grow at the national pace. Over the last decade, the age distribution of New York births has shifted only within the 20- to 35-year-old group, with declines in the fertility of 20- to 25-year-olds and gains in the 25- to 30- and 30- to 35-year-old groups. This shift accompanied a large increase in the national female labor-force

Table 5-4. Total Fertility Rate, United States

Year	Projected	Census Bureau Middle Series (Series II)	Difference
1981–82	1.764	1.825	−.061
1982–83	1.793	1.830	−.037
1983–84	1.781	1.847	−.063
1984–85	1.765	1.865	−.100
1985–86	1.757	1.883	−.126
1986–87	1.762	1.901	−.139
1987–88	1.784	1.916	−.132
1988–89	1.812	1.929	−.117
1989–90	1.848	1.939	−.091
1990–91	1.898	1.946	−.048

participation rate from 43.4 percent in 1970 to 51.5 percent in 1979. The fertility patterns resulting from these changes are likely to persist during the 1980s. The assumption of an unchanging ratio of New York to U.S. fertility rates is even easier to justify, as New York's total fertility rate has remained consistently 11 percent below the national rate from 1971 to 1977. Thus, differential state fertility rates may be related to tastes and other noneconomic factors, while trends in age-specific fertility are national.

Lack of sufficiently long annual data series for states prevented the modeling of New York's total fertility rate econometrically. Although estimates of state total fertility rates by age are available for 1970–77 through an unpublished Census Bureau report, earlier data are available through the National Center for Health Statistics for census years only. The method used here removes any possibility of accounting directly for the effects of the local economy on New York fertility by age group, but it does recognize the effect of net migration on births via the age distribution of young females, a process referred to as the "demographic multiplier" (Alonso 1980).

Simulations

Sample-period simulation of a new model provides a means of checking both its coding and its specification as a complete model. This type of simulation can take any or all of several particular forms. Once coded into its simulation package,[5] a model can be solved as a set of independent equations, using the historical values of all the regressor variables during a given interval of time. This procedure can be implemented to generate predicted values of the endogenous variables comparable to those originally generated by the individual regression equations, thus permitting the model code to be checked for coding errors. Alternatively, the model can be solved one period at a time, using as independent variables the historical values of both the exogenous and the lagged endogenous variables. Finally, the model can be solved dynamically, using the historical values of the exognous variables and the earlier predicted values of the lagged endogenous variables. A dynamic solution can be compared to the historical values of the endogenous variables in order to attempt to determine the predictive accuracy of the model. Alternatively, such a dynamic solution of the model can be compared with an alternative solution of the model for the same time period that involves different assumed values for at least one of the model's exogenous variables. This procedure permits the model to be examined in terms of the simulated impact of changing economic policies or other exogenous conditions.

In order to illustrate some of the properties of NYEDM, the results of two types of model simulation tests are presented in this section. As a first test, NYEDM was simulated dynamically from the first quarter of 1971 to the first quarter of 1979, corresponding to the estimation range of the net migration model. This process involved the use of the actual values of the model's exogenous variables and, after the initial periods of simulation, the model's predicted values of the lagged endogenous variables as they were generated by the model. This ex-post, sample-period simulation was conducted without applying any form of model adjustments and is commonly understood to be a test of model validity, notwithstanding the results presented by Howrey and Kelejian (1969) that call into question the degree to which a linear or approximately linear model can be validated by nonstochastic sample-period simulation.

The second type of test presented is an impact simulation and involves the comparison of alternative simulations with the model. The first (baseline) simulation takes as given the historical values of the exogenous variables. The second (impact) simulation uses the historical values of the exogenous variables, except in the case of the effective personal income-tax rate, which is assumed to be reduced.

Table 5-5. Sample Period Simulation Error Stastistics, Selected Major Variables

	Root Mean Square Percentage Error
Total nonresidential employment	1.60
Total nonagricultural employment	1.63
Manufacturing employment	2.25
Government employment	3.87
Services employment	3.77
Wholesale and retail trade employment	2.46
Finance and insurance employment	1.14
Contract construction and real estate employment	4.81
Other (TCPUM) employment	2.21
Unemployment	12.80
Total disposable personal income	6.74
Manufacturing wage bill	2.77
Nonmanufacturing wage bill	6.52
Total population	0.66
Population, 5–17	4.21
Population, 18–44	1.42
Population, 45–64	0.64
Population, 65 and over	1.44

Model Performance

The results of the historical simulation of NYEDM are presented in table 5–5. This table shows error statistics for a selection of the major endogenous variables of the model computed for the period from the first quarter of 1971 through the first quarter of 1979. The error statistics shown are the percent root mean square errors.

Generally speaking, these results are satisfactory. What is most interesting about them is not that they exhibit the magnitudes of percentage error normally associated with quarterly regional models, but rather which particular variables exhibit the greatest percentage error. Relatively high percentage errors are associated with the nonmanufacturing wage bill and, consequently, total disposable income and the number of unemployed.

The entire set of exploratory model simulation experiments that have been conducted so far indicates that the entire model is quite sensitive to errors in particular sectors. In the case of the nonmanufacturing wage bill, for example, errors propagate through both nonmanufacturing employment and personal income, affecting unemployment, total labor force, and total employment. The categories of nonmanufacturing employment that are most directly affected by the unemployment rate and by income generally exhibit the largest percentage root mean square errors.

Total employment exhibits a relatively smaller percentage error than a number of its subcomponents, indicating that subcomponent errors are to some degree offsetting. Similarly, total population exhibits a smaller percentage error than any of its components. The small magnitude of the population errors contrasts with the large errors obtained for net migration. These large migration errors can be attributed to a combination of factors, the most important being the dominant influence of the unemployment rate on migration. Some of the errors also can be ascribed to the construction of quarterly migration figures from the annual data.

Impact Simulation

The impact simulation incorporates a 20 percent reduction in the effective New York state personal income-tax rate. All other exogenous variables are held at their historical values, thus assuming that the tax cut is financed from a revenue surplus and necessitates no cut in government services and employment. Figure 5-2 illustrates the major channels through which a change in personal income taxes will affect the New York economy. A reduction in personal income taxes will affect both the supply side of the economy through the labor force and the demand side through the positive effect on disposable income and population.

The demand side effects are most immediate. As shown in figure 5-2, during the first year of the tax cut, the increase in disposable income (2) stimulates local demand for goods and services, increasing nonmanufacturing employment. The finance, insurance, and service industries are directly stimulated by this increase in disposable income (3), while construction, real estate, and trade sectors are affected indirectly via higher levels of housing starts and retail sales (4, 5). In the longer run, increased population resulting from net migration also augments services and government employment (9). These new jobs created by the initial increase in disposable income in turn produce additional wages, further stimulating disposable income through the multiplier effect (10, 11). Total resident

AN ECONOMETRIC-DEMOGRAPHIC MODEL OF NEW YORK STATE   121

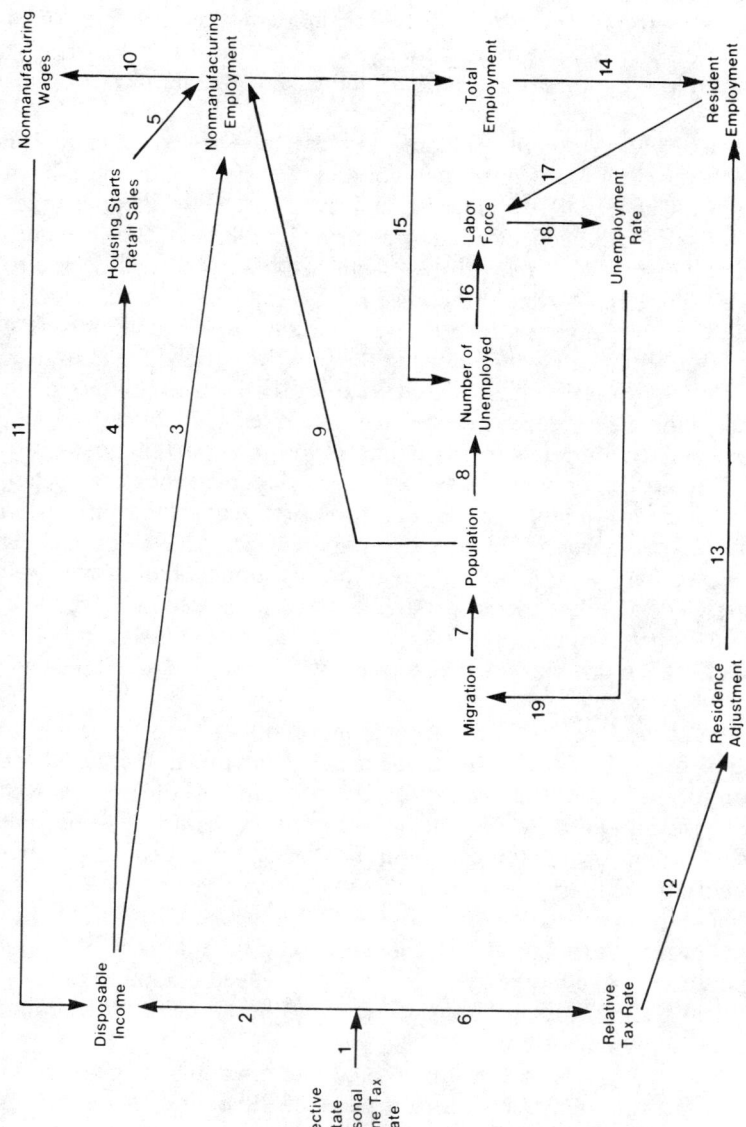

Figure 5-2. Effect of a change in the New York personal income tax rate on the New York economic–demographic model

employment rises by twice the increase in nonmanufacturing employment for two reasons. First, the self-employed and farm workers, excluded from payroll employment, are included in total resident employment. Improved economic conditions can be expected to result in the opening of new businesses and professional associations, increasing the number of self-employed.

Second, the New York state income tax can be viewed as a factor influencing the commuting decision by workers who have obtained jobs in the New York City area. A reduction in New York state income taxes relative to those of Connecticut or New Jersey (6) will mean that a higher proportion of persons obtaining employment in New York will decide to reside in New York than would otherwise have been the case (12, 13, 14). The relative tax term appears in the residence adjustment equation as a distributed lag over five quarters. During the current period, the tax cut is likely to influence primarily those who have recently obtained employment and not yet made a residence decision. As time goes on, a lower level of relative taxes will encourage some commuters to move into the state.

Since the majority of the migration effect occurs only with a lag, however, the increase in labor force during the first year of the simulation can be attributed primarily to the re-entry into the work force by previously discouraged workers as a result of their expectations of improved job opportunities. The absolute increase in the labor force exceeds the decline in the number of unemployed, indicating that not all immediately find jobs, but the net effect is a drop in the unemployment rate relative to the baseline (15, 16, 17, 18).

During the second year of the tax cut, the improved job outlook and lower cost of living begin to attract out-of-state migrants. Increased job competition does lessen the reduction in the number of unemployed compared to the baseline, but the unemployment rate continues to decline. Employment expansion continues to outpace labor force growth for five years, when an increase in the number of unemployed causes the unemployment rate to rise slightly above the baseline. This rise in the unemployment rate signals both residents and potential migrants that labor market conditions have worsened, resulting in reduced net migration the following year (19). This mechanism tends to keep New York labor markets in relative equilibrium.

The net result of this process is an impact which reaches its peak in the middle of the period, then levels off to the end of the period. The long-run effect of a 20 percent reduction in the effective personal income tax rate is a 1.8 percent increase in disposable personal income and a 0.4 percent increase in total employment. Although both employment and income remain above their baseline levels over the entire simulation period, the eventual rise in the unemployment rate suggests that tax cuts stimulate the New York economy's supply of workers to a greater extent than its ability to provide jobs.

Conclusions

The main strengths of NYEDM are its conceptual appeal as a sophisticated representation of the workings of a state economy and its tendency to increase the degree of consistency between the economic and demographic indicators simulated. The endogenous role of population as both a result and determinant of state economic activity broadens the potential use of the model for alternative policy simulations. In addition, the inclusion of a relatively detailed tax sector allows for some degree of interaction between changes in tax rates and yields and economic variables such as employment, prices, and personal income. The integration of demographic and economic activity tends to insure consistency between simulated population and economic growth rates through the feedback mechanism discussed above; changes in employment, to the extent that they lead to changes in unemployment, induce migration, which leads to population growth or decline and subsequent changes in employment and unemployment.

The weaknesses of the model are characteristic of particular equations rather than of the structure as a whole. Further development of the model will concentrate on improving the explanatory power of the stochastic equations, in particular the number of unemployed and migration. One approach toward solving simulation problems is the further disaggregation of employment by industry. In the case of manufacturing, separate treatment of each two-digit SIC industry or, at the very least, durables and nondurables, is expected to reveal growth patterns disguised by the aggregate. For nonmanufacturing, a further division of sectors into those primarily export-oriented and those more locally oriented would be useful, especially in the case of services employment. The revenue sector will be another focus for further development, particularly with respect to the flexibility of the income-distribution algorithm for the calculation of personal income-tax revenue and the explicit treatment of local as well as state taxes.

Notes

1. The net migration equations appear in the model in quarterly form in order to allow full integration of the population sector into the economic core of the model, but they are

estimated with annual data. In the case of an equation involving no lagged dependent variables, this procedure will result in estimates of the parameters of the analogous quarterly equations, at least if the quarterly values are stated at annual rates. To see that this statement is true, consider the "quarterly" equation:

$$y_t = \alpha + \beta x_t + u_t \tag{5.1}$$

and the quarterly-to-annual transformation of variables:

$$(1/4 \sum_{i=0}^{3} y_{t-i}) = \alpha + \beta (1/4 \sum_{i=0}^{3} x_{t-i}) + (1/4 \sum_{i=0}^{3} u_{t-i}). \tag{5.2}$$

where the u_t are assumed to be individually, independently distributed variates with a zero mean and a constant variance, distributed independently of the x_t. Note that the "annual" equation 5.2 involves the same parameters as the "quarterly" equation 5.1. Furthermore, provided that the moving averages of the variables involve no temporal overlap (which they will not in this instance), the annual form will preserve all the statistical properties of the quarterly form, except that it will involve a fourfold decrease in the degrees of freedom. In contrast, if the quarterly data were to be manufactured by interpolation, ipso facto, this interpolation would involve the introduction of (increased) measurement error. The increase in the degrees of freedom brought about by the use of quarterly data will thus destroy any possibility of the parameter estimates having optimal properties; in this case, in particular, the parameter estimates could not be best linear unbiased estimates. These results can be generalized to cases in which lagged dependent variables are present, but the particular characteristics of that situation are obviously more complicated.

2. The terms *postcensal* and *intercensal* are employed by the Census Bureau in classifying various types of population estimates. A post-censal estimate is any annual estimate based upon a previous decennial census prior to the release of the results of the next census. Intercensal estimates apply to time periods between two censuses which are benchmarked to both censuses.

3. Consumer price indices for New York state are constructed by weighting CPI components for the Buffalo and New York-New Jersey metropolitan areas by their respective shares of population in 1970.

4. There are a number of possible reasons why youth migration is more highly correlated with the movement of the 45–64 age group than the younger adult group. During the 1970s, New York City attracted a number of young people, many of these single and recent college graduates. While this flow of inmigrants did not reverse the direction of net migration, it did affect its pattern. Also, this inmigration has created a pool of potential migrants who may be more likely to remain childless than the national average. Another factor is the dramatic decline in birth rates, which would tend to increase the importance of migration by teenagers, compared to that of younger children.

5. The term *simulation package*, while historically meaningful, is somewhat misleading as a description of the software that supports the construction and use of NYEDM. This model was estimated and is solved using XSIM, a high-level, free-format, econometric modeling language. This language provides the ability to estimate equations and easily compile them in a model in a coded format that closely approximates the written notational conventions of econometrics (Drud 1983). XSIM is the modeling language of a substantial online data economic data-base system that is made available to subscribers to the time-sharing services of Chase Econometrics (Renfro 1980).

References

Alonso, W. 1980. Population as a system in regional development. *American Economic Review* 70:405–409.

Drud, A. 1983. A survey of model representation and simulation algorithms in some existing model systems. *Journal of Economic Dynamics and Control* 5, 2:

Easterlin, R.A. 1969. The American baby boom in historical perspective. *American Economic Review* 51:869–911.

Greenwood, M.J. 1975. Research on internal migration in the United States: a survey. *Journal of Economic Literature* 13:397–433.

Howrey, P., and Kelejian, H.H. 1969. Simulation versus analytical solution. In *The design of computer simulation experiments*, ed. T.H. Naylor, Durham, NC: Duke University Press.

Isserman, A.M.; Plane, D.A.; and McMillen, D. 1982. Internal migration in the United States: an evaluation of federal data. *Review of Public Data Use* 10:285–311.

National Center for Health Statistics. 1975. *U.S. decennial life tables for 1969–71: state life tables, 1969–71*, Vol. II. Rockville, MD: U.S. Department of Health, Education and Welfare.

Renfro, Charles G. 1980. Econometric data base systems: some reflections on the state-of-the-art. *Review of Public Data Use* 8:121–139.

U.S. Bureau of the Census. 1979. Population profile of the United States, 1978. *Current Population Reports*, Series P-20, No. 336. Washington, D.C.: U.S. Government Printing Office.

———. 1982. Projections of the population of the United States. *Current Population Reports*, Series p. 25, No. 922. Washington, D.C.: U.S. Government Printing Office.

6 THE EFFECTS OF REFINING DEMOGRAPHIC-ECONOMIC INTERACTIONS IN REGIONAL ECONOMETRIC MODELS

Carol Taylor

Introduction

The interdependence of economic and demographic growth in a local economy is generally recognized, but its implications for appropriate regional econometric model structure have not been systematically evaluated. Theoretical correctness is extremely difficult to establish in regional models. Given the joint presence of classical economic aggregation error, measurement error, specification error, and stochastic regressors, it is virtually impossible to determine a priori the theoretically correct level of aggregation (see, e.g., Grunfeld and Griliches' 1960 analysis of Theil's 1954 aggregation results). Furthermore, in constructing regional econometric models for forecasting, theoretically precise structural specification is only one component of model accuracy. A particular equation for variable X as a function of vector Z_1 may correctly embody our theoretical understanding of the determination of X, and yet still not perform well within the context of an entire model. An alternative specification formulating X as a function of Z_2 may be preferable if either (1) the variables in Z_2 are more accurately predicted than the variables in Z_1 or (2) predicted X based on Z_2, compared with predicted X based on Z_1, more effectively counteracts structural error in other model equations which use variable X as a determinant. That is, in deciding model structure, the nature of "reverberative" or "interactive" error has to be considered in addition to single-equation structural error (Charney and Taylor 1983).

Recognizing these problems that prohibit theoretical, a priori determination of optimal model structure, the purpose of this chapter is to examine empirically the benefits to refining economic-demographic linkages in regional econometric models. Eight model structures which vary substantially in the sophistication of these linkages are examined. Since local areas are so diverse economically and demographically, it is difficult to draw conclusions on model structure from one area alone. Consequently, the eight models are estimated for each of six substate areas that together encompass considerable variations in size, economic base, demographic and economic growth, and labor-market tightness. The areas covered are the San Francisco-Oakland Standard Metropolitan Statistical Area (SMSA), Phoenix SMSA, mid-Cumberland Tennessee Economic Development District (EDD),[1] Springfield-Chicopee-Holyoke SMSA, Tucson SMSA, and southeastern Utah EDD.[2] They are abbreviated, respectively, as SF, PH, MC, SC, TU, and UT. Some of the major economic and demographic features of the areas are summarized in table 6-1.

The construction and evaluation of the models focus on the major variables of population, personal income, and total employment.[3] In analyzing the effects of economic-demographic refinements, we look at (1) overall simulation accuracy of the major summary variables; (2) consistency of economic-demographic estimates as measured by the simulation accuracy of the employment to population ratio and per capita income; (3) the impact of differences in structural economic-demographic characteristics across areas on optimal model structure; and (4) the effect of time horizon of simulation—in particular, accuracy over three-year simulations compared with a nine-year simulation period.

The second section describes the eight different model structures. They are summarized in table 6-2 for easy reference. Briefly, the first three models are not simultaneous in specification and solution; model IV is simultaneous in specification, but not solution; and models V through VIII are simultaneous in both specification and solution. Model I is a simple time trend, model II incorporates non-area-specific, but variable-specific aggregate U.S. growth trends, and model III includes exogenous determinants of export-base activity. Model IV disaggregates total employment into export-base and local-serving sectors and separately estimates net migration and natural increase components of population change. Local population and employment are determinants of local income and the latter is a determi-

Table 6-1. Area Comparisons

Area	1974 Population (1,000s)	Percent Population Growth 1960–74	Ratio of Absolute Net Migration to Natural Increase 1960–74	Average Unemployment Rate 1960–74	Percent 1974 Non-agricultural Wage and Salary Employment			Percent 1974 Manufacturing Employment in Durable Goods
					Mining	Manufacturing	Government	
U.S.	211900.0	17.3	.19	4.98	.9	25.6	18.1	59.3
SF	3129.0	17.4	.56	7.67	.13	14.8	20.9	51.2
PH	1180.0	74.7	1.96	4.56	<.1	18.8	17.4	79.1
MC	850.6	24.4	.64	3.54	<.1	27.7	15.7	47.2
SC	524.2	3.6	.68	5.94	<.1	32.6	14.6	43.7
UT	40.5	−3.6	1.16	8.37	25.3	5.1	23.6	na
TU	427.3	58.8	2.64	4.73	5.8	8.6	26.8	71.8

Table 6-2. Summary of the Eight Model Structures

Model Structure	General Description
I	Trend extrapolations of population, employment, and income
II	Sector-specific but not area-specific exogenous variables added to equations from Model I (such as the U.S. employment growth rate)
III	Area-specific exogenous variables added to explain export demand
IV	Population change disaggregated into natural increase (function of U.S. population growth) and net migration (function of change in export or total employment); total employment disaggregated into export and local; and population affecting both local employment and local income
V	Same as Model IV but economic and demographic variables determined simultaneously
VI	Refinement of economic-demographic linkages: incorporation of wage determination and wage effects on employment and migration and incorporation of economic factors affecting natural increase
VII	Model VI with disaggregation of local employment with sector-specific refinements
VIII	Model VIII with disaggregation of income determination

nant of local-serving employment. Natural increase is a function of U.S. population growth (which is almost entirely natural increase), and net migration is determined by change in export-base or total employment. Model IV is solved using equation right-hand variable estimates from model III. Model V is a simultaneous solution of model IV. Model VI specification introduces local wages (and local labor-market determinants of those wages), relative economic condition determinants of net migration, and economic determinants of natural increase. Model VII disaggregates local-serving employment allowing for both subsector variations in specification of the effects on employment of population, income, and relative labor cost, and subsector differences in export-base components of local-serving employment. Finally, model VIII disaggregates personal income determination, allowing for potential reduction of aggregation error by differentiating economic-demographic specifications of income subcomponents.

A sequence of seven three-year simulations and one nine-year simulation was performed to test comparative model accuracy. The third section presents and evaluates the simulation results, and a concluding section summarizes the findings of the research.

Alternative Economic/Demographic Model Linkages

Model I—Simple Trend Extrapolations

Model structure I, the simplest formulation, ignores sector-specific determinants of economic-demographic change. It is a pure trend model. For each area i (i = SF, PH, MC, SC, UT, and TU) and variable L_j [L_j = ET (total employment), POP (population), and Y/DF (nominal income, Y, deflated by a regional consumer price index, DF)]:

$$L_j^i = \alpha_{ij,1} + \alpha_{ij,2}(L_j^i)_{-1} + \alpha_{ij,3} T \quad (6.1)$$

$$(E/P)^i \equiv ET^i/POP^i \quad (6.2)$$

$$(Y/P)^i \equiv (Y/DF)^i \cdot DF^i/POP^i \quad (6.3)$$

where T = time (1950 = 1, 1952 = 2, and so on). When its coefficient was clearly insignificant (coefficient t-ratio less than one), T was dropped from the specification. This result occurred only for POP in Tucson and Y/DF in San Francisco and Springfield.

Model II—Trend Extrapolations with Exogenous Variables

In model structure II, sector-specific, but not area-specific, exogenous determinants of ET, POP, and Y/DF are introduced. In particular, T in equation 6.1 is replaced by the ratio of year t to $t - 1$ of corresponding U.S. variable L_j (total employment, population, or real income). The equations are estimated in log-linear form, implying L_j^i in year t is a multiplicative function of L_j^i in year $t - 1$ and the U.S. growth in variable L_j from $t - 1$ to t. In particular:

$$L_j^i = \alpha_{ij,5}(L_{j,-1}^i)^{\alpha_{ij,6}}(L_j^{US}/L_{j,-1}^{US})^{\alpha_{ij,7}}. \quad (6.1')$$

In estimation, if specification 6.1' did not represent an improvement over its counterpart from model I, the latter was retained. That is, structural equation deterioration was not built into the movement from model I to II. It is interesting to note the number of instances in which inclusion of the U.S. trend did not improve specification. In particular, model I was retained in its entirety for Tucson and southeastern Utah and for the population equations of Phoenix and mid-Cumberland. Thus, inclusion of U.S. population-growth rates did not improve population estimation for four of the six areas, making clear the structural difference in population determination at the national and local levels.

Model III—Area-Specific Exogenous Variables

One of the simplest and most extensively written about models of regional growth is the export-base model in which export-base industrial expansion drives regional economic-demographic development (see, e.g., Isard (1960), Richardson (1969, 1978), Gerking and Isserman (1981), and references therein). This concept is embodied in model structure III which expands specification 6.1' (or 6.1 if the latter was used in model II) to include non-sector-specific, but area-specific, exogenous determinants of export-base output. For example, demand for output from the dominant export sector of machinery manufacturing in Phoenix is primarily a function of U.S. real investment, so specification 6.1' for this SMSA was expanded to include real U.S. fixed investment. Again, clearly insignificant variables were not retained. Typical specifications in model III include:

$$L_j^i = \alpha_{ij,8} + \alpha_{ij,9} L_{j,-1}^i + \alpha_{ij,10}(L_j^{US}/L_{j,-1}^{US}) + \alpha_{ij,11} X^i \qquad (6.1'')$$

and

$$L_j^i = \alpha_{ij,12} + \alpha_{ij,13} L_{j,-1}^i + \alpha_{ij,14} X^i \qquad (6.1''')$$

where X^i is an exogenous variable (or vector of exogenous variables) specifying output demand in the export-base sector of area i. Thus, model III merely expands the single-equation specifications to include export-base demand determinants. For 4 of the 18 equations, no export-base demand variables were significant: population in Phoenix and mid-Cumberland and real income in San Francisco and Springfield.[4]

Models IV and V—Economic-Demographic Linkages

Model III introduced the first rudimentary intra-area economic to demographic linkage in the models, but model IV refines that linkage by separating net migration and natural increase so that the impact of employment growth on population is isolated to the net migration component of population change. The model includes additional simple economic-demographic interdependencies among local-serving employment, total employment, income, and population. In particular, model structure IV is:

$$(NM/POP)^i = \beta_{i,0} + \beta_{i,1}\%\Delta ET^i + \beta_{i,2}TR \text{ or} \qquad (6.4)$$

$$(NM/POP)^i = \beta_{i,3} + \beta_{i,4}\%\Delta EX^i + \beta_{i,5}TR \qquad (6.4')$$

$$(NI/POP)^i = \beta_{i,6} + \beta_{i,7}(NI/POP)^i_{-1} + \beta_{i,8}(POP^{US}/POP^{US}_{-1}) \qquad (6.5)$$

$$POP^i \equiv POP^i_{-1}/[1 - (NI/POP)^i - (NM/POP)^i] \qquad (6.6)$$

$$EX^i = \beta_{i,9} + \beta_{i,10}EX^i_{-1} + \beta_{i,11}X^i \qquad (6.7)$$

$$EL^i = \beta_{i,12} + \beta_{i,13}POP^i + \beta_{i,14}(Y/P/DF)^i \text{ or} \qquad (6.8)$$

$$EL^i = \beta_{i,15} + \beta_{i,16}(Y/DF)^i \qquad (6.8')$$

$$ET^i \equiv EL^i + EX^i \qquad (6.9)$$

$$(Y/DF)^i = \beta_{i,17} + \beta_{i,18}POP^i + \beta_{i,19}ET^i + \beta_{i,20}(W/DF)^{US} \text{ or} \qquad (6.10)$$

$$(Y/DF)^i = \beta_{i,21} + \beta_{i,22}ET^i + \beta_{i,23}(W/DF)^{US} \qquad (6.10')$$

$$E/P^i \equiv ET^i/POP^i \qquad (6.11)$$

$$(Y/P)^i \equiv (Y/DF)^i \cdot DF^i/POP^i \qquad (6.12)$$

$$(Y/P/DF)^i \equiv (Y/P)^i/DF^i \qquad (6.13)$$

where NM = net migration, NI = natural increase (births minus deaths), $\%\Delta L$ denotes percent change in variable L over the previous year, TR specifies trend (either directly or via a lagged dependent), X^i is from 6.1" and 6.1''', EX = export-base employment, EL = local-serving employment, and $(W/DF)^{US}$ is a U.S. real wage index. Export-base employment is defined to be manufacturing employment for all areas except Tucson and southeastern Utah. For the latter two areas, export-base employment is manufacturing and mining. EL is the difference between ET and EX. Note that model IV contains: (1) separate specification of net migration and natural increase with derivation of total population by identity; (2) disaggregation of total employment into export-base and local-serving with the latter a function of local population and income, and (3) local population and employment impacts on local income.

Note the U.S. population growth variable in equation 6.5. Recall that this variable was allowed in model II for estimating *total* population but that it was not significant in that specification for four of the six areas. When the dependent variable is rate of natural increase, however, the aggregate U.S. population growth rate is significant in five of the six area equations (all areas except southeastern Utah). Since aggregate U.S. population growth is predominantly natural increase (see table 6–1), the estimation results suggest similar trends in natural increase over otherwise diversified local areas. This similarity can be used effectively in regional modeling, but only if it is correctly restricted to the specification of natural increase.

Model IV is simultaneous in structure, but not in solution. Estimates of population, income, and total employment used to forecast equations 6.4, 6.8 or 6.8′, and 6.10 and 6.10′ are derived from model III above. The purpose of this solution method is to attempt to isolate the effect of the new economic-demographic specification interdependencies from any potential interactive errors which might be generated in a simultaneous solution of the model.

Model V introduces simultaneous determination of economic and demographic variables. It is the same equation set as model IV, but it is solved using Gauss-Seidel numerical iteration.

Model VI—Refinement of Economic-Demographic Linkages

The major criticism of model V is that although economic and demographic variables are determined simultaneously, there is a clear ordering of "the chicken" and "the egg" (Muth 1970). Employment change determines migration. Conditions of the local labor market, wages in particular, do not affect employment, either export-base or local. Model VI refines the economic-demographic linkages to remove this ordering bias. Assuming cost minimization and using Shephard's Lemma determination of EX^i may be derived generally as:

$$EX^i = f_1(q_x^i, W_x^i/W^{US}, W_x^i/P_0^i) \qquad (6.14)$$

where q_x^i is a vector (or variable) specifying output (X^i in 6.7 above), W_x^i = wage in area i (relevant to the export-base industry), W^{US} = corresponding wage elsewhere (taken to be that in the U.S. as a whole), and P_0^i = price of non-labor inputs used in export-base production in area i. Since there were no data on P_0^i, relative cost of labor was measured by W^i/WPI where WPI is the U.S. wholesale price index. The theoretical dependent variable in equation 6.14 is manhours, but in estimation it is number of employees. Hours per employee tend to rise in a cyclical upswing and fall in a decline. Consequently, with annual data it is sometimes necessary to adjust equation 6.14 for this theoretical/empirical discrepancy. In general, this adjustment may be accomplished in one of three ways: (1) respecification of equation 6.14 as a partial adjustment model;

(2) inclusion of q_x^i lagged as well as current q_x^i in equation 6.14; (3) direct inclusion in equation 6.14 of a cyclical measure.

Specification of EL^i may be derived analogously to equation 6.14, yielding an equation similar to the latter except W^i/W^{US} is omitted:

$$EL^i = f_2(q_1^i, W_1^i/P_0^i). \qquad (6.15)$$

For some low-wage sectors, the relevant wage variable is the legislated minimum wage.

Equations 6.14 and 6.15 require the inclusion of local wage equations in the models. In addition to national wage impacts, Phillips effects (Phillips 1958) and regional price variations are assumed to affect the local wage rate:

$$W^i = f_3(W^{US}, U^i/U^{US}, P^i/P^{US}), \qquad (6.16)$$

where U^i = unemployment rate in area i, U^{US} = U.S. unemployment rate, and P^i/P^{US} is relative local to national prices measured as the ratio of a regional CPI to the overall U.S. CPI. Again, for some W^i, the relevant W^{US} may be the minimum wage. In many wage equations, fit was improved by allowing a lag on the Phillips effects and the relative price effects. In some areas, sufficient local average hourly earnings data were available to permit a wage-contour specification of non-manufacturing wages. For example, average hourly earnings in wholesale trade in San Francisco are estimated as a function of the minimum wage and the manufacturing wage in San Francisco, and the latter wage is estimated using equation 6.16.

The breadth of available local non-manufacturing average hourly earnings data which characterize San Francisco does not characterize all areas. In some cases, there were no non-manufacturing average hourly earnings data, creating a problem for estimation of equation 6.15. It was necessary to replace the direct relative labor-cost variable in that equation by a vector of variables specifying this relative cost. The appropriate vector was obtained from equation 6.16.

The use of local wages in the model was extended beyond employment determination to real income specification in equation 6.10 (or 6.10′). The real U.S. wage in those equations was replaced by a real local wage, a vector of real local wages, or a vector specifying real local wage determination.

The significant impact of Phillips effects in local wage determination requires the estimation of local unemployment rates in model VI. Because of the high inaccuracy of residual estimation of unemployment rates (from independent estimates of number of unemployed and labor force), local unemployment-rate determination uses the increasingly common stochastic formulation (see, e.g., Glickman 1977; Ledent 1978; and Rubin and Erickson 1980):

$$U^i = f_4(U^i_{-1}, U^{US}, \%\Delta POP^i, \%\Delta ET^i). \qquad (6.17)$$

For areas with clearly established cyclical and/or trend relationships to the United States, inclusion of a trend or cyclical measure improved specification in equation 6.17.

Equations 6.14 through 6.17 represent a significant alteration in structural specification over the previous models. The inclusion of local wages and Phillips effects in determination of these wages alters the simplistic exogenous determination of export-base employment in previous models. Population growth which can affect local labor-market tightness impacts employment and income via an indirect route of local wage determination. Similarly, in model VI, we also refine the export-base driven, labor-shift emphasis of net migration determination. Rather than assuming that population change responds directly to export-base or aggregate employment change, it is recognized that net migration decisions, being economic choices from a set of alternatives, are made in response to relative economic conditions. In particular, equation 6.4 or 6.4' is replaced by

$$(NM/POP)^i = \beta_{i,24} + \beta_{i,25} W^i/W^{US} + \beta_{i,26} U^i/U^{US} \\ + \beta_{i,27} h(EX^i) \qquad (6.4'')$$

with typically a logical lag in response of migration to actual shifts in relative economic conditions. The final term in equation 6.4" recognizes that although export-base employment may not singularly drive net migration, it can still have a role in migration determination in one of several ways. Percent change in local export-base manufacturing employment relative to percent change in U.S. manufacturing employment is itself a measure of relative local economic conditions. Furthermore, if export-base production requires specialized skills, its expansion may directly cause importation of labor embodying these skills. Thus, it is not surprising that percent change in export-base employment still affects migration in areas in which export-base employment is heavily impacted by specialized mining activities—Tucson and southeastern Utah. In fact, for southeastern Utah, the percent change in export-base activity is the only significant variable affecting net migration even in model structure VI. It is a small, rural area, heavily dominated in economic base by particular coal and uranium mining activities. Although perhaps not the usual situation, it is useful to recognize that there do exist small areas tied to particular industries whose expansion and contraction in fact drive local economic-demographic development.

Unlike W^i in equation 6.14 and 6.15, W^i in equation 6.4″ is implicitly a representative local wage, not necessarily a particular industry wage. For some areas, a specific industry wage may be a good measure of general local wage levels. However, in other cases, it was necessary to replace W^i/W^{US} by relative per capita incomes, recognizing that the dominance of labor income as a percent of personal income makes this a reasonable measure of relative earnings opportunities.

Finally, refinement of economic to demographic impacts in model VI was not limited to the net migration component of population change. Equation 6.5 for natural increase was expanded to include economic factors affecting birth decisions: unemployment rate, real per capita income, and real wage rates. As only logical, these factors have a lagged effect on birthrate. One or more of these economic variables was significant for four of the six areas. Economic conditions did not significantly affect rate of natural increase in the Springfield or southeastern Utah models.

Model VII—Disaggregation of Employment

In the sequence of models, model VI completes refinement of economic-demographic linkages among broadly aggregated variables. Models VII and VIII look at the benefit of refining the links first by disaggregating local-serving employment and second by disaggregating personal income. Equation 6.15 (the expansion of 6.8 and 6.8′) implicitly assumes that all local-serving sectors can appropriately be modeled as being identically influenced by changes in local population, local income, and local relative labor costs—identical in the sense that, except for size of coefficient, the appropriate structural equation for all subsectors is the same as 6.15. To the extent that this assumption is incorrect, there is aggregation error in the specification and estimation of 6.15. Several factors may contribute to the invalidity of the assumption. Both labor cost and the potential for substituting other inputs for labor differ across local-serving sectors yielding different appropriate wage variables and different estimated elasticities of labor demand with respect to relative labor costs (e.g., Cox and Oaxaca 1981, Appendix A).

Furthermore, per capita income and population elasticities of employment across trade, services, government, etc., are not equal. Three separate conditions cause this inequality. First, production functions differ across sectors yielding different elasticities of employment with respect to sector output (e.g., Cox and Oaxaca 1981, Appendix A). Second, underlying consumer income elasticities of demand differ across various commodities and services yielding different derived elasticities of output and employment with respect to local income. (For variations in income elasticities across consumption categories, see, for example, Houthakker and Taylor 1970.) Third, not all local-serving sectors are equally local-serving. Perfect separation of export-base and local-serving components of employment cannot be achieved by aggregation of one-digit (or even two-digit or three-digit) categories of employment (see Isserman 1980). Any definition separating the two components inevitably leaves some local-serving employment in the sector defined as export-base and vice versa. For some areas, significant export-base components in particular local sectors reduce local population and income elasticities of employment compared with other almost exclusively local-serving sectors.

Finally, while *level* of population is the appropriate demographic variable in determining trade, service, and government employment, it is less clearly the sole appropriate demographic variable for the sectors of construction, transportation-communications-utilities, and finance-insurance-real estate. Local area residential construction and real estate activities are typically particularly sensitive to population *growth* as opposed to level. The labor-intensive facets of communications and utilities tend to be concentrated in installation, the latter being determined by construction activity and hence, population growth or change.

The model VII disaggregation of local-serving employment into one-digit categories permits incorporation of these sector-specific refinements. In particular, equation 6.8 (or 6.8′) is eliminated and replaced by an identity:

$$EL^i \equiv ECC^i + ETCPU^i + ETRAD^i + EFIRE^i + ESERV^i + EGOV^i \tag{6.8″}$$

with separate equations estimating ECC = employment in construction; $ETCPU$ = employment in transportation, communication, and public utilities; $ETRAD$ = employment in trade; $EFIRE$ = employment in finance, insurance, and real estate; $ESERV$ = employment in services; and $EGOV$ = employment in government. For San Francisco, there is also a separate equation for mining employment, $EMIN$, and this component is included in the identity in equation 6.8″. The very small mining sector in Phoenix (< 400 persons) is aggregated with construction employment since the mining sector there is primarily composed of firms related to local construction. The data aggregate the very small mining sectors of

Springfield and mid-Cumberland Tennessee with services. Mining is part of the export-base sector in Tucson and southeastern Utah.

For all areas except southeastern Utah, there were variations across sectors in appropriate relative labor-cost variables and elasticity of employment with respect to labor cost.[5] Lower wage labor-cost variables were concentrated in service, finance, and trade local-serving sectors. Elasticities of employment with respect to relative labor costs tended to be higher in transportation-communication-public utilities compared with services and trade (approximately −.5 in the former compared with −.1 to −.4 in the latter). Similarly, population and real per capita income elasticities varied across sectors. Employment elasticities with respect to population were approximately one for services, trade, and government and generally less for transportation-communication-public utilities. Similarly, real per capita income elasticities were less in transportation-communication-public utilities than in trade and services. Per capita income was a significant determinant of government employment only for Tucson, and there its elasticity of .4 was less than its 1.2 elasticity for trade employment and .8 for services.

Export-base components of local-serving sectors were important in the San Francisco and southeastern Utah models. Since San Francisco is a major shipping and trade port, its large transportation sector (approximately 85,000 employees) is substantially export-base in nature. The city is also a national financial center and a popular tourist and business convention location. Consequently, national as well as local variables were significant in determination of San Francisco's employment in the one-digit sectors of finance-insurance-real estate and trade. Both utility and construction employment in southeastern Utah have large export-base components. Coal-mining and power generation are part of a unified, exogenously determined development. Furthermore, much of the construction in the area is related to mining and utility-plant expansion. Finally, there were clear export-base tourism impacts in the southeastern Utah trade sector generated by visits to the various national parks and monuments in the region.[6]

Finally, *changes* in population were significant determinants of construction employment in all areas except southeastern Utah. They were furthermore significant either directly, or indirectly through a construction employment variable, in determining transportation-communication-utility employment in four of the six areas. The local population change variable was not significant in the two areas discussed above which have large export-base components in this one-digit sector (San Francisco and southeastern Utah). Finally, for three of the six areas (San Francisco,

Phoenix, and Tucson), the change in demographic specification was significant in the determination of employment in finance-insurance-real estate.

Model VIII—Disaggregation of Income

Similarly to the model VII disaggregation of equation 6.8 (or 6.8'), model VIII disaggregates income determination (equation 6.10 or 6.10'). The latter retains the previous model's employment disaggregation and hence is an extension of disaggregation and not a substitution. Just as specification of income and population variables differ among subcomponents of local-serving employment, the role of employment, population, and wages varies among major categories of personal income: labor and proprietors income (LI), transfer payments (TP), dividends, interest, and rent (DIV), residence adjustment (RA), and personal contributions to social insurance (PERCONT). For four of the six areas with industrially disaggregated data on labor and proprietors' income available, LI is further divided into high wage (LIHIWAG) and low wage (LILOWAG) sectors. The former is defined (admittedly arbitrarily) as labor and proprietors' income from mining, manufacturing, and construction. Letting $EHIWAG$ and $ELOWAG$ denote corresponding employment levels:

$$LIHIWAG^i = \gamma_{i,1} (EHIWAG^i)^{\gamma_{i,2}} (W_{hi}^i)^{\gamma_{i,3}} \qquad (6.18)$$

$$LILOWAG^i = \gamma_{i,4} (ELOWAG^i)^{\gamma_{i,5}} (W_{lo}^i)^{\gamma_{i,6}} \qquad (6.19)$$

$$LI \equiv LIHIWAG + LILOWAG \qquad (6.20)$$

where W_{hi}^i and W_{lo}^i are wage variables (or vectors) specifying wages in the high and low wage sectors, respectively. Two variants of equations 6.18 and 6.19 appear in the models. First, in income determination based on number of employees instead of hours, there can be the same problem of cyclical variation in hours per employee discussed earlier with regard to equation 6.14. Thus, it may be necessary to adjust 6.18 or 6.19 to include a cyclical variable (e.g., capacity utilization in manufacturing). Second, $\gamma_{i,2}$, $\gamma_{i,3}$, $\gamma_{i,5}$ and $\gamma_{i,6}$ all are expected to be near one. However, sometimes multicollinearity among the independent variables in equation 6.18 and 6.19 resulted in illogical magnitudes on these coefficients. Often this problem was correctable by substituting a single multiplicative variable, e.g., $EHIWAG^i \cdot W_{hi}^i$, for the two separate variables.

Transfer payments are estimated on a per capita basis as a function of the corresponding U.S. variable and the relative local to national unemployment rate:

$$(TP/POP)^i = \gamma_{i,7} + \gamma_{i,8}(TP/POP)^{US} + \gamma_{i,9}(U^i/U^{US}). \quad (6.21)$$

The unemployment rate term allows for differing levels of welfare-type transfer payments in the local economy as a result of differing relative economic conditions.

The other two major components of personal income in the six areas are:

$$(DIV/POP)^i = \gamma_{i,10} + \gamma_{i,11}(DIV/POP)^{US} + \gamma_{i,12}(LI/POP)^i \quad (6.22)$$

$$(PERCONT)^i = \gamma_{i,13} + \gamma_{i,14}LI + \gamma_{i,15}CR + \gamma_{i,16}CB \quad (6.23)$$

where CR = FICA contribution rate and CB = ceiling on income subject to FICA payments. Specification of the residence adjustment varies across areas as a function of LI and/or U and/or a trend term, depending upon the nature of the commuting pattern in the region.

Model structures I–VIII were estimated for each of the six areas using annual data. Substate data base limitations generally restricted the period of estimation to the late 1950s or 1960 through 1974. Because of the shortness of the data bases, simultaneous equation techniques were not used on models IV–VIII. The decision to use ordinary least-squares estimation on all models reflects results of two sets of studies in the literature: (1) general Monte Carlo studies of small sample properties of different estimators are conflicting and inconclusive (e.g., Cragg 1967; Johnston 1972; Quandt 1962; Summers 1965; and Wagner 1958); and (2) regional modelers who have experimented with different estimation procedures have found ordinary least-squares estimation yields models as accurate, or more accurate than, simultaneous equation techniques (e.g., Glickman 1971; Hall and Licari 1974; and Latham, Lewis, and Landon 1979).

Model Comparisons

The models were tested for short-run accuracy by performing a sequence of seven three-year simulations and for long-run accuracy by conducting a single nine-year simulation, 1966–74. All simulations are in-sample. Several series revisions and area definition changes prevented evaluation of

Table 6-3. Mean Absolute Percent Error of Estimate Over Seven Three-Year Simulations[a]

Variable	Model Type and MAPE							
	I	II	III	IV	V	VI	VII	VIII
San Francisco-Oakland								
POP	.40	.65	.39	.32*	.36	.33	.34	.33
ET	2.20	1.24	.67	1.38	1.30	.95	.56	.50*
Y	1.01	.68	.68	.48	.47	.39*	.43	.41
E/P	2.13	.89	.76	1.37	1.18	.88	.50	.46*
Y/P	.79	.41	.59	.53	.50	.38	.32*	.41
Phoenix								
POP	2.27	2.27	2.27	1.68	1.68	.77*	.94	.89
ET	2.30	2.57	.97*	2.17	2.71	1.21	1.65	1.34
Y	2.18	2.36	2.44	1.30*	2.83	1.43	1.70	1.59
E/P	1.55	2.98	2.07	1.08	1.61	1.48	1.20	.89*
Y/P	1.87	3.14	2.47	1.40	1.27	1.60	1.38	1.15*
Mid-Cumberland								
POP	.34	.34	.34	.55	.55	.25*	.25*	.25*
ET	1.89	2.14	2.14	.96	1.38	.49*	.87	.96
Y	1.92	1.45	1.43	1.90	1.45	.56*	.74	.87
E/P	1.65	2.02	2.02	.62	1.04	.34*	.72	.84
Y/P	1.92	1.48	1.34	1.40	1.22	.55*	.70	.79
Springfield-Chicopee-Holyoke								
POP	.90	.59	.73	.56	.56	.34	.34	.33*
ET	1.90	1.02	.73	.88	1.13	.56	.31	.30*
Y	2.31	1.71	1.71	2.21	1.98	1.02	1.00	.45*
E/P	2.63	1.50	1.16	1.21	1.38	.54	.44*	.45
Y/P	2.68	1.58	2.42	1.80	1.54	.99	.98	.39*
Southeastern Utah								
POP	1.05*	1.05*	1.66	2.60	1.41	1.41	1.41	1.41
ET	3.48	3.48	2.04*	3.00	2.97	2.80	2.18	2.33
Y	4.90	4.90	3.78	2.26*	3.69	3.81	3.10	2.80
E/P	3.11	3.11	1.70*	2.86	2.74	2.38	2.20	2.36
Y/P	4.56	4.56	3.61	2.62	2.87	2.18	2.00*	2.66
Tucson								
POP	2.03	2.03	1.07*	1.79	2.74	1.24	1.34	1.64
ET	2.19	2.19	2.30	2.98	6.42	2.06	1.35*	2.37
Y	2.53	2.53	2.02	2.21	4.99	1.33	.82*	2.56
E/P	1.60	1.60	1.62	2.39	3.93	1.69	1.02*	1.28
Y/P	1.58	1.58	1.60	1.47	3.37	1.35	.98*	1.76

[a] An asterisk denotes lowest MAPE in the row.

a post-sample test for all variables. It would have been possible to examine employment simulation accuracy for the six areas for 1975–76. While the latter is interesting for economic turning-point analysis, this topic has been treated elsewhere (Taylor 1982a). Rather than repeat material from that study, this chapter focuses on economic-demographic interactions and the consistency of economic-demographic estimates over different lengths of simulation. Consequently, testing is restricted to periods with full economic-demographic information available.

The mean absolute percent error of estimate (MAPE) over the three-year simulations are presented in table 6–3 for each major economic-demographic variable by area and by model structure. An asterisk denotes the lowest MAPE across model structures for a given variable in a given area.

Looking at the pattern of asterisks in table 6–3, there are two immediate observations to be made. First, no single model structure dominates as most accurate either overall or for any single variable for all areas. This result clearly confirms the necessity of examining structural methodological issues in regional modeling with diverse areas. Second, excluding southeastern Utah, almost all of the asterisks, 21 of 25, occur in the last three columns, model structures VI to VIII. Some level of careful simultaneous specification and solution is generally necessary for minimizing short-run economic-demographic simulation error. This finding is especially important with respect to the variables measuring consistency of economic-demographic forecasts, E/P and Y/P. Again except for southeastern Utah, the minimum MAPE for these two variables for all areas occurs in models VI, VII, or VIII. Even for southeastern Utah in which each of $ET, Y,$ and POP is individually most accurately simulated in one of model structures I to IV, the lowest MAPE on Y/P is in model structure VII, and the E/P MAPE's for models VI, VII, and VIII are lower than those for any other structure except III.

Before turning to a closer discussion of models VI through VIII, the anomalous result of southeastern Utah should be put in perspective. Very little is added to the accuracy of modeling this area beyond the inclusion of exogenous determinants of export-base activity (model III)—which is not surprising given the regression results discussed in the second section. First, recall that none of the relative economic conditions refinements to the net migration specification were significant for this area. Only the percent change in export-base employment has a significant impact on migration to the area. Second, relative labor-cost variables were not significant in determination of employment, not for export-base employment or aggregated local-serving employment or disaggregated local-serving employment. These first two empirical results substantially negate the theoretical attraction of models VI and VII for this area. Finally, three of the one-digit local-serving sectors in southeastern Utah have major export-base components. The conclusion from all of these empirical results taken together is that for this small, rural area, activity in the export-base mining-power generation industry effectively determines most characteristics of the local economy. Little is gained in modeling accuracy by the more sophisticated specification refinements appropriate for larger, more diversified, metropolitan areas.

Turning to the other five regions, it is fairly easy to select optimal model structure from table 6–2 for four of the areas: San Francisco (model VIII), mid-Cumberland (model VI), Springfield (model VIII), and Tucson (model VII). The results for Phoenix are somewhat more mixed, but in balancing trade-offs in accuracy across variables, one would probably select VI or VIII for a single structure choice. Beyond the earlier observation that the same structure is not optimal for all areas, three major points stand out in comparing models VI through VIII for these five regions: (1) the progression from VI to VIII has relatively little or no impact on population-estimation accuracy for any of the areas; (2) except for population, accuracy of the mid-Cumberland simulations sharply declines in structure VII compared with structure VI (an average 62 percent increase in MAPE in model VII over model VI for ET, Y, E/P, and Y/P); and (3) except for population, accuracy of the Tucson simulations sharply declines between model structures VII and VIII (an average doubling of MAPE in model VIII over model VII for ET, Y, E/P, and Y/P).

Point one is interesting because the refinements in demographic to economic impact embodied in structures VII and VIII, compared with structure VI, do clearly affect employment and income accuracy. However, significant feedback from changes in the simulation accuracy of the latter two sectors to population determination is not apparent empirically. Part of the reason for this result may be the short simulation time horizon, three years. Economic determinants of population change generally enter with a lag in the net migration and natural increase equations, so only in the second and third periods of simulation is there even any scope for feedback effects. Evidence of this phenomenon can be seen by comparing MAPE's individually for the first, second, and third years of the simulations. For example, in going from model VII to model VIII in Tucson, the increase in population MAPE of only 22 percent is not nearly as large as the 75 percent increase in employment MAPE and tripling of the income MAPE. However, the 22 percent is an average of very different first, second, and third year increases in population simulation MAPE's. The two model's

MAPE's are identical for the first year of simulation, the model VIII MAPE exceeds the model VII MAPE by 16 percent in the second year of simulation, and by the third year of simulation, the model VIII MAPE exceeds the model VII MAPE by 44 percent. For the Phoenix area in table 6-2, the model VIII population MAPE exceeds the model VI MAPE by 19 percent. Again the MAPE's are identical for the first year of simulation, but the model VIII MAPE exceeds the model VI MAPE by 12 percent in the second year of simulation and by 33 percent in the third year of simulation. Similar differences can be perceived even for the almost identical model VI, VII, and VIII population MAPE's for San Francisco and Springfield. The San Francisco model VII population MAPE in the third year of simulation is more than 6 percent that of models VI and VIII, but only 3 percent greater for the average of the three years. In the Springfield sequence of models, the structures VI and VII three-year population MAPE's are only 3 percent over that of model VIII. However, restricted to the third year of simulation alone, the population MAPEs in models VI and VII exceed that of model VIII by 13 percent and 9 percent, respectively.

For most of the areas, the model VII structure simulates generally more accurately than model VI. The clear exception, however, is mid-Cumberland. Of all the areas, this one has the least variation in structure among local-serving subsectors. The simulation results clearly show the costs to disaggregation when there is not substantial inherent aggregation error in a total sector specification. With data-measurement errors, specification errors, and stochastic regressors, it is not true even theoretically that greater disaggregation improves estimation accuracy (see, e.g., Grunfeld and Griliches 1960; or for a theoretical application specific to regional modeling, Taylor and Charney 1983). When there is no clear aggregation error, "detail for detail's sake" can notably reduce model simulation accuracy.

The change from model structure VII to VIII, inclusion of income disaggregation, typically has small effects on simulation accuracy. Only for Springfield is there a substantial improvement in estimation of Y and Y/P, and even for this area, the feedbacks to ET and E/P accuracy are minimal. For San Francisco and Phoenix, model VIII is fairly consistently more accurate than VII, but the improvements are small in magnitude. Model VIII is marginally poorer than model VII for mid-Cumberland. For southeastern Utah, neither model structure is consistently more accurate than the other, but the differences between the two models are consistently small. A consistent, non-marginal difference between models VII and VIII characterizes only one area, Tucson, where model VIII performs more poorly than model VII. The result can be traced entirely to the disaggregation of high-wage and low-wage labor and proprietors' income. Tucson's high wage employment, mining, manufacturing, and construction generally simulates with less accuracy than the other areas for which labor and proprietors' income was disaggregated (i.e., San Francisco, Phoenix, and mid-Cumberland). The 4.4 percent Tucson MAPE on high-wage employment is two to five times that of the other three areas. As a consequence, the high-wage labor and proprietors' income MAPE of 5.1 percent in Tucson is also two to five times that of the other regions. The greater inaccuracy of the Tucson model reflects structural economic-demographic differences among the areas. Tucson's concentration of mining employment in a cyclically sensitive industry (copper) and concentration of manufacturing employment in the difficult to estimate, defense-related ordnance industry result in high simulation errors in the export-base sector. These problems are further compounded by sectoral concentration of employment in one or a few firms and the resulting small sample problems of specifying a single firm's activity. Finally, construction employment is particularly difficult to specify in Tucson because the area's average high, but uneven, population growth generates speculative cycles in residential construction superimposed on the usual cyclical variability of the housing industry (Taylor 1982b).

Although these structural factors explain why Tucson's high-wage employment simulates less accurately than that of other areas, it does not by itself explain why model VIII has such notably higher errors than model VII in this SMSA. The high-wage employment does not simulate any more accurately in the Tucson model VII than the Tucson model VIII, but in model VII the high wage employment has an impact on income-determination equivalent to other employment categories, whereas in model VIII this relatively inaccurately estimated employment component is given larger weight in income determination. Consequently, the relatively large high-wage employment errors are magnified in the income sector, tending to increase error on total personal income, which, through model feedbacks, increases the error on local-serving employment sectors. In summary, income disaggregation in conjunction with unusually large errors in high-wage employment determination can significantly raise interactive or reverberative error in the model resulting in an overall deterioration of model-simulation accuracy.

Thus far, the focus of discussion of empirical results has been on model structures VI, VII, and VIII. Although these were generally the most accurate models, a more complete perspective on the impact of economic-demographic refinements requires a broader survey of the simulation performance of all model structures. Consequently, it is instructive to review the empirical accuracy of models I through V. Only for two areas, San Francisco and Springfield, does the inclusion of U.S. economic-demographic trends in model II compared with model I improve simulation accuracy. Recall that for southeastern Utah and Tucson, these refinements were not even significant at the regression-estimation stage and, hence, for these two areas, model II is identical to model I. Furthermore, inclusion of aggregate U.S. demographic trends was not significant at the regression-estimation phase of model development for population determination in Phoenix and mid-Cumberland. Except for population, model II simulates less accurately than model I for Phoenix, and a comparison between the two model structures yields mixed results for mid-Cumberland. Poorer model II empirical simulation results in these two areas derives from the fact that weight on the lagged dependent variable tends to increase in moving from model I to model II. This shift causes increased intertemporal simulation error. For example, in the two Phoenix models, the coefficients on lagged ET and lagged Y/DF are .76 and .85 in model I regressions, but rise to over 1 (1.06 and 1.01) in model II. The same phenomenon occurs in the mid-Cumberland employment and real income regressions. Going from model I to II, estimated coefficients on the lagged dependent variable rise from .47 to 1.02 (employment) and 0 to 1.12 (real income). Although the model II intertemporal error compounding in mid-Cumberland income determination is not apparent from the three-year simulations alone, it does become clear in the nine-year simulation discussed below. In particular, over the nine-year simulation period, the model I MAPE on mid-Cumberland variable Y is 1.88 and the model II MAPE is 7.97! In short, model structure II is an improvement over model structure I only if a region is *very* similar to the U.S. in economic-demographic growth (e.g., San Francisco) *and* the transition from model I to model II does not significantly increase the estimated coefficient on the lagged dependent variable.

Generally, inclusion of exogenous determinants of export-base activity in specification of local variables improves employment simulation accuracy (model III compared with models I and II). The improvement is clear for four of the areas, San Francisco, Phoenix, Springfield, and southeastern Utah. For these regions, the ET MAPE declines an average of 44 percent between models II and III. However, there is no consistent improvement in income and population accuracy between models II and III. This latter result conflicts with theoretical models of regional development in which all local economic-demographic characteristics are directly derived from local export-base employment growth. Model IV separates net migration and natural increase estimation, disaggregates total employment into export-base and local-serving, and is simultaneous in structure but not solution. This set of refinements yields very mixed results compared with the first three models. For all areas, simulation accuracy of some variables improves and that of others deteriorates. Furthermore, for the same variable across areas, there is little consistency in the simulation accuracy of model IV compared with models I through III.

The empirical results of simulating model V are especially interesting. In the sequence of models, it is the first one that is simultaneous in both structure and solution. It allows for simple simultaneous interactions: local population and employment determine local income which in turn impacts local-serving employment; change in either total or export-base employment is the primary variable affecting net migration. Despite its theoretically more attractive economic-demographic simultaneity compared with models I to IV, model V does not simulate very accurately relative to these simpler model structures. Model V improves population-estimation accuracy over model IV for only one area, southeastern Utah; and in this case, both models IV and V are less accurate than the time-trend model I. For five of the six areas, employment-estimation accuracy is less in model V than model III. Income estimates have higher errors in model V than model III and/or IV for five of the six regions. In the sixth area, San Francisco-Oakland, the income accuracies of models IV and V are almost equivalent (a MAPE difference of only .01). Economic-demographic consistency as measured by errors on the E/P variable is less in model V than III and/or IV for all regions. Only in the simulation of Y/P is there any evidence of increased accuracy in model V. For four of the six areas, the MAPE's on Y/P are less in model V than models III and IV.

The relatively high errors in the simulation of model V make clear the need for careful wording on the earlier conclusion about simultaneity and model accuracy. In particular, it was not concluded that simultaneous models are *always* more accurate than non-simultaneous models, but rather that "some level of careful simultaneous specification and solution is generally necessary for minimizing short-run economic-demographic simulation error." It is apparent from the model V results that an incorrectly specified simultaneous model is less accurate in simulation than other nonsimultaneous structures. The increase in interactive error in model solution outweighs any benefits of partial improvement in structural specification. The role of interactive error is particularly clear in comparing models IV and V, which are identical in equation specification and differ only in that the latter is solved simultaneously, but the former is not. For example, the average MAPE reported in table 6–3 for Phoenix rises 32 percent between models IV and V and for Tucson 98 percent. The average

MAPE increases are less dramatic, but still present, for heavily export-base-dominated southeastern Utah and the inherently more accurately estimated mid-Cumberland. Model V reverberative error does not appear to be a simulation problem in only two of the areas, San Francisco and Springfield. These two regions have structural economic-demographic characteristics which permit comparatively high accuracy for all model structures.

In general, the economic-demographic refinements of model structure VI, inclusion of local wages (and local labor-market determinants of wages) and inclusion of relative economic conditions in determination of net migration, are critical components of simultaneous model structure if the latter is to simulate more accurately than non-simultaneous models.[7] Note the clear improvement in accuracy between models V and VI in table 6-2. Average MAPE for the five reported variables declines 23 percent for San Francisco, 36 percent for Phoenix, 61 percent for mid-Cumberland, 48 percent for Springfield, 8 percent for southeastern Utah, and 64 percent for Tucson.

Nine-Year Simulation

Table 6-4 presents the MAPE's for the nine-year simulation, 1966 through 1974. As expected, the MAPE's are generally higher over the longer simulation period. Between tables 6-3 and 6-4, increases in MAPE's outnumber declines two to one. There is a difference among models in comparative long-run versus short-run MAPE increase. Model structures III and VIII have the lowest average increase in MAPE—.13 and .12, respectively. Long-run instability is most apparent in model structures V and II. The high interactive error of model V results in an average MAPE increase of .68 between the three-year and nine-year simulation periods. The average increase in MAPE is almost one full point, .93, between tables 6-3 and 6-4 for model II. Recall that the intertemporal error compounding in this model resulting from high estimated coefficients on lagged dependent variables was apparent even in the three-year simulations. Not surprisingly, the problem becomes exaggerated in a nine-year simulation.

Optimal model structure for a particular area does not appear to be generally affected by the change in time horizon of simulation. Recognizing some trade-offs among variable MAPE's, the best model structure still is VI for mid-Cumberland, VIII for Springfield, III for southeastern Utah, and VII for Tucson. In the three-year simulations, choice between VI and VIII was not clear for Phoenix, but in the nine-year simulation, structure VIII definitely dominates for this area. Only for San Francisco do the long-run

Table 6-4. Mean Absolute Percent Error of Estimate over a Nine-Year Simulation Period[a]

	Model Type and MAPE							
Variable	I	II	III	IV	V	VI	VII	VIII
San Francisco-Oakland								
POP	.48	.50	.38	.18*	.26	.51	.63	.55
ET	2.15	.89	.56*	1.25	1.21	.78	.76	.71
Y	1.23	.67	.67	.62	.47*	.61	.87	.70
E/P	1.96	.60	.66	1.17	1.02	.70	.51	.40*
Y/P	1.60	.29*	.61	.68	.54	.53	.51	.46
Phoenix								
POP	2.96	2.96	2.96	2.84	2.84	.60	.57	.48*
ET	2.24	2.49	.81*	3.35	4.36	2.37	1.30	1.24
Y	2.58	2.89	2.67	1.15	4.18	2.68	1.30	1.09*
E/P	1.89	3.53	2.48	3.13	3.01	2.40	1.41	1.02*
Y/P	1.95	3.70	2.55	2.47	3.00	2.68	1.53	1.00*
Mid-Cumberland								
POP	.34*	.34*	.34*	.77	.77	.55	.55	.55
ET	1.89	2.55	2.55	1.10	1.52	.56*	1.00	.73
Y	1.88	7.97	1.98	2.16	1.55	.74*	1.09	.75
E/P	1.63	2.40	2.40	1.43	1.05	.57*	.99	.87
Y/P	1.87	8.08	2.10	1.58	1.04	.68*	1.05	.91
Springfield-Chicopee-Holyoke								
POP	.42	2.29	.33*	.74	.74	.55	.60	.46
ET	1.94	1.02	.84	1.05	1.59	.73	.24*	.36
Y	4.09	2.63	2.63	.88	3.17	1.02	1.00	.33*
E/P	2.27	3.09	.79	.80	1.48	.85	.69*	.77
Y/P	4.34	2.54	2.81	1.29	2.56	.98	.95	.39*
Southeastern Utah								
POP	1.28	1.28	.86*	2.59	2.59	2.59	2.59	2.59
ET	2.72	2.72	1.77*	2.64	2.62	2.53	2.77	2.61
Y	4.36	4.36	3.80	2.23	4.13	4.39	5.08	3.18*
E/P	3.66	3.66	1.39*	3.01	2.67	2.41	2.08	2.26
Y/P	4.49	4.49	3.57	3.48	2.62*	2.77	2.84	2.66
Tucson								
POP	4.24	4.24	1.14	1.92	5.08	1.00*	1.41	2.56
ET	1.88	1.88	2.25	2.77	9.10	1.80	1.18*	2.55
Y	2.50	2.50	2.22	1.87	6.85	1.17	.81*	2.56
E/P	5.31	5.31	2.03	2.70	5.41	1.40	1.18*	1.62
Y/P	4.13	4.13	2.63	2.73	4.28	1.23	1.06*	1.99

[a] An asterisk denotes lowest MAPE in the row.

simulation results present an obviously different pattern from the short-run results. Although model VIII generally yielded the lowest errors for this area in the three-year simulations, the MAPE on each of the five variables in table 6-4 is minimized by a different model structure in an almost random pattern. All of models II, III, VI, VII, and VIII yield highly accurate long-run empirical simulations for San Francisco.

Conclusions

The results of this study permit the following major conclusions:
1. Generally, some level of careful simultaneous specification and solution is necessary for minimizing all model simulation errors, especially those on the variables measuring economic-demographic consistency. For five of the six areas, optimal model structure is one of models VI through VIII. The exception is southeastern Utah, a small, rural area whose economic-demographic characteristics are essentially determined by changes in activity of its dominant export-base (mining and power generation). For this area, little is gained in modeling accuracy beyond structure III which includes exogenous determinants of export-base activity.
2. Simultaneous models which do not incorporate the economic-demographic refinements of model VI (local wages, local labor-market determinants of wages, relative economic conditions as determinants of net migration, economic determinants of natural increase) do not perform as well as alternative, non-simultaneous models. The increase in interactive or reverberative error in model V outweighs any benefits of the partial improvement in structural specification embedded in that model.
3. Optimal simultaneous structure (the choice among models VI, VII, and VIII) differs across areas. There is no single dominant structure for all regions. In particular, lack of significant structural differences among local-serving employment sectors can cause an increase in error between models VI and VII. Relatively large simulation errors in high-wage employment can become magnified in the disaggregated income-determination sector of model VIII, resulting in a decline in simulation accuracy for all variables over model VII.
4. Choice among model structures VI to VIII for short-term simulations is primarily based on differences in employment and income accuracy. In three-year simulations, population-estimation accuracy is almost equivalent across the three structures for all areas. The lack of feedback from changes in accuracy of the economic variables to population determination

is a result of the short time horizon of the simulation and the fact that economic variables generally enter demographic specification with a lag.

5. Inclusion of aggregate U.S. trends in model specification (model II) does not improve simulation accuracy unless the area is *very* similar to the United States in economic-demographic growth *and* the transition from model I to model II does not significantly raise the coefficients on lagged dependent variables causing increased intertemporal simulation errors. However, trends in natural increase appear to be similar across areas, and use of aggregate U.S. population trends does improve regional specification if restricted to natural increase specification alone.

6. Inclusion of exogenous determinants of export-base employment (model III over model II) typically improves employment and per capita employment simulation accuracy, but has less notable effects on other model variables. This result conflicts with theoretical models of regional development in which all local economic-demographic characteristics are directly derived from local export-base employment growth.

7. Generally, for each area, optimal model structure does not change between three-year and nine-year simulation time horizons. Model structures III and VIII exhibit the least decline in accuracy with the longer time period. Average MAPE increase is only .13 and .12 for these models between the two sets of simulations. The high interactive error of model V and the high intertemporal error compounding of model II result in the most substantial MAPE increases between short-run and long-run simulation periods (average MAPE increases of .68 and .93, respectively).

Regional econometric modelers are faced with a sequence of choices—sector coverage, disaggregation within a sector, intersectoral links, functional form, parameter estimation technique, and so on. In making decisions many issues must be balanced—economic-demographic theory, data limitations, model purpose, model accuracy, and model cost. However, scientific choices cannot be made without systematic analysis of alternatives. Construction of a new data series, increased detail in a sector, introduction of a different form for a production function—these choices cannot be evaluated logically in isolation. Just because an innovation does not yield inaccurate estimates or forecasts in one context does not imply that it (1) significantly improves upon a model which does not incorporate the innovation, (2) contributes to a model with a different time horizon or different forecasting versus policy analysis focus, or (3) is appropriate for a structurally very different economic-demographic region. Only systematic comparison of alternatives on a set of regions will yield insight into these issues. The present study has focused specifically on such an analysis of alternatives. Economic and demographic variables have been linked (or not linked) in regional econometric models for some time, but there has been little attempt to evaluate the appropriate level of sophistication of these links. Although this study has provided some insight, it too has its obvious limitations in terms of number of areas covered and types of linkages examined. Certainly the specific conclusions cited above require further research. The general result, that the systematic analysis tended to yield qualified conclusions and sometimes counterintuitive conclusions, is the most significant methodological outcome of the study and indicates the need for further analyses.

Notes

1. The mid-Cumberland EDD is a 13-county area centered on the Nashville-Davidson SMSA.
2. The southeastern Utah EDD is the rural four-county area of Carbon, Emery, Grand, and San Juan counties.
3. Total employment is measured as total nonagricultural, wage and salary, establishment employment. This variable is used both because its data series has fewer historical inconsistencies than total employment and because it can be disaggregated by one-digit industry. None of the areas is predominantly agricultural nor does any have significant in or out commuting patterns that cause establishment employment to deviate substantially from resident employment. Total nonagricultural wage and salary employment as a percent of total resident employment is approximately 80 percent for southeastern Utah, 85-90 percent for Springfield-Chicopee-Holyoke and mid-Cumberland Tennessee, 90-95 percent for Phoenix and Tucson, and 98 percent for San Francisco-Oakland. The lower percentage for southeastern Utah reflects primarily constant Indian reservation, non-commercial agricultural and non-salary employment.
4. Recall that for population estimation in Phoenix and mid-Cumberland, equation 6.1' was poorer than 6.1. Thus, for models I–III, population specification for these two areas is the simple time trend in 6.1. For model III, the real income equation in San Francisco and Springfield is 6.1'.
5. No wage variables were significant in southeastern Utah local-serving sectors. This result probably in part reflects lack of appropriate area-specific wage data (only average hourly earnings in coal mining were available) and the extreme smallness (and hence probably lesser scope for labor substitution) of some one-digit sectors. (For example, finance, insurance, and real estate averaged only 200 employees over the period of estimation.)
6. Other areas in the study besides San Francisco and southeastern Utah are also impacted by tourism. However, while these export-base factors show up in models that disaggregate trade and services to isolate the heavily tourist-impacted two-digit sectors (e.g., SIC 58, restaurants and bars, and SIC 70, hotels and motels), significant effects of national tourism-determining variables were not found empirically at the one-digit level other than in San Francisco and southeastern Utah.
7. To avoid confusion with conclusions in Taylor (1982a), it should be noted that the simple simultaneous structure of that study is essentially model VI, not model V, of the present study.

References

Charney, A.H., and Taylor, C.A. 1983. Decomposition of *ex ante* state model forecasting errors. *Journal of Regional Science*, 24:229–248.

Cox, J.C., and Oaxaca, R.L. 1981. Effects of minimum wage policy on inflation and output prices, employment, and real wage rates by industry. *Report of the minimum wage study commission.* Vol. VI-The minimum wage and the macro economy, pp. 171–210. Washington, D.C.: U.S. Government Printing Office.

Cragg, J.C. 1967. On the relative small sample properties of several structural equation estimators. *Econometrica* 35:89–110.

Gerking, S., and Isserman, A. 1981. Bifurcation and the time pattern of impacts in the economic base model. *Journal of Regional Science* 21: 451–467.

Glickman, N.J. 1971. An econometric forecasting model for the Philadelphia region. *Journal of Regional Science* 2: 15–32.

———. 1977. *Econometric analysis of regional systems.* New York: Academic Press.

Grunfeld, Y., and Griliches, Z. 1960. Is aggregation necessarily bad? *Review of Economics and Statistics* 42: 1–15.

Hall, O.P., and Licari, J.A. 1974. Building small region econometric models: extension of Glickman's structure to Los Angeles. *Journal of Regional Science* 14: 337–53.

Houthakker, H.S., and Taylor, L.D. 1970. *Consumer demand in the United States: analyses and projections.* Cambridge, MA: Harvard University Press.

Isard, W. 1960. *Methods of regional analysis: an introduction to regional science.* Cambridge, MA: M.I.T. Press.

Isserman, A. 1980. Estimating export activity in a regional economy: a theoretical and empirical analysis of alternative methods. *International Regional Science Review* 5: 155–184.

Johnston, J. 1972. *Econometric methods*, 2nd ed. New York: McGraw-Hill Book Co.

Latham, W.R.; Lewis, K.A.; and Landon, J.H. 1979. Regional econometric models: specification and simulation of a quarterly alternative for small regions. *Journal of Regional Science* 19: 1–14.

Ledent, J. 1978. Regional multiplier analysis: a demometric approach. *Environment and Planning A* 10: 537–60.

Muth, R.F. 1970. Migration: chicken or egg? *Southern Economic Journal* 37: 295–305.

Phillips, A.W. 1958. The relation between unemployment and the rate of change of money wage rates in the United Kingdom. *Econometrica* 25: 283–99.

Quandt, R.E. 1962. Some small sample properties of certain structural equation estimators. Research Memorandum No. 48, Econometric Research Program, Princeton.

Richardson, H.W. 1969. *Regional economics.* New York: Praeger Publishers.

———. 1978. The state of regional economics: a survey article. *International Regional Science Review* 3: 1–48.

Rubin, B.M., and Erickson, R.A. 1980. Specification and performance improvements in regional econometric models: a model for the Milwaukee metropolitan area. *Journal of Regional Science* 20: 11–36.

Summers, R. 1965. A capital intensive approach to the small sample properties of various simultaneous equation estimators. *Econometrica* 33: 1–41.

Taylor, C.A. 1982a. Econometric modeling of urban and other substate areas: an analysis of alternative methodologies. *Regional Science and Urban Economics* 12: 425–48.

———. 1982b. Regional econometric model comparisons: what do they mean? *Annals of Regional Science* 16: 1–15.

Taylor, C.A., and Charney, A.H. 1983. State-substate multiarea modeling: the case for non-rigid aggregation rules. *Review of Public Data Use*, 11:315–330.

Theil, H. 1954. *Linear aggregation of economic relations*. Amsterdam: North-Holland.

Wagner, H. 1958. A Monte Carlo study of estimates of simultaneous linear structural equations. *Econometrica* 26:117–33.

III INTERREGIONAL ECONOMIC-DEMOGRAPHIC MODELING

7 ECONOMIC-DEMOGRAPHIC LINKAGES IN AN INTERREGIONAL MODEL
Walter Isard and Christine Smith

Introduction

This chapter examines procedures for estimating linkages between the economic and demographic modules within an integrated multipolicy, multiregional model. This model is designed to identify the joint and interdependent impacts of a set of policies—in areas such as environment, employment, energy, housing, and transportation—and the impact of one policy on another. The economic-demographic linkages discussed represent part of a larger set of linkages required to make this integrated model operational. Because of limitations of space, the fully integrated model is sketched quickly, thereby enabling the demographic-economic linkages to be developed more fully. Although there may still be skepticism about the operationality of the fully integrated model, the demographic and economic modules and linkages between them are operational given available data and the data processing required. The focus here will be on the Australian multiregional system, since Smith (1982) has made a comprehensive survey of the data available to support implementation of such a model.

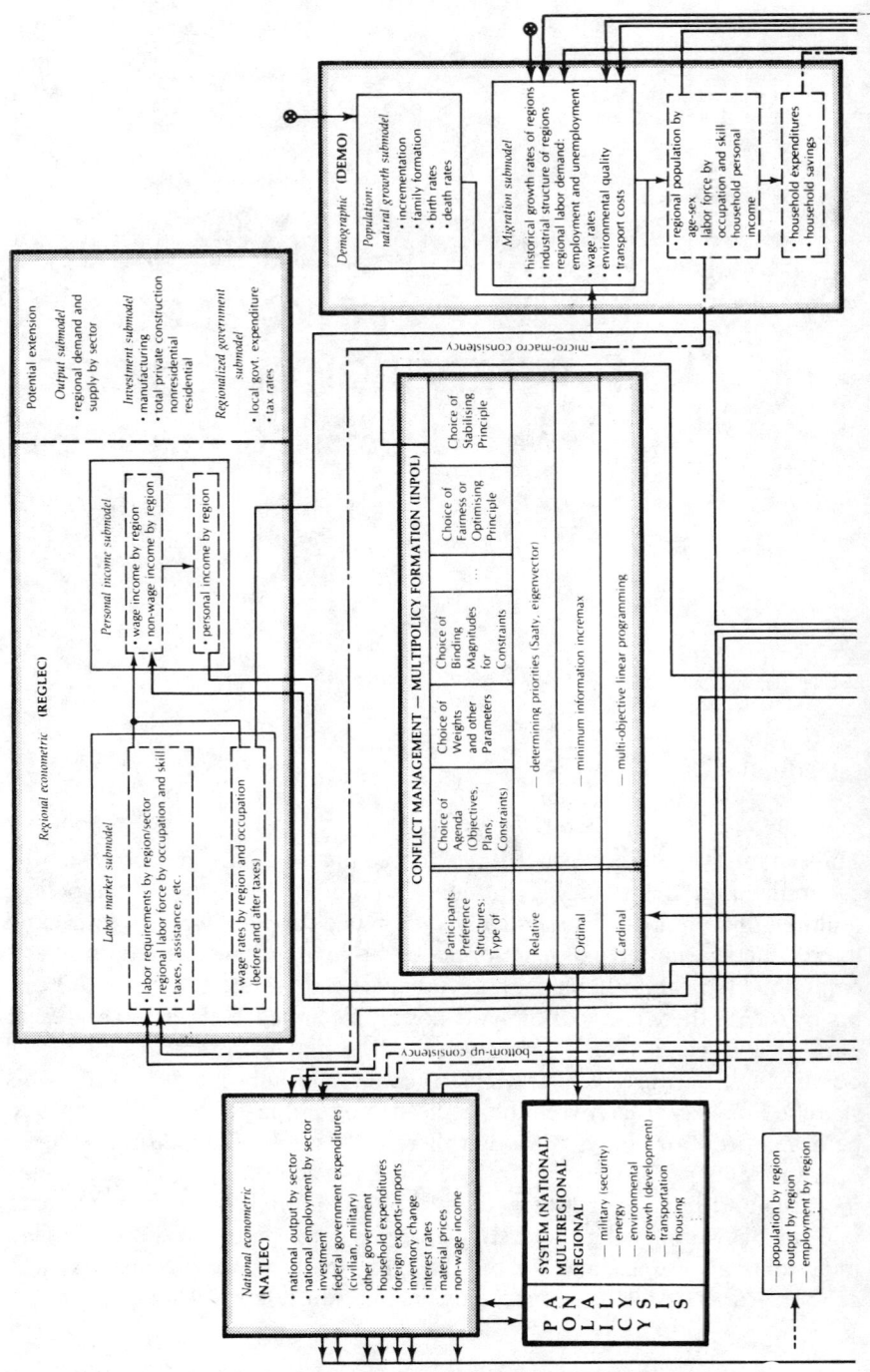

Figure 7-1. An integrated multiregional model

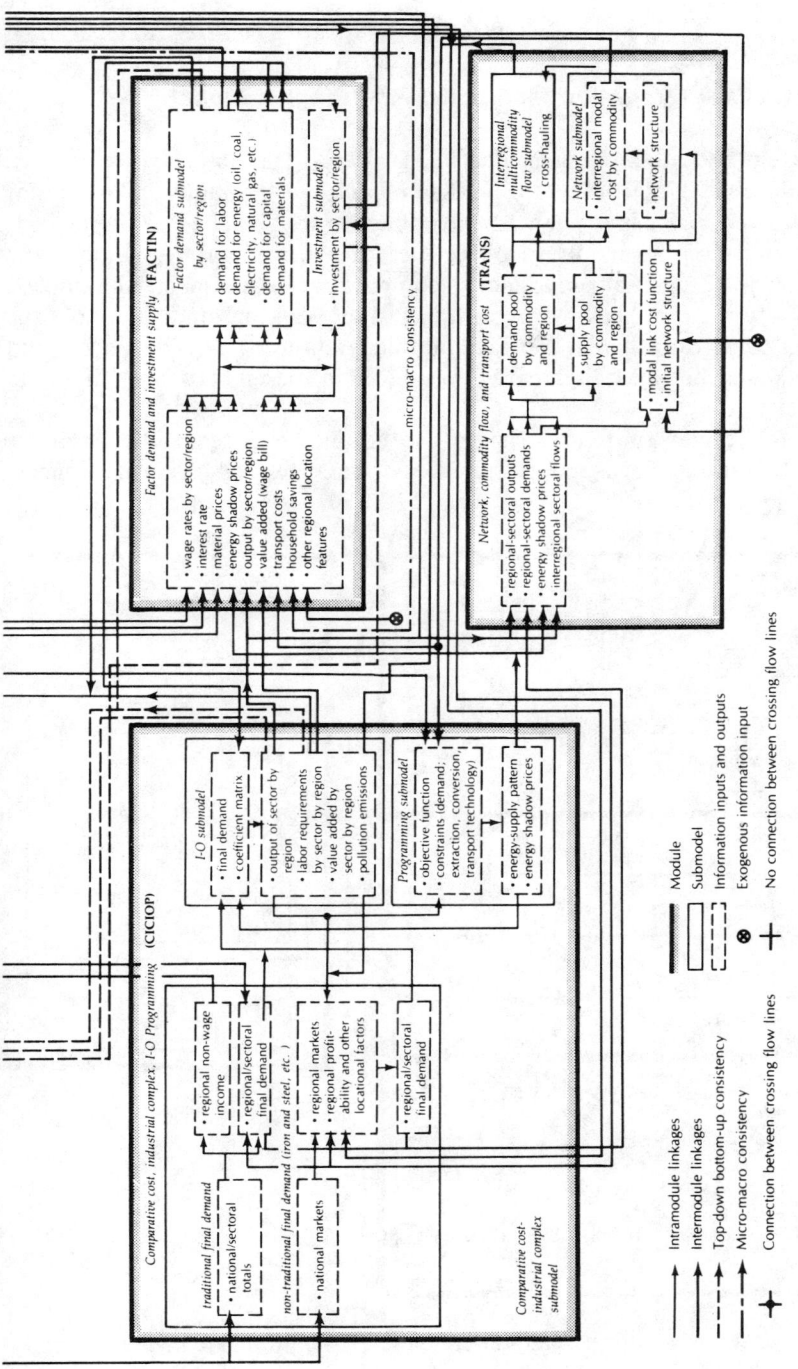

Sketch of the Integrated Multipolicy, Multiregion Model

The integrated model is presented in Isard and Anselin (1982) and Isard and Smith (1982a, 1982b, 1983). The model and the many linkages that are involved between its component modules are sketched in figure 7–1. Those parts of the model to be discussed in this chapter—namely, the demographic, regional econometric, comparative cost, industrial complex, input-output, and linear programming modules—are indicated by the boxes and arrows therein. To facilitate understanding, these modules and the linkages between them are reproduced in simplified form in figure 7–2.

At the center of figure 7–1 is the conflict management-multipolicy formation module designated INPOL. Given current or base year policies,

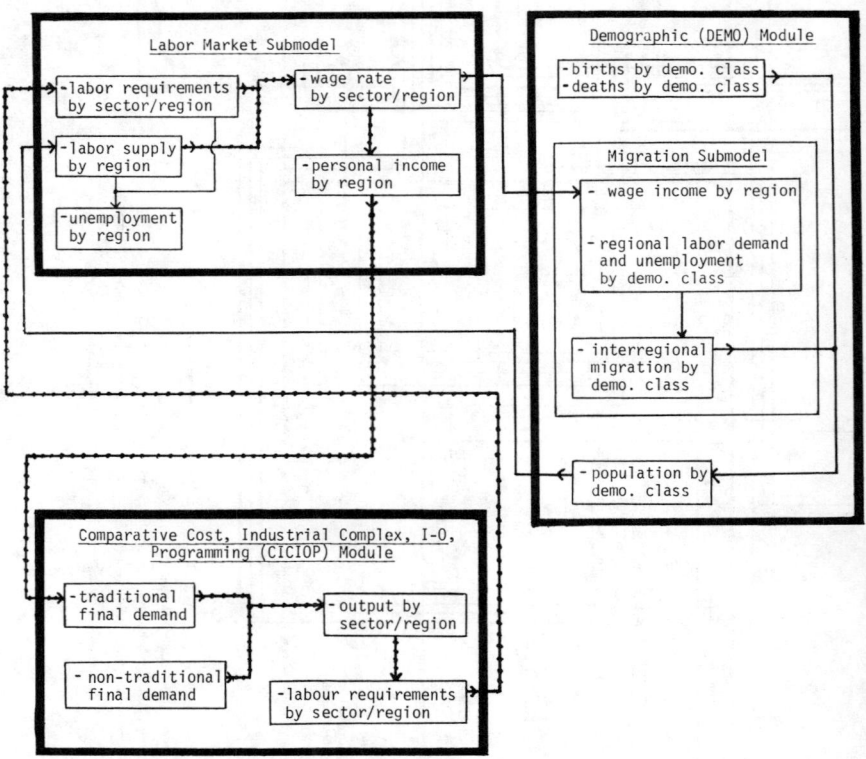

Figure 7-2. Selected economic-demographic linkages

the module is designed to project likely policy changes for a given year in the future, say 1990. These policy changes cover many programs (including tax rate and deficit financing decisions) and reflect the influence of many interest groups (sectoral, regional, etc.) at all levels of government. A number of procedures may be used to yield a most likely pattern of policy compromises. One procedure that may be employed to estimate these policy changes is the Saaty eigenvector approach for determining priorities (see Isard and Smith 1983, ch.5). Others are listed in figure 7–1. Moreover, the analyst is free to introduce other consistent alternative sets of policy changes.

To put these policy changes into place, consider an appropriate comparative cost, industrial complex, input-output, linear programming framework as indicated in the CICIOP box at the lower left-hand side of figure 7–1. The specific characteristics of this framework will depend, at least in part, on the multiregional system considered.

In the interregional input-output submodel, many policy changes can be represented as a set of changes in the several government programs (or components) of the final demand vector. The impact of such policy changes can then be derived in standard fashion via use of the Leontief inverse. However, for some sectors in certain situations input-output can be improved upon. The addition of a linear programming submodel dealing with the energy sector in the United States is a case in point (Isard and Anselin 1982). In Australia, a linear programming model for the major agricultural sectors, which is already in operation, can with minor modifications be fruitfully fused with the interregional input-output submodel. Smith (1982, ch. 3) discusses procedures which may be used in constructing such an interregional input-output model for Australia, and Longmire and others (1979) present a detailed description of the agricultural model. Combining them, in essence, requires removing the relevant agricultural sectors from the I-O structural matrix. A set of agricultural end-products can then be specified for each region. The output in physical units is available to meet foreign export demand, intermediate demands from nonagricultural sectors, the demands of the agricultural sectors themselves, and final demands from all regions. The final demand vectors required for operation of the combined model contain as components the set of inputs required to effect the level of each government program initially forecast as a result of analysis of likely compromises, legislation, and other policy decisions in the INPOL box. See Smith (1982, appendix 5A) for further discussion.

Before specifying demographic-economic linkages in our model for Australia, one more critical step must be taken. Given its mineral endowment (including abundant resources of coal, bauxite, and iron ore), it is absolutely essential to project changes in the regional pattern of mineral exploitation and the associated basic industry. This step can be done by conducting appropriate comparative cost and industrial complex analyses. Since these analyses have been discussed in the literature, including Isard and others (1960) and Smith (1982), the nature of the steps involved will not be spelled out here. Once the pattern of regional changes in these economic activities is projected, we remove the set of coefficients relating to each of these activities from the I-O structural matrix and treat each of these sets as components of nontraditional final demands. Isard and Kuenne (1953) and Isard and others (1960, ch. 12) present further details on this procedure in applied studies.

An integrated model also must confront the interface of the economic-demographic system with the transportation system. Hence figure 7–1 includes a TRANS module, which projects transportation costs, commodity flow, and network change. The transportation system is of critical importance for many industrializing and industrialized nations. Figure 7–1 also contains a factor demand and substitution module, an essential element of any model for a competitive-market system. Processes embodied in this module are discussed somewhat in the fourth section of this chapter.

Finally, the integrated model contains a national econometric module. This module is necessary because (1) for some variables, say employment, the sum of regional projections must equal the national; and (2) national variables such as interest rates and foreign exchange rates affect regional developments. These two categories of relations justify the use of a simultaneous bottom-up, top-down approach.

Demographic Module

The Australian Bureau of Statistics (1980) regularly publishes forecasts of the natural increase component of the population change of its states; they shall be used here as initial forecasts of national and regional populations. However, such forecasts are regarded as only crude beginning points, since migration projections should be made and used to modify the bureau's population projections. The level of overseas migration is treated as prespecified by policy, so attention is given to internal migration only.

Migration Submodel Employing a Simple Gravity Model Approach

Using a set of fixed output to employment coefficients, an input-output computation can easily be extended to produce employment-demand projections by sector for each region, and for each demographic class by age, sex, and occupation. In addition, historical labor-force participation rates can be used together with the initial crude population projections referred to above to yield labor-supply estimates by demographic class. Contrasting the labor requirements (demands) derived from input-output with these supply estimates yields regions of deficit and surplus for each demographic class. A nonbehavioral technical-type of gravity model may then be employed to eliminate deficits in the deficit regions.

This model is introduced simply to provide a reasonable fallback in case none of the other models based on the best available theoretical analyses of migration behavior produces reasonable results and in case no historical data are available on origin-specific, destination-specific migration (designated interregional migration). This point is important. For some multiregion situations reasonable results may be obtained from the best theoretical analyses, but sometimes reasonable results are obtained only with illegitimate changes in the theory to fit the data.

This model begins with the simple formula frequently used in the past:

$$M_d^{LJ} = G(S_d^L/d^{JL}) \tag{7.1}$$

where M_d^{LJ} is net migration of the labor force in age-sex-occupational (demographic) class d from region L to J; S_d^L is surplus labor-force members in demographic class d in region L (the excess of supply over demand); d^{JL} is a relevant measure of distance between J and L; and G is an arbitrary conversion constant with distance as units.

As a first step it is required that labor-force deficits D_d^J in each region be eliminated. If this is not the case initially for region J, the constant G is to be adjusted by a factor α^J. However, outmigration from any region must be checked against its surplus to ensure that net outmigration does not exceed the surplus. If this constraint is not met, then additional adjustment factors β^L must be introduced for surplus regions. Equation (7.1) thus becomes

$$M_d^{LJ} = G\alpha^J\beta^L(S_d^L/d^{JL}). \tag{7.2}$$

In general, several rounds of adjustments will need to be made to achieve convergence to a solution in which all deficits are met without exceeding the surplus of any region. The above assumes that the deficits in total do not exceed the surpluses. Should this assumption not be met, the initial crude population estimates can be revised upwards.

Fortunately, in the case of Australia, data do exist on interregional migration classified by age, sex, and occupation. Hence equation 7.2 can be given some "scientific" character. Data are available from the last three population censuses (1971, 1976, 1981). In this case, the term M_d^{IJ} refers to migration flows between periods $t - 5$ and t, which raises the obvious question of to which time period the surpluses and deficits refer. For this adjusted formula to work it is implictly assumed that there is no structural change in the population composition of regions during the five-year period and that in a sense the new industrial structure of year $t + 5$ is instantly achieved and the migration instantly occurs. Then given the observations for M_d^{IJ}, S_d^L, D_d^J, and d^{JL} in a given year, an estimate can be derived of the constant term $G\alpha^J\beta^L$ in equation 7.2 from standard calibration procedures. [See Batty (1976), Batty and Mackie (1972), Evans (1971), and Hyman (1969) for discussions of the process of calibration.] Then for projected surpluses, and assuming constant distances and parameters, migration flows to deficit regions can be projected. If projections are made for a nonfull-employment economy in year 1990 and a best estimate of a national unemployment rate is specified, then another constraint may be added which sets a maximum range on unemployment rate differences between each pair of regions. The binding magnitude for this constraint can be based (at least in part) on historical experience.

Since the above method does not effectively use all the relevant demographic data available for Australia, the remainder of this chapter will explore possibilities of doing better and will discuss the feedbacks between the economic and demographic modules.

Migration Submodel Employing a Combined Econometric-Gravity Approach

A richer behavioral approach which can be used to model interregional migration flows in the Australian context would include: (1) a set of econometric equations for inmigration by members of the labor force in each demographic class d, (2) a set of econometric equations for outmigration by members of the labor force in each demographic class d, and (3) a doubly constrained gravity model for projecting interregional migration flows. The gravity model may appear redundant since it does not affect the level of outmigration or inmigration projected for any region's labor-force members. However, for many purposes a knowledge of the pattern of interregional migration flows is required, thereby justifying the inclusion of the above-mentioned gravity model.

Inmigration Equations. Gross regional inmigration flows of persons of each demographic (age-sex) class in the labor force are determined as functions of: (1) the wage income per employee in region L relative to the nation (a proxy for the potential gains from migration out of L); (2) the change in employment demand in region L compared with the nation (a proxy for the change in employment opportunities in L relative to elsewhere); and (3) the ratio of employment demand relative to employment supply in region L compared to the nation (a proxy for the probability of obtaining employment in L relative to elsewhere). The dependent variable is expressed as the ratio of inmigration of a demographic class to the labor-force supply of that class in L. Smith (1982, ch. 6) contains a full presentation and discussion of these equations and others discussed below.

There are several problems associated with modeling inmigration in this way. The first involves the question of timing. The migration flows take place between the two points of time $t - 5$ and t, so that one has a choice as to which year the at-risk population in the denominator of the dependent variable refers. Is it $t - 5$ or t, or some intermediate point in this time span? Similarly, while the change components of the independent variables clearly refer to the change in employment demand between $t - 5$ and t, the other components can once again refer to conditions at either $t - 5$ or t or some other point in between. To keep things manageable, a simple average of conditions between t and $t - 5$ (or conditions at year $t - 3$) may be used wherever such a problem arises.

Second, while use of equations for each age-sex group is desirable, this practice raises the question of whether people consider just the benefits from migration accruing to members of their present demographic class or whether they take into account the possibility of changes in their demographic class affiliation over their life-time—because of either natural progression from one age group to another or increases in skill levels over time. The latter type of calculations are suggested by the human capital theory of migration. They can be introduced into the model by defining for each demographic class d a set of classes $\bar{d}$ which could reasonably be expected to be reached from d (and which are not so distant as to be eliminated from consideration once a reasonable discount factor is employed). The independent variables in the equations are then changed to be a weighted average of the corresponding variables in all demographic classes $\bar{d}$.

Third, since internal migration questions have only been asked on the last three population censuses in Australia, time-series and cross-sectional data must be pooled in order to be able to derive meaningful results from econometric analysis. Doing so does not permit regional differences in inmigration relationships, although one or more regional dummies may be introduced in order to get around this problem somewhat. Since so few observations exist even after pooling, care must be taken that the addition of dummies does not use up too many degrees of freedom. This pooling of data also provides the rationale for the use of the ratio-dependent variable rather than simply the flow in order to avoid the problem of heteroscedasticity that would otherwise arise because of regional differences in population sizes, and hence inmigration absorption potential.

Outmigration Equations. A similar set of econometric equations is proposed for modeling gross regional outmigration by members of the labor force aged 15–64, again in ratio form. Gross outmigration is hypothesized to increase (1) as wage rates decline relative to the nation, (2) as the percent of increase in wage rates declines relative to the nation, and (3) as unemployment rates increase relative to the nation.

A parallel set of problems arises with respect to this formulation. The question of timing arises, as does the question of the set of demographic classes to which the independent variables refer. Once again regional differences are ignored since we must pool time-series and cross-sectional data, and the dependent variable is expressed in ratio terms because of the problem of heteroscedasticity which would otherwise arise. Many of the same types of variables appear in both inmigration and outmigration equations. As a result, one or both of these equations may give nonsensical results (such as wrong signs) when confronted with the actual data.

The problem of ensuring that the sum of regional outmigration projections is equivalent to the sum of regional inmigration projections must also be resolved. We do so by taking a simple average of these two sums as a binding control total, and then proportionally adjusting the individual regional projections until this constraint is met.

Interregional Migration Flows. Net interregional migration flows for members of the labor force aged 15–64 are modeled via the use of a gravity model of the form:

$$M_d^{JL} = k^L l^J M_d^{J\cdot} M_d^{\cdot L} f(d^{JL}) \qquad (7.3)$$

with the double set of constraints:

$$\sum_{J \neq L} M_d^{JL} = M_d^{\cdot L} \qquad (7.4)$$

$$\sum_{L \neq J} M_d^{JL} = M_d^{J\cdot} . \qquad (7.5)$$

The first set of constraints expresses the requirement that the net number of migrants coming into L must be equal to the level of inmigration ($M_d^{\cdot L}$) estimated econometrically, and the second set expresses the symmetrical requirement that the net number of migrants leaving region J must be equal to the level of outmigration ($M_d^{J\cdot}$) estimated econometrically.

The solution of this distribution problem (i.e., the assignment of migrants among regions) is well known in the regional science literature. It requires that the conversion factors k^L and l^J be determined iteratively and that a specific form for the interaction impedance function $f(d^{JL})$ be determined. Batty (1976), Evans (1971), Kau and Sirmans (1979), and Wilson (1970), for example, present detailed discussion of this problem.

Interregional net migration rates for demographic classes comprising persons aged 15–64 who are not members of the labor force and demographic classes comprising persons aged 0–14 are assumed to change over time in the same proportion as those for members of the labor force. The interregional migration patterns of persons aged 65 and over may be determined using a set of fixed destination-specific migration rates for each region determined on the basis of the results of the latest population censuses or of time trends implied by the censuses. Where region-specific changes occur in other relevant factors such as in tax conditions or social welfare programs, ad hoc adjustments may be made.

Migration Submodel Employing an Econometric Approach Only

An exclusively econometric approach for modeling labor-force migration flows was considered under the hypothesis that a behavioral equation for origin-specific, destination-specific migration flows would perform better than a gravity model formulation. An equation for gross regional inmigration could be estimated as discussed previously. Then an equation for origin-specific migration shares ($M_d^{JL}/M_d^{\cdot L}$) could be estimated. Two of the independent variables would be the same as in the inmigration equation, i.e., relative wages and the relative employment demand-supply ratio, but relative change in wages would replace relative change in employment demand; however, all these variables would refer to the origin region J rather than the inmigration destination L. The level of gross regional outmigration could then be derived via a set of identities summing the migration from J to each destination.

A number of problems arise when trying to estimate migration flows in this fashion. There are the problems with respect to the appropriate timing of observations and the inclusion of migration gains in related demographic classes. In addition, the conventional ordinary least-squares regression technique cannot be employed, since it will not guarantee that the migration shares fall between 0 and 1. One useful transformation which can be used under the circumstances is that underlying the multinomial logit model, but although it guarantees that the shares each fall between 0 and 1, it does not guarantee that they sum to 1. Thus, since the demographic module includes an equation for estimating the total migration into region L, one of the share equations must be dropped and this region's share determined as a residual. In general, however, the results can be expected to vary depending on which share is treated as a residual—not a highly satisfactory state of affairs. After some iterations we may be able to identify a share that can be dropped and projected satisfactorily as a residual, but not when time-series and cross-sectional data have to be pooled in order to yield reasonable parameter estimates. It is difficult to interpret what one is really estimating when one attempts to calibrate a multinomial logit model using pooled time-series and cross-sectional data. Hence the analyst may feel more comfortable dismissing this type of approach until a reasonable time-series of interregional migration data become available.

Introduce Labor Market and Factor Substitution

With Fixed Output to Labor Demand Coefficients and Fixed Labor-Force Participation Rates

Wage rates are an important variable, and the use of a set of regional econometric equations for wage rates by demographic class by sector may improve demographic and economic projections. In particular, these equations will allow wage rates to be adjusted to reflect labor-market conditions in each region.

To keep the problem simple, begin by continuing to assume that labor demand for demographic class d by sector i in region J is determined from CICIOP output projections via the use of a set of fixed coefficients. Also continue to assume that labor-force participation rates by demographic class by region are constant, and hence that labor supply can be derived as an identity from population.

Wage rates in many countries are determined in a market, but in Australia wage rates by demographic class by sector are composed of two major components: (1) a basic wage component which is determined in the arbitration courts when national and state wage decisions are handed down; and (2) an above-award wage component, which is determined for each region on the basis of its local labor-market conditions. The rate of change of the national *basic* wage rate for demographic class d in sector i is modeled as a linear function of the change in the consumer price index (lagged) and the change in labor productivity in sector i (lagged). The rate of change for each region is a function of the national rate of change and a time trend included to reflect the increasing proportion of wage decisions covered by national rather than state awards, i.e., the convergence of basic wage rates toward the national average in each state. [The agricultural and defense sectors are modeled differently; see Smith (1982, ch. 7) for further discussion.]

The relationship between total wage rates and basic wage rates in any sector is then determined for each region as a function of local labor-market conditions (the employment supply-demand ratio) via a partial adjustment model. A partial adjustment model is used to reflect inertia and stickiness in the labor market.

The revised set of demographic-economic linkages is depicted in figure 7-2. The total wage rates when multiplied by employment demand and summed over all sectors yield wage income by demographic class. Recall that wage income by demographic class was a major explanatory variable in our migration equations, and hence a major factor determining regional population levels. Thus a feedback loop exists with (1) population levels leading to labor supply, (2) labor supply relative to labor demand determining wage rates, and (3) wage rates and other labor-market conditions determining the interregional migration and hence, in part, regional population levels. See the light arrows in figure 7-2.

In addition, wage income in a region is a major component of personal income in that region, and personal income is a major determinant of the household consumption component of the traditional final demand vector of the input-output model. Thus another feedback loop exists with (1) final demand determining output by sector by region via operation of the

CICIOP module, (2) output by sector by region determining labor demand by demographic class via a set of fixed output to employment coefficients, (3) labor demand relative to labor supply partially determining wage rates in each region, and (4) wage income forming a major component of personal income and hence partially determining the household consumption component of final demand (see the bold arrows in figure 7-2). In a fuller version of the integrated multiregional model the link between personal income and household consumption expenditures is made operational via the inclusion of a set of consumption equations within the regional econometric module (Smith 1982, ch. 7).

With Labor-Force Participation Rates Endogenous

Regional labor-force participation rates are influenced by labor-market conditions. A set of regional econometric equations is estimated for labor-force participation rates by demographic class. For males aged 26–64 the rate is a function of lagged wage rates (a proxy for gains from employment) and the lagged unemployment rate (a proxy for the probability of finding employment upon entering the labor force). The form of this equation differs somewhat for other demographic classes, but lagged wage rates and lagged unemployment rates appear in all equations. For example, for persons in age-groups 15–24 the proportion of the population that is full-time students is included as an explanatory variable, and for females aged 15–64 the median years of school completed, the number of dependents (persons under 15 years of age) per capita, and an index of the femininity of employment demand are included.

With these labor-force participation equations, a more involved set of demographic-economic linkages emerges. Wage rate changes in the current period not only lead to (1) changes in regional populations due to interregional migration but also to (2) changes in labor-force participation rates and hence (3) changes in the labor supply in the next period. Those changes in labor supply in turn lead to changed wage rates, but, as just discussed, changed wage rates lead also to (1) changed personal incomes, (2) changed consumption final demand, and hence (3) changed output levels and employment demand, and so on through many rounds of effects.

With Factor Substitution Permitted

Although the assumption of fixed output to employment ratios may be useful as a first approximation, another refinement is to recognize that, when wage rates change relative to the prices of other factors of production, profit-maximizing producers can be expected to engage in factor substitution.

One approach is to determine the relative inputs of different factors of production via duality principles and to employ a translog production function. If the analyst is prepared to assume that the production function for the given sector is weakly separable in the major categories of factors (i.e., the marginal rate of substitution between the various classes of labor, for instance, is independent of the level of capital, energy, and material inputs) and that the factor aggregates are homothetic in their components, then the shares of the different classes of labor in total labor costs can be derived (see Lakshmanan 1979). From these shares the regional demand for each labor class by the given sector can then be derived.

With this procedure, the demographic-economic linkages have become even more involved. Wage rate (labor price) changes in the current period lead not only to (1) changes in regional populations due to interregional migration and (2) changes in labor supply by demographic class due to revised labor-force participation rates in the next period, but they also lead to (3) changes in the demand for labor relative to other factors of production and to substitution among the different classes of labor. The other linkages already discussed still remain.

Substitution among factors of production also suggests the need for revisions in corresponding input-output coefficients for the given sector. Procedural rules by which these input-output coefficients might be revised are developed in Smith (1982, ch. 8).

Conclusion

We have developed a set of equations based on our best theory and subject to data limitations. We would like to investigate them further in the Australian context. They may or may not yield reasonable results. In addition, for the U.S. economy the possibility of employing a microsimulation approach is being explored. This flexibility in our thinking on the demographic module is consistent with the very flexible design of the integrated multiregion model. For each module in that model an analyst may introduce an approach best designed for his or her needs. Moreover, for many purposes and where resources are severely limited, only some of the modules may be developed. That is, only partially integrated models may be required or possible.

If demographers, economists, and regional scientists are to be as effective as possible in assisting political leaders, decision-makers, and others in formulating appropriate policies, they must develop the full range of linkages among the modules of figure 7-1 (and perhaps others to be added with time). Only then can they trace the impact of any one policy in a given policy area (say, housing, employment, transportation, or social welfare) upon the outcome of policies in other areas. In short, they must aim at analysis for wise joint or multipolicy formulation. That is why the INPOL box is at the center of figure 7-1.

References

Australian Bureau of Statistics. 1980. *Projections of the population of the states and territories of Australia.* Canberra: Australian Government Printing Service.
Batty, M. 1976. *Urban modelling.* New York: Cambridge University Press.
Batty, M., and Mackie, S. 1972. The calibration of gravity, entropy and related models of spatial interaction. *Environment and Planning A* 4: 131–150.
Evans, A. W. 1971. The calibration of trip distribution models with exponential or similar cost functions. *Transportation Research* 5: 15–38.
Hyman, G. M. 1969. The calibration of trip distribution models. *Environment and Planning A* 1: 105–112.
Isard, W., et al. 1960. *Methods of regional analysis: an introduction to regional science.* Cambridge, MA: M.I.T. Press.
Isard, W., and Anselin, L. 1982. Integration of multiregional models for policy analysis. *Environment and Planning A* 14: 359–376.
Isard, W., and Kuenne, R. E. 1953. The impact of steel upon the greater New York-Philadelphia industrial region: a study in agglomeration projection. *Review of Economics and Statistics* 35:289–301.
Isard, W., and Smith, C. 1982a. Linked integrated multiregion models at the international level. *Papers, Regional Science Association* 51: 3–19.
_____. 1982b. The world system, summary article IV: toward an integration of multiregional analysis and regional development approaches. *Man, Environment, Space and Time* 2, 2.
_____. 1983. *Conflict analysis and practical conflict management procedures.* Cambridge, MA: Ballinger Publishing Co.
Kau, J. B., and Sirmans, C. F. 1979. The functional form of the gravity model. *International Regional Science Review* 4, 2: 127–136.
Lakshmanan, T. R. 1979. A multiregional policy model of the economy, environment and energy. Working Paper NSF-79-1, Department of Geography, Boston University, Boston, MA.
Longmire, J. L., et al. 1979. *A regional programming model of the grazing industry.* Canberra: Bureau of Agricultural Economics.

Smith, C. 1982. Integration of multiregion models for policy analysis. Unpublished Ph.D. dissertation, Cornell University.

Wilson, A. G. 1970. *Entropy in urban and regional modelling.* London: Pion.

8 MULTISTATE DEMOECONOMIC MODELING AND PROJECTION

Andrei Rogers and Pamela Williams

Introduction

Demographic and economic change are intricately and simultaneously linked, and the usefulness of regional population projections is enhanced if they incorporate consistently the relationships between demographic and economic variables, including those policy variables over which decision-makers have control. Given the wide variety of uses and users of regional population projections, the relevance of the projections will also be increased by the maintenance of a high degree of disaggregation for important variables such as sex, age, marital status, and, where relevant, race.

In this chapter, a possible framework for multistate demoeconomic projection that incorporates these dimensions is presented. This framework makes use of several techniques currently available for the modeling and projection of demographic variables, including:

1. *multistate mathematical demography*, which imposes standard demographic accounting identities on the projections and incorporates the impacts of preceding demographic events by allowing for simultaneous and consistent determination of the effects on the projected size and distribution

of the population of all the rates of transition that are assumed to occur in the projection period;

2. *a two-sex model of marriage, divorce, and widowing*,[1] which takes into account the parallel transitions among individuals of each sex and ensures that there are no inconsistencies between such transitions;

3. *model schedules*, which parsimoniously describe the age distributions of demographic transitions ensuring consistency across age distributions and reducing the information to be projected to a few descriptive and interpretable parameters for each schedule of transition; and

4. *an economic model*, which determines the projected parameters of the demographic transitions by incorporating explicitly the assumptions that are made regarding the demographic and economic environment underlying the projection and by clearly specifying the relationships that exist between this environment and population change.

This framework ensures that population projections will be disaggregated, consistent, and policy-relevant. To our knowledge, it is the first multistate population projection model that contains not only fertility, mortality, and migration schedules but also considers marriage and divorce patterns and includes a two-sex model that ensures consistency in the determination of the future number of transitions between the married, divorced, and widowed states.

At this stage, the framework considers only one side of the joint interaction between the demography and economy of regions, namely, the effect of economic change upon regional populations and their distribution. It does so, however, in a more comprehensive manner than is normally provided within studies of joint interactions between economic and population growth. Population change, via its impact on consumer demand, housing demand, and labor supply, will affect the economic environment of regions, which will simultaneously affect the various components of that population growth. The framework presented here could readily be incorporated into a wider model of simultaneously determined economic and demographic growth. [See Powell (1982) for a prototype of such a model for Australia and Ledent (1978) for a model of Tucson, Arizona.]

This chapter represents a joint effort between two research groups that have been closely involved in the development of these techniques. The International Institute for Applied Systems Analysis (IIASA) has played a significant role in the development of the techniques and applications of multistate demography (Rogers 1980, 1981) and in the estimation of model schedules of many facets of demographic behavior for a large number of countries (Rogers and Castro 1981a). The IMPACT Project, in its efforts to construct a set of economy-wide models that will provide a systematic framework for the analysis of a large number of policy issues, has developed a facility for the consistent projection of the Australian population disaggregated by age, sex, and marital status (Sams 1979a; Sams and Williams 1980, 1982; Williams 1981). This facility employs model schedules and a two-sex marriage and divorce model and is driven by an economic model that relates marriage, divorce, fertility, and female labor-force participation behavior to their economic determinants. The framework described here combines aspects of these developments in demographic techniques at IIASA and IMPACT.

A schematic representation of the proposed framework for the consistent projection of a population disaggregated by age, sex, marital status, and region of residence is given in figure 8–1. For simplicity of representation, only two regions, A and B, are assumed to exist. We consider each of the features of this framework in turn.

The Projection Algorithm

Multistate population projection techniques are used to determine simultaneously the projected population from migration flows by sex, age, and marital status, marital status changes (becoming married, divorced, remarried, and widowed), deaths, and fertility.[2] For each year of projection, transition probabilities calculated from multistate life tables generated separately for each sex may be used to determine the projected level and distribution of the population. The projected populations can then be augmented by the expected numbers of international migrant arrivals and departures (disaggregated by sex, age, marital status, and region of arrival or departure) to give the projection of male and female populations by age, marital status, and region of residence.

These projections are consistent in the sense that the assumed transitions are used to determine the population, one sex at a time. However, the concept of consistency also relates to the harmony between the assumed demographic transitions themselves. For example, research suggests that families tend to migrate together; thus the probability that a child will migrate should be consistent with the probability that persons of the age of his or her parents will migrate. Similarly, the likelihood of a woman giving birth is higher when she is married and in the prime child-bearing ages, and also reflects the number of children she has already borne and expects to bear in the future; thus fertility projections should be consistent with these characteristics of the female population. Also, at various times, usually as

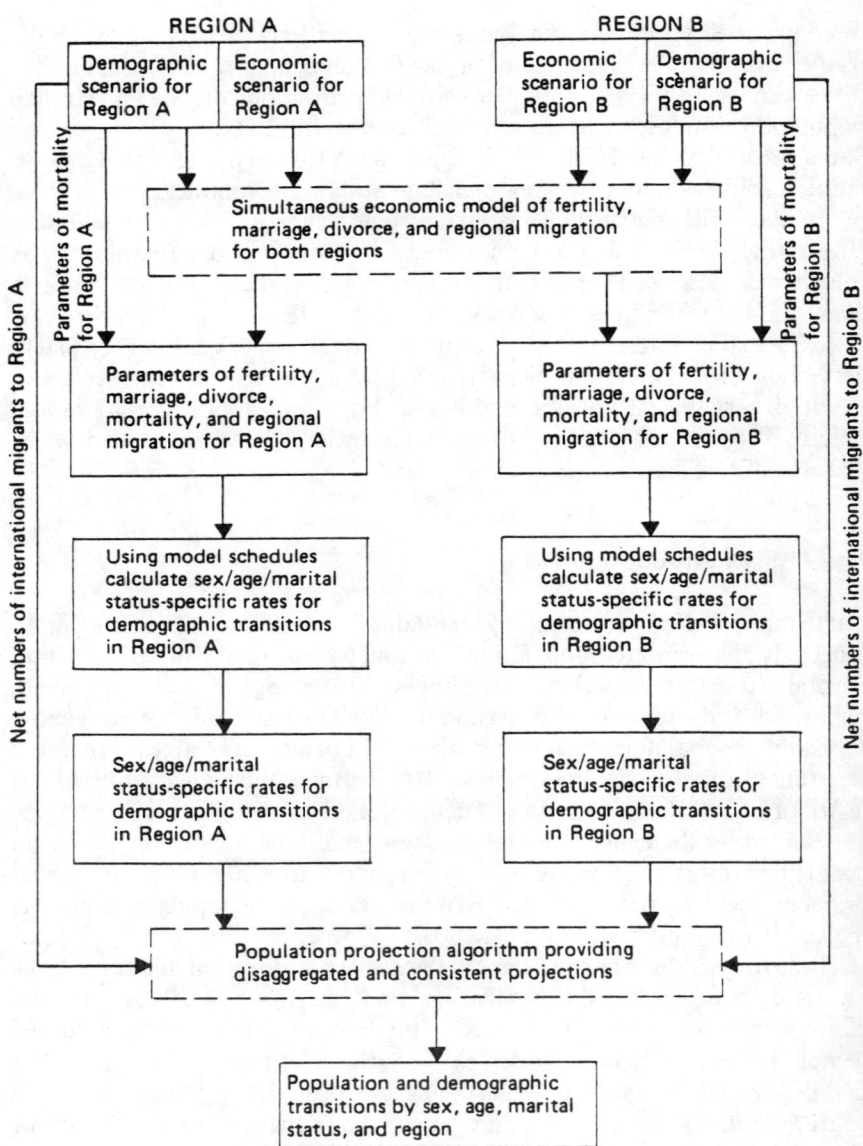

Figure 8-1. Schematic representation of a proposed framework for the consistent projection of a population disaggregated by age, sex, marital status, and region of residence

the result of large-scale migration or of war, the number of men and women of prime marriageable ages can become seriously unbalanced; thus it is necessary to ensure that the projected marriages of men and women are consistent with the likelihood of finding suitable partners.

Normally these consistencies can be approximated by the thoughtful projection of the required flows. In our framework, it is achieved partly by the use of model schedules to ensure consistency across age distributions, and partly by the use of an economic model to estimate the important features of demographic flows on the basis of their economic and demographic determinants. Consistency in the marital status changes of males and females requires special treatment. It is not realistic to project the transitions among individuals of one sex without taking into account parallel transitions among individuals of the other sex. The separate projection of the evolution of the male and female populations in our framework could lead to inconsistencies, such as the number of marriages or divorces of males not coinciding with the number of marriages or divorces of females over a given period, and the number of new widows during the year not coinciding with the number of deaths among married men in that year, and so on.

Operational resolutions to the problem of two-sex interaction are few; this chapter adopts one proposed by Sams (1981a) and incorporated into the population projection algorithm developed at IMPACT. The Sams procedure rests upon a matrix of married couples disaggregated by the age of each partner, which is updated from year to year over the projection period. The updating of this matrix requires the establishment of four sets of consistent demographic flows disaggregated by the age of the male and the age of the female involved in the transition—becoming married, divorced, and widowed, and married migrant arrivals and departures (both regional and international). In general, these consistent cross-tabulated flows are established by a two-stage process. First, the number of marriages, divorces, deaths, and arrivals and departures are calculated at each age for each sex on the basis of projected model schedules and the at-risk population for each event. Second, the consistent cross-tabulations by the age of each party to the event are established, sometimes leading to the adjustment of the initial numbers of marriages, etc., for each sex and, consequently, to changes in the implied age-specific rates.

For marriages, the Sams approach makes use of the possible difference between the number of marriages to men (women) of a given age *desired* by women (men) of that or some other age, *independent* of the supply of men (women) available, and the number of marriages which actually take place.

This divergence may occur for either or both of two reasons: there are physically not enough eligible men (women) of that given age available for marriage or the desires of eligible men (women) of that age are such that they do not wish to marry women (men) of the other age. The numbers of men and of women at each age desiring to marry are determined from model schedules of desired marriage and an economic model that projects, among other things, the parameters of those model schedules. We assume that these model schedules (in fact gamma distributions) for each sex are the marginal distributions of a bivariate gamma function whose parameters are those of the model schedules for males and females plus a correlation coefficient which can be estimated from cross-tabulated data. From this bivariate distribution it is possible to determine the number of marriages of couples of given ages desired by men and desired by women.

We then set up a constrained minimization problem which minimizes the differences between desired and actual marriages of men and women at each pair of ages, subject to the constraints that the number of marriages between women and men of any ages be not less than zero and that the total number of marriages of all women (men) to men (women) of a particular age does not exceed the stock of men (women) of that age. It is possible that not all of the total stock of men or women of a given age eligible for marriage would be willing to marry; in such cases, we could assume that only a proportion of the supply of women (men) of that particular age would be available for marriage. Such proportions would need to be determined by observation and intuition, since there would be little information available to estimate them systematically. Now, if none of these constraints were binding, the numbers of marriages between men and women of given ages would be simply the weighted sum of the number of marriages for couples of these given ages desired by men and desired by women. The weights could be expected to be equal, except in cases where the desires of one sex were found to be dominant. In such cases, the weights for the other sex could be set to lower values, even as low as zero. In situations where the constraints are binding, it is possible to establish a linear programming technique to determine consistency between the marriages of males and females at each pair of ages, as explained in Sams (1981a). Once the number of marriages by the age of each spouse is determined, consistency-adjusted age-specific marriage rates for men and women can be calculated using the populations at risk.

So far, we have ignored the complication that there are three types of marriages for each sex, depending on previous marital status, and therefore nine combinations of marriages between the sexes. In fact, the numbers of men and women at each age desiring to marry are determined separately for each previous marital status, and these are added together for each sex to form the desired level of marriage by the age of the partners. Once the reconciled cross-tabulation of marriages by the age of the partners is established, the number of marriages at each age for each sex by previous marital status is derived by distributing the reconciled number of marriages at each age in proportion to the original desired distribution of marriages by previous marital status at that age. Details of this procedure can be found in Sams (1981a).

Consistent cross-tabulations of transitions into the divorced and widowed states by the age of each spouse are calculated on the basis of a matrix of married couples by age of wife and age of husband. It is assumed, quite plausibly, that the death of a married male (female) is independent of the age of his (her) wife (husband). Thus, the widowing of married females (males) of a given age is equal to the number of those females (males) married to males (females) of any given age multiplied by the death rates of those males (females). For divorces, as for marriages, the numbers of married men and women at each age desiring to divorce are determined from model schedules and an economic model that projects the parameters of these model schedules. The number of divorces of married couples is then determined by the matrix of married couples by age and the arithmetic average of the desired divorce rates for each partner at their given ages. A scaling factor may also be introduced to take account of the higher probability of divorce for couples with wider age differences [as suggested by several studies, including Day (1963)]. Consistency-adjusted age-specific divorce rates for men and women can then be calculated using the populations at risk. Finally, consistency must be imposed on the arrivals and departures of married male and female migrants, both regional and international. In general, this is achieved by the iterative adjustment of a standard matrix of the relative ages of migrant couples to agree with the age profiles of migrants of each sex.

Procedurally, two-sex consistency must be incorporated into the multistate projection algorithm in an iterative manner. First, the desired number of marriages and divorces must be determined from the model schedules and the populations at risk and the numbers of new widows from the couples matrix and the death rates of married persons. Two-sex consistency is then imposed upon these marital status changes. Although consistency is imposed separately for each region, this may be inadequate when the regions under consideration have substantial demographic interaction, particularly where marriages occur between persons initially residing in different regions. In such cases, the reconciliation process which adjusts desired marriage rates should incorporate the possibility that some of those desiring marriage, but unable to find a suitable partner in their region of residence, may find a partner in another region. Once two-sex consistency has been imposed, the consistency-adjusted rates of marital status change can then be used within the multistate projection algorithm to determine consistent population projections. At the same time, the stocks of married couples by age of husband and age of wife must be updated in each period according to the transitions occurring to married persons.

The Model Schedules

The basic starting measure for most demographic analyses is a central rate that is defined for a population in a given region during a particular time span. In our projection framework, these occurrence or exposure rates are used wherever possible, as the projection of rates allows for the automatic response of projected demographic transitions to changes in the age and marital status profile of the regional populations. As indicated by figure 8–1, the ultimate inputs to the projection algorithm for each region are fertility rates, death rates, marriage and divorce rates, and regional migration rates. The use of occurrence or exposure rates is less valid for international migration, where the region of origin is the rest of the world.

The use of parametric functions to smooth and describe parsimoniously sets of age-specific rates is a common practice in demography. A variety of mathematical formulas has been proposed and fitted to mortality, fertility, marriage, divorce, and migration schedules; and the results have been widely used for such applications as data smoothing to eliminate irregularities, interpolating rates given for five-year age groups to single years of age, comparing different growth regimes, inferring rates from partial or inaccurate data, and forecasting future populations. The relevant literature is vast, and entry into it can be made from such representative publications as Brass (1971), Coale and Demeny (1966), Coale and Trussell (1974), Heligman and Pollard (1979), Hoem and others (1981), Rogers and Castro (1981a, 1981b), Rogers, Raquillet, and Castro (1978), United Nations (1967), and Williams (1981).

In our population projection framework, the role of model schedules is twofold. First, if highly disaggregated population projections are to be made, the transitions between states of existence, or the vital flows, in each year must retain a similar degree of disaggregation. Model schedules allows us to condense this enormous amount of information into a few parameters for each transition in each year. Second, if the model schedules are chosen wisely, they provide a manageable number of interpretable descriptive statistics for each demographic transition in each year, the time series of which can capture changes in the underlying determinants of that demographic transition and thereby provide the basis for econometric estimation. The model schedules chosen will vary according to the transitions under analysis and the population under consideration; the criteria for such choice should emphasize the interpretability of the parameters, their success in characterizing the important features of demographic behavior, and the goodness-of-fit of the schedules to available data.

We propose the use of model schedules to characterize, in each year of projection, the age distributions of the necessary demographic transitions: (1) fertility rates by the age and marital status of the mother for each region; (2) rates of first marriage, divorce, remarriage of divorcees, and remarriage of widows by sex and age for each region; (3) death rates by sex, age, and marital status for each region; and (4) rates of regional migrant outflows by sex, age, and marital status for each region. There are two exceptions to the use of model schedules: widowing (the remaining marital status change) by sex and age for each region, which can be determined by the stock of married couples by age of spouse and the deaths of married persons; and international migrant arrivals and departures by sex, age, and marital status for each region, which, particularly in the case of arrivals, are more difficult to express in terms of occurrence or exposure rates—the normal data base for model schedules.

In the remainder of this subsection, we present details of some model schedules that have been used in an illustrative projection reported in Rogers and Williams (1982).

Fertility

The demographic literature has concentrated on the modeling and projection of age-specific fertility rates of all women of child-bearing age. However, our framework allows us to consider separately marital and nonmarital fertility rates, thus enabling us to capture the effects on fertility of changes in the age and marital status distributions of women, and to consider the different economic and demographic influences on marital and nonmarital fertility. In the illustrative projection, a double-exponential function [developed and used by Coale and McNeil (1972) for first marriages] was used to describe, separately for women of each marital status in each region, fertility rates at age x:

$$f(x) = gae^{-\alpha(x-\mu)-e^{-\lambda(x-\mu)}} \tag{8.1}$$

where the shape of the curve is defined by three parameters, α, μ, and λ, and the level of the curve is defined by a, the scaling parameter, and g, the gross fertility rate, which is the sum of the age-specific fertility rates. Although these parameters (apart from g) are not easily interpretable, it is possible to derive the propensity, mean, variance, and mode of the double-exponential function in terms of them (Coale and McNeil 1972; Rogers and Castro 1981a; and Sams 1981b). We are thus able to identify four potentially estimable parameters of marital and of nonmarital fertility—the propensity to have a confinement, and the mean age, variance in age, and modal age of women having confinements.[3]

However, it is with some reservations that we have adopted this approach. Certainly the numbers and age distributions of married and unmarried women of child-bearing age should influence fertility, and analysis of movements over time in the parameters of these model schedules of fertility would shed some light on past and expected future fertility behavior. This approach may be adequate in the case of nonmarital fertility, but for marital fertility the decision to have a child is also strongly influenced by the number and timing of previous children born to the mother. This aspect of marital fertility could be incorporated via the use of separate model schedules for the age distributions of the fertility rates of women having confinements of different birth orders. Analysis of the changes over time in the parameters of these age and birth order-specific model schedules would give insights into the influences on marital fertility of the past experiences of the cohorts of women of child-bearing age and of the decisions made by parents with respect to family size. A time-series of such parameters would provide an excellent basis for economic modeling.

Marital Status

Although Coale and McNeil's (1972) double-exponential model schedule of first marriage rates was introduced a decade ago, parametrized schedules of other changes in marital status have been produced only recently. Williams (1981) fitted gamma distributions to Australian rates of first marriage, divorce, remarriage of divorcees, and remarriage of widows, for each year from 1921 to 1976. Using the gamma distribution, the rate of first marriage, of divorce, or of remarriage for males or females of age x is given by:

$$p(x) = p \left\{ \frac{1}{\beta^\alpha \Gamma(\alpha)} (x - x_0)^\alpha e^{-(x-x_0)\beta} \right\} \quad (8.2)$$

where P is an index of the propensity to first marry, to divorce, or to remarry; α and β are the parameters of the gamma distribution which can be expressed in terms of the mean age and variance in age of first marriage, of divorce, or of remarriage; x_0 is exogenously set equal to the last age at which a zero rate occurs; and Γ is the gamma function. Thus the distribution across ages of age-specific rates of each marital status change can be expressed in terms of three easily interpretable parameters—the propensity, mean age, and variance in age—whose time-series can then be modeled and projected using an economic model.

These model schedules provided adequate descriptions of Australian marital status changes, although some difficulties arose with age distributions that exhibited steep rises in early ages, in particular, the age distributions of first marriages. This difficulty was overcome by the addition of a second, time-invariant, gamma distribution. Functions based on the Coale-McNeil double-exponential distribution seem better able to cope with the problem of steeply rising age distributions than the gamma distribution. Although the parameters of both functions can be expressed in terms of a propensity, mean age, and variance in age, the double-exponential function requires a further parameter, the modal age, whose movements over time may be more difficult to model and project. In the specification of model schedules, some sacrifice in accuracy across the age distribution may be necessary in order to allow for improved modeling and projection of movement over time in the schedule.

Mortality

Three principal approaches have been advanced for summarizing age patterns of mortality: functional descriptions in the form of mathematical expressions with a few parameters (Benjamin and Pollard 1980), numerical tabulations generated from statistical summaries of large data sets (Coale and Demeny 1966), and relational procedures associating observed patterns with those found in a standard schedule (Brass 1971). Because numerical tabulations have proved to be somewhat cumbersome and inflexible for applied analysis, the relational methods first proposed by Brass have become widely adopted. With two parameters and a standard life table, it has become possible to describe and analyze a large variety of mortality regimes parsimoniously.

Recently Heligman and Pollard (1979) identified several mathematical functions that appear to provide satisfactory representations of a wide range of age patterns of mortality. We adopt the slightly modified Heligman and Pollard formula suggested by Brooks and others (1980):

$$d(x) = d_I(X) + d_A(x) + d_S(x) \quad \text{for } x = 0, 1, \ldots, 100+ \quad (8.3)$$

where

$$d_I(x) = \begin{cases} \Omega_0 & \text{for } x = 0 \\ \Omega_1^{x^\gamma} & \text{for } x > 0 \end{cases}$$

$$d_A(x) = \Omega_A e^{-(\frac{\ln x - \ln X_A}{\sigma})^2} \quad \text{for } x \geq 0$$

and

$$d_S(x) = \Omega_S \frac{e^{x/X_S}}{1 + \Omega_S K e^{x/X_S}} \quad \text{for } x \geq 0.$$

These three terms can be interpreted as representing infant and childhood mortality, mortality due to accidents, and mortality due to aging.

Death rates can be shown to differ markedly not only among ages but also between sexes, among marital states and, perhaps, among regions. At the IMPACT Project, model schedules based on equation 8.3 have been successfully fitted to Australian age-specific data for the death rates of persons of each sex and marital status. In practice not all components of the Heligman-Pollard curve are used, with the first component being omitted for married males and females and divorced and widowed females, and both the first and second components being omitted for divorced and widowed males. The IMPACT study is not region-specific, but, given availability of data, such model schedules could be fitted in each region. Movements over time in the parameters of such schedules could then be analyzed and used to project future mortality by age, sex, marital status, and region.

Regional Migration

In a recent study of age patterns in migration schedules, Rogers and Castro (1981a) have shown that such patterns exhibit a profile that can be adequately described by the mathematical expression:

$$m(X) = a_1 e^{-\alpha_1 x} + a_2 e^{-\alpha_2(x-\mu_2) - e^{-\lambda_2(x-\mu_2)}} + R + c \qquad (8.4)$$

where

$$R = a_3 e^{-\alpha_3(x-\mu_3) - e^{-\lambda_3(x-\mu_3)}}$$

if the curve has a retirement peak,

$$R = a_3 e^{\alpha_3 x}$$

if the curve has an upward retirement slope, and

$$R = 0$$

if the curve has neither and is approximately horizontal at the post-labor-force ages. The migration rate, therefore, depends on values taken on by 11, 9, or 7 parameters, respectively. The shape of the second term, the labor-force component of the curve, is the double-exponential formula put forward by Coale and McNeil (1972). The first term, a simple negative exponential curve, describes the migration age profile of children and adolescents. Finally, the post-labor-force component is a constant, another double-exponential, or an upward sloping, positive exponential.

In our framework, model migration schedules must be determined for the age distributions of regional migrant outflows for each sex and marital status. The model schedule given in equation 8.4 can be used, but for the married and previously married states, the first term does not need to be included, since children and young adolescents do not enter these marital states. The schedule has been found to be flexible enough to fit adequately age-specific migration rates disaggregated by sex and marital status. However, Rogers and Castro (1981b) have shown that model migration schedules can also be applied to migration flows disaggregated by the cause of movement. Similar to the birth-order fertility schedules discussed earlier, cause-specific model schedules of rates of migrant outflow could provide sets of parameters that more adequately capture the underlying determinants of migration and that can be more successfully integrated into an economic model of migration behavior.

The Economic Model

To produce population projections, some assumptions must be made about the transitions expected to occur over each year of the projection or, as in our framework, about the parameters of those transitions. Here future movements in demographic variables are related to changes in the economic and social structure of the region under analysis. Marriage and divorce are affected, for example, by changing incomes, relative wages, unemployment, and contraceptive usage. Fertility is also affected by these factors and by the changing patterns of marriage and divorce. Movement between regions is closely tied to economic developments within those regions inasmuch as people will move to regions with higher incomes, better employment opportunities, and better housing, as well as for personal reasons, such as marriage and divorce. International migration is also a response to relative economic opportunities. Policy analysis will be greatly aided if the relationships between demographic, economic, and social variables, some of which are amenable to policy control, are expicitly incorporated into population projections.

In this section, we consider the features of an economic model which could be used to determine simultaneously the future time paths of the parameters of fertility, marriage, divorce, and regional migration on the basis of scenarios of the future economic and demographic environment. In our framework, future values of the parameters of mortality and the net numbers of international migrants are assumed to be specified exogenously. Patterns of mortality are undoubtedly related to the economic environment and, for example, to changes in the provision of health care services. If the exogenous specification of future mortality were considered inadequate (for instance, in the case of population projections for a developing country), the relationship between economic variables and the parameters of mortality could be directly specified and incorporated in the economic model. The endogenization of mortality has not been attempted here, but there are several examples of this within demoeconomic models of developing countries (Food and Agriculture Organization 1976; Rodgers, Hopkins, and Wéry 1976; Simon 1976). Future international migration will also be related to relative changes in the economic climates of origin and destination countries, as well as to changes in costs of migration and in government policies toward migration. Although no attempt has been made to endogenize international migration in this framework, there are several examples of such modeling attempts: for instance, Kelley (1965), Kelley and Schmidt (1979), Pope (1976), Quigley (1972), Wadensjö (1977), and Wilkinson (1970).

In this chapter we do not fully specify a simultaneous model of fertility, marriage, divorce, and regional migration, but we draw upon models already developed and attempt to identify their important features and provide suggestions for a possible model. In particular, we draw upon work done at the IMPACT Project in specifying a simultaneous model of fertility, marriage, divorce, and labor-force participation and consider how this model could be linked with models of regional migration developed elsewhere [for example, those developed at IIASA by Kelley and Williamson (1980) and Gordon and Ledent (1981)]. First, we will discuss the theoretical basis for, and the empirical specification of, the IMPACT model. Second, we will provide a brief survey of migration models, and, finally, we will consider how these could be combined to provide a simultaneous model of fertility, marriage, divorce, and regional migration.

Fertility, Marriage, Divorce, and Labor-Force Participation[4]

The IMPACT economic model (Brooks, Sams, and Williams 1982; Filmer and Silberberg 1977) incorporates the essential features of the new home economics, which is an extension of consumer theory to incorporate nonpecuniary aspects of consumption, such as the utility derived from children and from leisure (see Becker 1960, 1965; Lancaster 1966; Willis 1974). The individual or the family is treated as a decision-making unit that maximizes its utility from the consumption of household commodities, which are produced by the household using its scarce resources of goods and services purchased in the market and of time of the individual or family members. Although children are not purchased in the market, inputs of market goods and services, and of time, are used by the household to "produce" child services, which is a function both of the number of children and the resources (including time) intensity or "quality" of these children. Children therefore have a shadow price, partly reflecting the time intensity of their production and the opportunity cost of that time. Thus, with regard to fertility, the family is faced with a decision concerning the allocation of its resources of time, especially of the mother, between child-rearing, labor-force participation, and leisure. If child services are normal goods, an increase in family income will tend to increase consumption of child services, which can imply growth in the number of children and/or in expenditures per child (that is, child quality). If the increase in family income derives from an increase in the female wage rate, however, the shadow price of the mother's time will have increased, implying that a larger part of the increase in child services will be directed toward increased child quality, rather than increased numbers of children (Butz and Ward 1979; Heckman 1974; Mincer 1963). The effect of fertility on non-economic variables, such as birth control and infant mortality rates, can be incorporated via their effect on the relative prices of the number and quality of children.

The new home economics approach has also been applied to explain marriage (Becker 1974) and divorce (Becker, Landes, and Michael 1977; Hutchens 1979). People are assumed to marry when both parties expect to enjoy a level of utility which is greater than that which they could receive if they remained single. Gains from marriage are related to the complementarity between the inputs to the household of the husband and wife, which is higher for large relative wage differentials between men and women. Since children provide an important source of utility to their parents, the demand for child services, and the complementarity of males and females in producing these child services, will act as an incentive to marry and to remain married. However, the decision to marry is not without cost, since a single person must spend resources searching for a spouse. Thus the decision to marry, the timing of that decision, and the duration of search will depend not only on the gains of marriage but also on the costs of search (Keeley 1977, 1979). Since divorce and separation are the result of conscious choice on the part of at least one spouse to terminate the marriage, the reverse of the factors discussed above are assumed to apply.

The new home economics also provides a consistent framework for dealing with female labor-force participation and its relationship to the female wage rate, the level of male earnings, and the fertility decisions of married women. The fertility decisions of earlier periods and the desired levels of child quality can influence the level of participation in the workforce, and in particular, rising levels of child quality can act as an inducement for married women to enter the workforce in order to supplement the family income.

The IMPACT economic model provides a practical application of these theories and also attempts to capture some of the dynamic elements of family formation, family size, labor-force participation, and their interactions. It explains the probabilities of marriage and divorce and their age profiles (that is, in our framework, the parameters of the model schedules of first marriage, remarriage, and divorce) as a function of variables such as the demand for child services (for marriage only), the female/male relative wage rate, real GDP per capita, an index of female educational attainment (for marriage only), the rate of oral contraceptive usage (for marriage only), the number of dependents per married female (for divorce only), real social security payments (for divorce only), dummy variables to account for the effects of war (for marriage only), and divorce legislation (for divorce only). In the model, marital confinements by birth order are determined by treating fertility decisions sequentially, beginning with the decision to have a first marital confinement and then to have higher order confinements (Sams 1979a, 1979b). First and higher order marital confinements (specifically, the crude first marital confinement rate and the mean and variance of implied completed family size) are related to the real female hourly wage rate, real GDP per capita, the rate of oral contraceptive usage, the real old-age pension rate, weighted first marriages per married female (for first marital confinements only), and dummy variables to account for the effects of war. Although labor-force participation rates are not directly relevant in our one-sided framework for regional population projections, the IMPACT model of labor-force participation rates (Brooks, Sams, and Williams 1982) could provide an important link in a fully simultaneous model of demographic-economic interactions. [See Ledent (1978) and Ledent and Gordon (1981) on this point.]

The IMPACT economic model has been moderately successful in explaining Australian marriage, divorce, fertility, and labor-force participation over the period 1921 to 1976. [See Brooks, Sams, and Williams (1982) for full details of the model specification, estimation, and performance.] Although the fertility equations are not directly related to the parameters of model schedules of fertility (and hence could not be used in our illustrative projection), aspects of this approach could be useful in the specification of the relationships between fertility parameters and economic and social variables [see Sams (1979b)]. Given this refinement and adequate data, the model could be estimated with separate equations specified for each region and, when combined with equations specifying regional migration and its relationship to economic and demographic variables in the source and destination regions (to be discussed next), would provide the simultaneous model of fertility, marriage, divorce, and regional migration necessary to complete our framework for multistate population projection.

Regional Migration

People choose to migrate when they expect to incur some positive gain, either of a pecuniary or nonpecuniary nature, and their choice of destination will be that region in which they can expect to incur the greatest net benefit.[5] The benefits associated with migration could include improved real income-earning potential for the migrant and/or his family, via higher wage rates, expanded and more secure employment opportunities, lower living costs, better educational facilities, less expensive housing, and greater availability and choice in housing. Nonpecuniary benefits of migration could include improved climate, better living environment, and enhanced personal relationships, where the migrant is moving to be closer to friends and family, or in response to changing marital arrangements, such as marriage, divorce, or widowhood. These benefits must be balanced against the costs of migration, which include transportation and relocation costs, costs of return trips to the home region, and the psychic costs of taking a risk and of moving away from family and friends.

Models of migration flows between regions have attempted to encapsulate the personal motivations of migrants by incorporating variables representing regional income, employment, and living environment differentials and measures of the costs, both real and psychic, as well as the uncertainty associated with migration. Early studies used regional population size as a proxy for income-earning potential and distance as a proxy for the transportation and psychic costs of migration as well as for the availability of information and the uncertainty involved in the move (Dodd 1950; Zipf 1946). Several studies improved upon the causal content of these gravity models by using indices of the relative attractiveness of regions to partition total migration into directional flows between each region (Lowry 1966; Somermeijer 1961). Lowry's model of migration inflows and outflows assumes that people migrate in search of jobs from low-wage to high-wage rates and from areas of labor surplus to those with labor shortages. According to this model, over time migration to areas of relative attractiveness will tend to reduce regional wage-rate and labor-supply imbalances and thereby reduce migration flows to those levels implied by the gravity model.

Many studies since Lowry have concentrated on improving the way in which economic variables are specified in migration models. Todaro (1969) has emphasized the role of the unemployment rate in the destination region as a proxy for the probability that the potential migrant will find employment in that region within a reasonable time. His model has been improved upon, for the special case of net rural-urban labor migration in developing countries, by Kelley and Williamson (1980); and a model incorporating features of both these studies has been suggested by Ledent and Gordon (1981). Ledent and Gordon assume that the propensity of an individual to move from one region to another depends on the relative attraction of the destination region, expressed as the percentage of the system's population living in that region, and on the earnings differentials between the regions, expressed by a quotient of the real expected wages one can expect to earn in those regions. The regional real expected wage rate is given by the product of the average wage rate and the ratio of total employment to total labor force, deflated by a cost-of-living index adapted from Kelley and Williamson (1980).

The effect of uncertainty and lack of information on the decision to migrate has been modeled by using past migration levels as a positive determinant of current inmigration (Greenwood 1975). The more persons who have migrated from a given source region to a given destination region, the greater will be the quantity of information sent back from the destination region, and the greater will be the likelihood that friends and relatives will be present in the destination region. Past inmigration levels may also determine future outmigration, since persons who have migrated once are more likely to migrate again (Greenwood 1973; Miller 1973). As for psychic costs, Schwartz (1973) has suggested that the psychic cost of migration can be directly measured by the cost of visits necessary to negate the effect of isolation from family and friends.

The decision to migrate will also vary according to the personal characteristics of the migrant. Adults are more likely to migrate when they are young, since they are less likely to be restricted by family, career, and community responsibilities (Gallaway 1969), and they can expect a longer working life over which to realize the advantages of migration (Becker 1964). Because very young children are more likely to have young, mobile parents, migration rates will be higher for young children than for adolescents. Unmarried or previously married people are less likely to have their freedom of movement restricted by family ties. Race and economic and social class may have some influence on the likelihood of migration (Greenwood 1975). Education may increase the likelihood of migration, since education tends to increase the awareness of other localities and the availability of employment information and opportunities. It also tends to reduce the importance of tradition and family ties (Greenwood 1975).

Ideally, a model of regional migration flows should incorporate these demographic, economic, and noneconomic determinants of migration. As such it should separately model migration inflows and outflows; there is no such person as a net migrant. It should also respond to changes in the demographic profile of the region of origin, since sex, age, marital status, race, social and economic class, and educational attainment have been shown to influence the likelihood that an individual will migrate. In our framework, we apply projected outflow migration rates by sex, age, and marital status to the sex, age, and marital status profile of the origin region, thus allowing for the automatic response of numbers of migrant outflows to changes in the demographic profiles of the regional source populations. Unfortunately, race, class, and educational characteristics of regional populations are not directly incorporated in this framework, since doing so would require projections of the populations disaggregated by all of these characteristics.

The specific rates of migration outflow are projected from the parameters of model migration schedules, which can be grouped as follows: (1) those parameters which determine the level of the model schedule—a_1, a_2, a_3, and c; (2) those parameters which determine the shape of the model schedule—$\alpha_1, \alpha_2, \alpha_3, \lambda_2$, and λ_3; and (3) those parameters which determine the location of the components of the model schedule—μ_2 and μ_3.

These eleven parameters are not all easy to interpret or model in terms of the economic and noneconomic determinants of migration, in particular those parameters which determine the shape and location of the model schedule. The majority of studies of regional migration have attempted to explain only gross migration levels, and the variables suggested in these studies can be used to model the level parameters. However, to maintain consistency across the age distribution of migration rates, it may be necessary to constrain the modeling of these parameters according to some simple empirically determined relationship.[6] In a model of migration levels, the determinants discussed above would vary in importance according to the level parameter being modeled. For instance, we could expect the level of retirement migration (as encapsulated by the parameter a_3) to be related more strongly to noneconomic determinants of migration, such as climate and lifestyle, than to employment factors. Thus, in comparison to the equation explaining a_2 (the level of labor-force migration), the coefficients relating to noneconomic variables in the equation explaining a_3 would be *relatively* greater than those relating to economic variables. The means by which the more poorly determined "shape" and "location" parameters would be projected could vary according to the particular characteristics of the country under analysis, with some being projected exogenously on the basis of simple time trends or as functions of the level parameters [as in Schmidt (1980)]. For instance, the location parameters could be projected using a simple time trend reflecting, say, for μ_2, a long-term decline brought about by the increased independence of young persons and, for μ_3, a long-term decline brought about by the declining age at retirement. This approach has the advantage of reducing the number of parameters necessary for modeling and projection.

Concluding Remarks

This system for multistate projections provides highly disaggregated projections of population by sex, age, marital status, and region within a tightly integrated framework that respects demographic accounting identities and that faithfully tracks through time the changes in the age and marital status profiles of regional populations. At the same time it allows reasonable latitude for demographic events to be influenced by changing economic and social conditions. This approach is made feasible by the condensation of the time series of changes in important demographic variables into a manageable set of descriptive statistics amenable to economic modeling, which are then available for forging links between demographic changes and wider economic influences. By allowing this technique to separate the effects of changes in behavior from changes in the demographic structure of the regional populations due to aging and previous history, the task of the economic model is simplified by limiting its role to accounting for behavioral changes alone and not those arising from the evolutionary dynamics of population growth.

This chapter has detailed the components of an economic model of fertility, marriage, divorce, and regional migration which could be incorporated into a framework for multistate population projection. Given sufficient data, the parameters of the model schedules of each of these demographic transitions for each region can be modeled on the basis of a number of economic and social variables which have been discussed above. Some of these variables, such as regional wage rates and income levels, would, in conjunction with other variables, jointly determine all of the demographic transitions, whereas other variables, such as climate and relocation costs, would figure in only one of the transitions. Unfortunately, time, data, and financial constraints have not allowed us to estimate such a model as yet, but parts of it have been implemented in the illustrative projection for Australia presented in Rogers and Williams (1982).

Research efforts are currently being directed toward the expansion of the economic model to incorporate the modeling of parameters of model schedules of fertility and regional migration. Such a model would complete the system outlined here and provide a tool for the analysis of the effects of economic variables upon demographic behavior. In this chapter, however, we have concentrated only on part of the relationship between economic and demographic variables. The changing demography of a region will undoubtedly affect the economy of that region via the impacts on consumer demand, housing demand, and labor supply. The framework presented here must therefore be incorporated into a wider model of simultaneously determined economic and demographic growth. Work is currently proceeding in this direction.

Notes

1. By *widowing* we mean the transition from the married to the widowed state.
2. Rogers (1980, 1981) may be consulted for a discussion of multistate population projection techniques.
3. The use of confinements, as opposed to births, appears appropriate since women do not make the decision to have a multiple birth.
4. This section borrows heavily from Brooks, Sams, and Williams (1982).
5. Greenwood (1975) provides an excellent survey of research on regional migration, and Long and Hansen (1979) provide an interesting study of the reasons for regional migration, both of which concentrate on the United States and have been referred to in the drafting of this section.
6. Exhaustive studies of model migration schedules in developed countries by Rogers and Castro (1981a) suggest at least the following relationship: $a_3 < a_1 < a_2$.

References

Becker, G.S. 1960. An economic analysis of fertility. In *Demographic and economic changes in developed countries*, a report of the National Bureau of Economic Research. Princeton, NJ: Princeton University Press.
―――. 1964. *Human capital*. New York: National Bureau of Economic Research, Columbia Press.
―――. 1965. A theory of the allocation of time. *Economic Journal* 75:493–517.
―――. 1974. A theory of marriage. In *Economics of the Family*, ed. T.W. Schultz. Chicago and London: University of Chicago Press.
Becker, G.S.; Landes, E.M.; and Michael, R.T. 1977. An economic analysis of marital instability. *Journal of Political Economy* 85, 6:1141–1187.
Benjamin, B., and Pollard, H.J. 1980. *The analysis of mortality and other actuarial statistics*. London: Heinemann.
Brass, W. 1971. On the scale of mortality. In *Biological aspects of demography*, ed. W. Brass, pp. 69–110. London: Taylor and Francis.
Brooks, C.; Sams, D.; and Williams, P. 1980. A time series of smooth approximations for age, sex, and marital status specific death rates in Australia, 1950/51 to 1975/76 with a projection to the year 2000. Research Memorandum. Melbourne: IMPACT Project, BACHUROO Module.
―――. 1982. An econometric model of fertility, marriage, divorce and labour force participation for Australian women, 1921/22 to 1975/76. Preliminary Working Paper BP-29. Melbourne: IMPACT Project.

Butz, W.P., and Ward, M.P. 1979. The emergence of counter-cyclical US fertility. *American Economic Review* 69:318–328.

Coale, A.J., and Demeny, P. 1966. *Regional model life tables and stable populations*. Princeton, NJ: Princeton University Press.

Coale, A.J., and McNeil, D.R. 1972. The distribution by age of the frequency of first marriage in a female cohort. *Journal of the American Statistical Association* 67:743–9.

Coale, A.J., and Trussell, T.J. 1974. Model fertility schedules: variations in the age structure of childbearing in human populations. *Population Index* 40, 2:185–258.

Day, L.H. 1963. Divorce in Australia. *The Australian Quarterly* 48, 2.

Dodd, S.C. 1950. The interactance hypothesis: a gravity model fitting physical masses and human groups. *American Sociological Review* 15:245–256.

Filmer, R., and Silberberg, R. 1977. Fertility, family formation and female labour force participation in Australia, 1922–1974. Preliminary Working Paper BP-08. Melbourne: IMPACT Project.

Food and Agriculture Organization. 1976. A systems simulation approach to integrated population and economic planning with special emphasis on agricultural development and employment: an experimental study in Pakistan. PA 4/1 INT/73/P02, Working Paper Series 11. Rome: Food and Agriculture Organization.

Gallaway, L.E. 1969. Age and labor mobility patterns. *Southern Economic Journal* 36, 2:171–180.

Gordon, P., and Ledent, J. 1981. Modeling the dynamics of a system of metropolitan areas: a demoeconomic approach. *Environment and Planning A* 12:125–133.

Greenwood, M.J. 1973. Urban economic growth and migration: their interaction. *Environment and Planning* 5:91–112.

———. 1975. Research on internal migration in the United States: a survey. *Journal of Economic Literature* 13, 2:397–443.

Heckman, J. 1974. Shadow prices, market wages and labor supply. *Econometrica* 42, 4:674–694.

Heligman, L., and Pollard, J.H. 1979. The age pattern of mortality. Research Paper 185. Sydney: Macquarie University, School of Economic and Financial Studies.

Hoem, J.M.; Madsen, D.; Nelson, J.L.; Ohlsen, E.M.; Hansen, H.O.; and Lennermalm, B. 1981. Experiments in modelling recent Danish fertility curves. *Demography* 18, 2:231–244.

Hutchens, R.M. 1979. Welfare, remarriage and marital search. *American Economic Review* 69, 3:369–379.

Keeley, M.C. 1977. The economics of family formation. *Economic Inquiry* 15:238–250.

———. 1979. An analysis of the age pattern of first marriage. *International Economic Review* 20, 2:527–544.

Kelley, A.C. 1965. International migration and economic growth: Australia, 1865–1936. *Journal of Economic History* 25, 3:333–354.

Kelley, A.C., and Schmidt, R.M. 1979. Modelling the role of government policy in post-war Australian immigration. *The Economic Record* 55, 149:127–135.

Kelley, A.C., and Williamson, J.G. 1980. *Modeling urbanization and economic growth*. Research Report RR-80-22. Laxenburg, Austria, International Institute for Applied Systems Analysis.

Lancaster, K.J. 1966. A new approach to consumer theory. *Journal of Political Economy* 74:132–157.

Ledent, J. 1978. Regional multiplier analysis: a demometric approach. *Environment and Planning A* 10:537–560.

Ledent, J., and Gordon, P. 1981. A framework for modeling interregional population distribution and economic growth. *International Regional Science Review* 6, 1:85–90.

Long, L.H., and Hansen, K.A. 1979. Reasons for interstate migration. *Current Population Reports*, Series P-23, No. 18. Washington D.C.: U.S. Department of Commerce, Bureau of the Census.

Lowry, I.S. 1966. *Migration and metropolitan growth: two analytical models*. San Francisco: Chandler Publishing Co.

Miller, E. 1973. Is out-migration affected by economic conditions? *Economic Journal* 39, 3:396–405.

Mincer, J. 1963. Market prices, opportunity costs and income effects. In *Measurement in economics: studies in mathematical economics and econometrics in memory of Yehuda Grunfeld*, ed. C. Christ. Stanford, CA: Stanford University Press.

Pope, D. 1976. The peopling of Australia: United Kingdom immigration from federation to the Great Depression. Ph.D. dissertation. Canberra: Australian National University.

Powell, A.A. 1982. Aspects of the design of BACHUROO, an economic demographic model of labor supply. In *Modeling growing economies in equilibrium and disequilibrium: proceedings of an IIASA meeting, 10–13 November 1980*, ed. A.C. Kelley, W.C. Sanderson, and J.G. Williamson.

Quigley, J.M. 1972. An economic model of Swedish emigration. *The Quarterly Journal of Economics* 86, 1:111–126.

Rodgers, G.B.; Hopkins, M.J.D.; and Wéry, R. 1976. Economic-demographic modelling for development planning. Bachue-Phillipines. Population and Employment Working Paper 45. Geneva: International Labour Organization.

Rogers, A. (ed.) 1980. Essays in multistate demography. Special issue of *Environment and Planning A* 12, 5:485–622.

———. 1981. *Advances in multiregional demography*. Research Report RR-81-6. Laxenburg, Austria: International Institute for Applied Systems Analysis.

Rogers, A., and Castro, L.J. 1981a. *Model migration schedules*. Research Report RR-81-30. Laxenburg, Austria: International Institute for Applied Systems Analysis.

———. 1981b. Age patterns of migration: cause-specific profiles. In *Advances in*

multiregional demography, ed. A. Rogers, pp. 125–59. Research Report RR-81-6. Laxenburg, Austria: International Institute for Applied Systems Analysis.
Rogers, A.; Raquillet, R.; and Castro, L.J. 1978. Model migration schedules and their applications. *Environment and Planning A* 10, 5:475–502.
Rogers, A., and Williams, P. 1982. A framework for multistate demoeconomic modeling and projection. Working Paper 82-69. Laxenburg, Austria: International Institute for Applied Systems Analysis.
Sams, D. 1979a. The demographic core of the IMPACT project, an overview. Preliminary Working Paper BP-18. Melbourne: IMPACT Project.
_____. 1979b. The performance of the births block of the demographic core. Research Memorandum. Melbourne: IMPACT Project, BACHUROO Module.
_____. 1981a. A two-sided marriage model for the IMPACT population projection facility. Research Memorandum. Melbourne: IMPACT Project, BACHUROO Module.
_____. 1981b. The double-exponential function. Research Memorandum. Melbourne: IMPACT Project, BACHUROO Module.
Sams, D., and Williams, P. 1980. The IMPACT project's facility for disaggregated population projections: a brief exposition and progress report. Preliminary Working Paper BP-22. Melbourne: IMPACT Project.
_____. 1982. Some projections of Australian population and labor force, 1980 to 2001. Preliminary Working Paper BP-30. Melbourne, IMPACT Project.
Schmidt, R.M. 1980. The demographic dimensions of economic-population modeling. Unpublished Ph.D. dissertation. Durham, NC: Duke University.
Schwartz, A. 1973. Interpreting the effect of distance on migration. *Journal of Political Economy* 81, 5:1153–1169.
Simon, J.L. 1976. Population growth may be good for LDCs in the long run: a richer simulation model. *Economic Development and Cultural Change* 24, 2:309–337.
Somermeijer, W.H. 1961. Een analyse van de binnen-landse migratie in Nederland tot 1947 en van 1948–57 (An analysis of the internal migration in the Netherlands until 1947 and from 1948–1957). *Statistische en Econometrische Onderzoekugen*.
Todaro, M. 1969. A model of labor, migration, and urban unemployment in less developed countries. *American Economic Review* 59:138–148.
United Nations. 1967. *Methods of estimating basic demographic measures from incomplete data*. New York: United Nations.
Wadensjö, E. 1977. Some factors determining international migration. In *Demographic, economic, and social interaction*, ed. A.E. Andersson and I. Holmberg. Cambridge, MA: Ballinger Publishing Co.
Wilkinson, M. 1970. European migration to the United States: an econometric analysis of aggregated labor supply and demand. *Review of Economics and Statistics* 52, 3:242–279.

Williams, P. 1981. Marriage and divorce in Australia: a time series of fitted distributions, 1921/22 to 1975/76. Working Paper B-20. Melbourne: IMPACT Project.

──────. 1982. Notes on illustrative projections of the Australian population disaggregated by age, sex, marital status and region using the IMPACT population projection facility. Research Memorandum. Melbourne: IMPACT Project, BACHUROO Module.

Willis, R.J. 1974. Economic theory of fertility behavior. In *Economics of the family*, ed. T.W. Schultz. Chicago and London: University of Chicago Press.

Zipf, G.K. 1946. The P_1P_2/D hypothesis: on the intercity movement of persons. *American Sociological Review* 11, 6:677–686.

9 THE ECESIS ECONOMIC-DEMOGRAPHIC MODEL OF THE UNITED STATES

Paul Beaumont, Andrew Isserman,
David McMillen, David Plane,
and Peter Rogerson

Introduction

ECESIS is an interregional economic-demographic model of the United States. It consists of 51 regional econometric models (one for each state and the District of Columbia) and a multiregional demographic model. Its distinguishing feature is the linking of sophisticated demographic accounts with sophisticated structural econometric models. Emphasis is on the linkages in order to assess the need for and benefits from modeling economic-demographic feedbacks.

The modeling strategy underlying ECESIS was to build complete economic and demographic models with only the detail necessary to measure the impacts of, including the linkages between, economic and demographic changes. Despite this concern for parsimony—only three industrial sectors and ten population groups—ECESIS is a very large system of models. Each state model has 142 endogenous variables, and the entire system has 7,400 endogenous variables and 884 exogenous variables. In addition, 25,500 state-to-state migration flows are modeled (including the District of Columbia): 2,550 for each of the ten population groups. Nevertheless, ECESIS was designed so that further demographic and economic disaggregation is feasible.

The creators of a large-scale regional systems simulation model concluded the description of their experience with an observation appropriate here:

> In terms of modeling research, one must face the fact that many people will judge a model by the sophistication of the model sector relating to the subject matter with which they are most familiar.... A demographer will usually study the demographic sector of the model first. If he finds it "uninteresting," perhaps only in the respect that he feels it does not make a contribution to his field, he is apt to judge the whole model on this basis (Hamilton et al. 1969, p. 282).

ECESIS, by its very size and scope, reflects compromises in both its economic and demographic components. As a demonstration project of modeling economic-demographic linkages, on the other hand, ECESIS achieves an uncommon level of integration. It also contains several innovations in regional economic and demographic modeling.

The modeling of migration and the demographic accounts are discussed in the following section; the economic models are presented in the third section; and the linkages between economic and demographic change are reviewed in the fourth section.

The Demographic Model

At the core of the demographic model is a set of population accounts. Changes in population due to migration, births, and deaths are calculated for each of the ten population groups in each of the 51 regions. In this section the methods used to project migration and births are discussed followed by a description of the accounts themselves.

Migration

The transition matrices (or Markov matrices) associated with multiregional demography are used to model migration. A transition matrix contains the probability that an individual in one region will remain in that region for another period and the probabilities that the individual will migrate to each of the other regions in the system. These probabilities usually are based on past rates. In aggregate terms estimated migration from region i to region j (M_{ij}) is based on the following equation:

$$M_{ij}(t) = P_i(t-1)\left[\frac{M_{ij}(b)}{P_i(b-1)}\right], \quad (9.1)$$

where $P_i(t-1)$ refers to the population in region i in year $t-1$ surviving to year t and b is a base year. The term in brackets is the migration rate observed in the base year. It is assumed to remain constant into the projection period.

Using the term *attractiveness* from the geography literature, a transition matrix can be modified so that the probabilities change with changes in the attractiveness of different regions. Attractiveness will remain undefined for the moment, but generally any factor considered to be a determinant of migration may be incorporated into a region's attractiveness index. Equation 9.1 can be modified to incorporate relative attractiveness:

$$M_{ij}(t) = P_i(t-1)\left[\frac{M_{ij}(b)}{P_i(b-1)}\right]\frac{A_j(t-1)/A_n(t-1)}{A_j(b-1)/A_n(b-1)}, \quad (9.2)$$

where A represents the attractiveness index and the n subscript the nation as a whole. Thus, the new term measures the attractiveness of region j relative to all other regions in period $t-1$ compared to $b-1$. If the relative attractiveness of j increased, migration from i to j would increase.

Equation 9.2 can be modified to assure that

$$\sum_k M_{ik}(t) = P_i(t-1),$$

where k includes the entire set of regions and M_{ii} refers to people who remain in i ("stayers"). Dividing the left side of equation 9.2 by $P_i(t-1)$ and the right side by $\Sigma M_{ik}(t)$, then substituting for the latter from equation 9.2 and collecting terms, the following equation results:

$$\frac{M_{ij}(t)}{P_i(t-1)} = \frac{M_{ij}(b)\left[\dfrac{A_j(t-1)}{A_j(b-1)}\right]}{\sum_k M_{ik}(b)\left[\dfrac{A_k(t-1)}{A_k(b-1)}\right]}. \quad (9.3)$$

Note that all transition rates are interdependent. Migration probabilities from i to j change when there are changes in the attractiveness of any other regions in the system, even if there are no changes in the attractiveness of both i and j. If there are no relative changes in attractiveness of any region, equation 9.3 simply becomes equation 9.1, the constant probability equation.

Equation 9.3 can be refined further by adding a parameter γ that measures the magnitude of the migration response to changing attractiveness:

$$\frac{M_{ij}(t)}{P_i(t-1)} = \frac{M_{ij}(b)\left[\dfrac{A_j(t-1)}{A_j(b-1)}\right]^\gamma}{\sum_k M_{ik}(b)\left[\dfrac{A_k(t-1)}{A_k(b-1)}\right]^\gamma}. \quad (9.4)$$

With two sets of migration flow matrices, γ can be estimated, for instance, to minimize the root mean-square error between estimated and observed transition rates in the second year. γ is a close approximation to an elasticity. Its derivation using a secant method is discussed in Rogerson (1981). When $\gamma = 0$, equation 9.4 is identical to the standard demographic, Markov approach, i.e., there is no migration response to changing attractiveness.

The attractiveness measure in ECESIS varies by age group. For the four population groups in primary labor-force ages (18–44 and 45–64), the attractiveness measure is related to regional labor-market conditions. It is a proxy for the probability of gaining employment:

$$A_j(t) = \frac{[E_j(t) - E_j(t-1)] + sE_j(t-1)}{U_j(t-1) + sE_j(t-1)},$$

where $E_j(t)$ is the employment in region j in t, $sE_j(t-1)$ the number of separations excluding layoffs, and $U_j(t-1)$ the number of unemployed. The number of separations is estimated using the national rate of separation (s), because this statistic is not available for all 50 states. The numerator can be considered a measure of opportunity (the number of jobs available) and the denominator a measure of competition (the number of people seeking employment). Although a crude proxy, this attractiveness variable proved effective in simulation exercises, which will be discussed later in this section.

Migration in the four population groups less than 18 years of age was modeled with migration of fecund females (18–44 years of age) as the attractiveness index. If migration of women increased from i to j, the migration of children would be expected to increase.

Migration of the elderly was modeled with no attractiveness measure, i.e., in the standard demographic manner with fixed transition rates and no linkages to economic conditions. Although an argument can be made that elderly migration is sensitive to economic conditions such as interest rates and transfer payments, migration of this group was not a focus of the ECESIS project.

The γ parameters for the four population groups in labor-force age were estimated using migration data based on federal income tax records. [See Engels and Healy (1981) and Isserman, Plane, and McMillen (1982) for discussions of these data.] Interstate migration is estimated by the U.S. Bureau of the Census for use in making population estimates to allocate General Revenue Sharing funds. An individual's tax return for one year is matched to the return for a subsequent year by social security number. If the addresses on the two returns are in different states, the individual and any dependents claimed are counted as interstate migrants. Annual migration flows for 1975–76, 1976–77, and 1978–79 were available but with no age detail. Therefore, the age distribution of migrants was estimated using the age distribution of 1965–70 migration flows from the 1970 population census adjusted for subsequent changes in the national population composition.

The 1975–76 matrices of transition rates for each of the four labor-force groups were modified to approximate the 1976–77 matrices using equation 9.4 and the opportunity/competition attractiveness index. The values of γ were chosen to minimize the root mean-square error between the estimated and observed transition rates for 1976–1977. These γ values then were held constant in ECESIS. With no other annual migration flow matrices available for consecutive years, it is not possible to estimate a time-series of γ in order to model γ endogenously.

Several alternative attractiveness indices were created and used to estimate the 1976–77 rates from the 1975–76 matrix. In particular, a measure of expected wages (the probability of gaining employment times the real wage) was examined, but it resulted in larger root mean square errors and, on occasion, negative γ's.

In a simulation exercise the 1976–77 matrix was used with the estimated γ's and the actual values for the attractiveness measures to estimate 1978–79 migration [see Isserman, Plane, Rogerson, and Beaumont (1985)]. For the four labor-force age groups this method was more accurate than the demographic approach by 20 percent in estimating net migration by state. The greatest improvement in projecting migration occurred for growing states in the West and South.

For the ECESIS model itself a set of 1957–58 migration flow matrices had to be created to be compatible with the economic data that began in 1958. These matrices were constructed from 1955–60 migration flows identified in the 1960 census, the 1965–70 age distribution of migration adjusted for changes in population composition from 1965–70 to 1958, and the ratio of one-year to five-year migration according to the Current Population Survey. The constructed matrices were used as base-year values in ECESIS. They are adjusted annually using their respective attractiveness indices and the estimated γ's. Thus in ECESIS equation 9.4 becomes:

$$\frac{M_{ij}(t)}{P_i(t-1)} = \frac{M_{ij}(t-1)\left[\frac{A_j(t)}{A_j(t-1)}\right]^\gamma}{\sum_k M_{ik}(t-1)\left[\frac{A_k(t)}{A_k(t-1)}\right]^\gamma},$$

with age group subscripts on every variable implied but not shown. The surviving population $P_i(t-1)$ is estimated in the demographic accounts. Note the change in time subscripts in the attractiveness indexes from equation 9.4. The labor-force attractiveness index in ECESIS incorporates employment change from $t-1$ to t to model migration between $t-1$ and t. Thus, population and economic change are simultaneous.

Summarizing, migration of the population in labor-force ages is modeled to change in response to employment change, employment (through the separations measure), unemployment, and the number of people in each age group. Migration into each state depends on economic conditions not only in that state but in every other state. The changing economic conditions in each state are weighted by the size of previously observed flows between the origin and that state. Migration of children is linked indirectly to economic conditions through the use of migration of females 18–44 as the attractivity index. At present, migration of the elderly in ECESIS is not related to economic conditions.

Births

Economic conditions can affect fertility both directly and through migration. Economists have analyzed fertility using the same conceptual framework applied to goods and services. Both price and income effects have been identified. The number of children desired by a family is expected to decrease with increases in the price of children. The main component of the price of children is considered to be the mother's time. The expected negative relationship between fertility and female wages or female labor-force participation has been found in several empirical studies. (See chapter 1 for a review of this literature.)

The relationship between income and fertility is more complex. One theory is that the income effect is positive (as postulated by Malthus), but other factors which change with income can offset the income effect. Among the offsetting tendencies postulated are the increasing cost of children accompanying rising income because of (1) the use of now more expensive parental time and (2) demand for higher quality children.

The link between fertility and migration is based on age. The highest rates of both fertility and migration generally are observed for those aged 20 to 29. Therefore, net migration may be expected to have a positive impact on fertility through its effect on the age structure of a state (Alonso 1980). Since the same conditions that encourage higher female wages and female labor-force participation also encourage inmigration, the negative impact on fertility of the former is countered by the positive impact of the latter.

Births can be modeled either stochastically or exogenously within ECESIS. The initial strategy was to model state general fertility rates as a countercyclical phenomenon using an approach similar to the national model of Butz and Ward (1979) and incorporating the effects of migration. Data limitations required the use of proxy variables once again, because all three variables in the Butz-Ward model—female unemployment, female wages, and male wages—are not available annually on the state level. The resultant equations were only satisfactory for a few states.

The next strategy was to model state general fertility rates as a function of both the national general fertility rate and state variables expected to explain the deviation between the national and state rates. Among the latter were female labor-force participation rates, unemployment rates, and wages. In this manner theoretically pleasing national models of fertility could be linked to ECESIS, since reasonably satisfying state models do not appear feasible.

This strategy is similar to that used in most regional econometric models in which regional output is a function of national output and such variables as relative wages and relative energy costs. Births, however, has proven more difficult to model than regional output. The equations combining the national general fertility rate and relative state-national variables proved unsatisfactory. Only the national fertility rate was significant. All other variables were dominated by the strong correlation between national and state rates (table 9-1). Although efforts will continue to model the linkage between fertility and economic conditions on the state level, at present a standard demographic approach is used in ECESIS. It is incorporated into the demographic accounts discussed in the next part of this section.

Demographic Accounts

Population changes as a result of births, deaths, and migration. The basic demographic equation summarizes this accounting relationship:

$$P_j^t = P_j^{t-1} + B_j^t - D_j^t + I_j^t - O_j^t,$$

where P_j^t represents the population of state j at time t, B_j^t the births in region j during time period $(t - 1, t)$, D_j^t deaths during the time period, I_j^t inmigration to j, and O_j^t outmigration from j.

Unfortunately, this equation does not hold when presently available data

Table 9-1. Birth Equations (General Fertility Rate)[a]

State	Constant	U.S. General Fertility Rate	ρ[b]	R^2
Arizona	.0299	.8116	.7187	.99
	(4.27)[c]	(11.38)		
Indiana	.0053	.9897	.3628	.99
	(2.38)	(47.12)		
Iowa	−.0226	1.2592	.5866	.99
	(5.52)	931.47)		
New York	−.0059	.9958	.8204	.99
	(.63)	(9.8)		
Texas	.0178	.9147	.6428	.99
	(3.97)	(20.59)		
Washington	−0.0167	1.131	.5782	.99
	(2.8)	(19.45)		
Utah	.078	.5185	.7410	.94
	(69.21)	(48.37)		

[a] These equations were estimated with a Cochran-Orcutt adjustment.
[b] ρ is the degree of first-order autocorrelation.
[c] The numbers in parentheses are t-statistics.

are used. The addition of births to the population in j incorrectly assumes that no infants migrate during the year of their birth. The subtraction of deaths fails to recognize that an inmigrant who dies was not part of the population of j in the beginning of the period and, therefore, should not be subtracted from it. Similarly, the outmigration figures do not include outmigrants between $t - 1$ and t who died before t. Because they died in another state, they are subtracted from its population as a death but not from state j's population as an outmigrant. These problems are discussed below in more detail.

ECESIS contains a set of demographic accounts which corrects the basic demographic equation. It should be stressed that the equation is only incorrect because of the characteristics of the data for births, deaths, and migration. With correctly defined data, the equation would hold. The problem then is designing a set of accounts which provide correctly defined estimates of the components of population change. The age and sex disaggregated accounts built into ECESIS are based on the work of Rees and Wilson (1977). Their system is modified to work on gross inmigration and outmigration totals, rather than place-to-place flows. This change considerably reduces the amount of data which must be processed without significantly reducing the amount of information obtainable from the full accounts matrix.

Migration statistics often do not include individuals who are born during the time period. For example, migration questions that ask, "Where did you live X years ago?" cannot include those of age under X. This deficiency can be corrected by estimating infant migrants. Infant migrants that inmigrate and survive are added to the inmigration total in ECESIS, and infant migrants that outmigrate are added to the outmigration total whether they survive or not.

Death statistics are inflated by the inclusion of deaths to inmigrants. Since the beginning period population is changed in the basic equation by subtracting deaths occurring to those people in the region at the beginning of the period, deaths of inmigrants must be estimated and subtracted from the actual death statistics. Deaths to inmigrants born during the period should also be subtracted from total deaths. Similarly, outmigration statistics only include those migrants who have survived until the end of the period. The number of outmigrants who die before the end of period must be estimated and added to the outmigration statistics. To illustrate, a person who moves from New York to Florida and then dies during the period incorrectly appears as a loss of population to Florida rather than to New York. The procedures used in ECESIS assign such deaths correctly.

The accounting equation in its correct form is:

$$P_j^t = P_j^{t-1} + B_j^t - (D_j^t - ID_j^t - IBD_j^t)$$
$$+ (I_j^t + IB_j^t) - (O_j^t + OB_j^t + OBD_j^t + OD_j^t),$$

where IB_j^t is the number of inmigrants to j born during the period $(t-1, t)$, OB_j^t is the outmigrants from j born during the period, ID_j^t is the inmigrants to j who die before t, OD_j^t is outmigrants from j who die before t, IBD_j^t is inmigrants to j born during the period who die before t, OBD_j^t is outmigrants from j born during the period who die before t, and the remaining variables are defined as before. No data are available on the terms, IB, OB, ID, OD, IBD, and OBD. Therefore, these so-called minor flows must be estimated for each age-sex group.

For many states, the magnitude of the minor flows is small. For particular states and age groups, however, the effects may be significant. For example, 7 percent of Florida's population over 65 in 1976 had moved there during the previous year. Given data on death rates, the implication is that over 3 percent of all deaths in the over 65 age group represent deaths to inmigrants.

The At-Risk Population

Another important contribution of the demographic accounts in ECESIS is to calculate the appropriate populations for use in calculating and applying the rates. In historical use with existing data on actual births and deaths, the demographic accounts compute accurate rates by dividing by an appropriate population. For projections, demographic rates, either from a model or from rates calculated by using the accounts historically, are applied to the appropriate population to obtain correctly defined projections of births, deaths, migration, and minor flows.

The appropriate population for the computation of rates in the historical mode and the application of rates in the projection mode is defined as the at-risk population. It includes anyone in the state at any time during the period multiplied by the fraction of the time period for which that person was in the state. For example, the at-risk population for deaths is estimated by including all surviving stayers, half of surviving outmigrants, half of surviving inmigrants, a fourth of nonsurviving inmigrants, a fourth of nonsurviving outmigrants, and half of nonmoving nonsurvivors. The fraction for inmigrants is half on the assumption that inmigrants on average spent half the year at the origin and half at the destination. The fraction one-fourth for nonsurviving inmigrants assumes that the person lived one-half year, equally divided between origin and destination. Since the population is disaggregated by age in ECESIS, care must be taken to account not only for individuals remaining in the same age group during the period (using the fractions above) but also for individuals entering and leaving the age group during the period (in both cases, by assuming that they change age groups halfway through the period).

As another example, the population at risk of giving birth in a state should include women of child-bearing age who migrate into a state. Migrating women who survive will appear, on average, in the at-risk population of both the origin and destination states for half of the time period. Migrating women who survive and are aged into a nonchild-bearing age group are at risk of giving birth in the destination region for one-fourth of the time period.

At-risk coefficients may be thought of as the product of three separate coefficients: (1) the proportion of the time period the individual was alive; (2) the proportion of the time alive spent in a given age group; and (3) the proportion of time alive in an age group spent in a given region. Special care must be taken in computing at-risk populations for the first and last age groups since individuals cannot age into the first age group or out of the last age group.

The Accounting Procedure

The demographic accounting procedure used in ECESIS is illustrated in figure 9–1. The process begins by calculating the number of migrants who change age groups during the year. For each year, the number of persons entering and leaving each age group must be estimated. Since no data are available by single year of age at the state level, U.S. population totals by sex for single-year age groups are used to determine the proportion of individuals changing age groups during the year. These proportions are then applied to the interstate flows obtained from the migration component of the model.

Births are estimated by applying the 1975 state birth rates to the at-risk population. State level births are then disaggregated by sex by applying the observed national sex ratio (51.33 percent males) to all states. State births (sex disaggregated) are then proportionally adjusted to be consistent with actual U.S. male and female births during the historical period or projected U.S. male and female births during the projection period. Thus, the 1975 rates are used as a base to calculate births in other years, but proportional adjustment of the resulting births serves to capture changing birth rates on both state and national levels. (Alternatively, state birth rates can be

INPUTS:

Population by state, age and sex from previous period $(t-1)$. In- and outmigrants for $(t-1, t)$ from migration model. Birth and death rates by state, age, and sex. U.S. controls for births and deaths. Coefficients for proportion of population changing age groups during period.

STEP ONE:

Estimate the number of migrants who change age groups during the period.

STEP TWO:

Estimate at-risk population for births and deaths (initially setting minor flows equal to zero) and calculate total births and deaths by applying appropriate rates. Adjust births and deaths to conform to U.S. totals.

STEP THREE:

Estimate minor flows: inmigrating births, outmigrating births, dying inmigrants, dying outmigrants, dying inmigrating births, and dying outmigrating births.

STEP FOUR:

Estimate major flows, and population by state, age, and sex for t. Estimate "survived" population for input into migration model.

Convergence of Minor Flows?
If not, return to STEP TWO.
If so, go to STEP FIVE:

STEP FIVE:

Allocate inmigrants to states by age and sex.

STEP SIX:

Estimates state populations by age and sex are inputs into the economic models. The economic and migration models are rerun, generating new migration values for $(t-1, t)$. Then the demographic accounts are rerun beginning with STEP ONE. This entire process continues until population converges.

Figure 9-1. Flow chart of ECESIS accounts

estimated stochastically as discussed previously.) In the next step, migration of infants born during the period is derived by assuming that the infants migrate at the same rates as females in the 18–44 age group.

Deaths are estimated by applying the observed 1975 age-sex specific state death rates to the at-risk population in each state. Like births, these figures are then proportionally adjusted to be consistent with U.S. male and female deaths. Because deaths are age-sex disaggregated and national controls are only sex disaggregated, this adjustment must be carried out in a two-step procedure. First, the difference between the estimated national total and the control is allocated for each sex to states in proportion to the state's share of national deaths. Next, the age-sex disaggregated deaths within each state are adjusted to conform with the new state level deaths for each sex by allocating the numbers from the first step to age groups in proportion to the state age group's share of total deaths in the state.

Deaths to migrants are estimated by applying age-sex disaggregated state death rates to the appropriate at-risk population. Migrants who changed age groups before they died are then estimated by applying age-sex specific coefficients to total state deaths in each age-sex group. The coefficients may be interpreted as the proportion of deaths in an age group that occurs to individuals who were in the previous age group at the beginning of the time period. These coefficients are not state-specific due to limited data, and hence the same national coefficient is applied to each state for each age-sex group. The usual assumption that migrants take on the death rate of the destination region is modified in ECESIS so that migrants take on a death rate whose magnitude is between the rates of the origin and destination states. It is initially assumed that inmigrants take on the death rate of their destination region and that outmigrants take on the death rate of their origin region. Since total deaths to inmigrants will not necessarily equal total deaths to outmigrants, the resulting difference is allocated to each state after it has been multiplied by the state's share of the national total of inmigrants and outmigrants who die. Deaths to migrants born during the period are calculated in similar fashion.

Accounting identities are then used to calculate the following major flows: (1) deaths to nonmigrating infants born during the period by state and sex; (2) deaths to nonmigrants changing age groups by state, age, and sex; (3) deaths to nonmigrants not changing age groups by state, age, and sex; (4) the population alive at the beginning of the period and still alive in the same state at the end of the period, which is further subdivided into: (a) surviving nonmigrants who change age groups, (b) surviving nonmigrants who do not change age groups, (c) surviving nonmigrants born during the time period, and (5) new population by state, age, and sex, including information on the totals in each group who are changing age groups.

State survived populations are computed for each age-sex group by subtracting deaths to nonmigrants and deaths to outmigrants from the population at the beginning of the period. This survived population represents the number of people at-risk of migrating and is used by the migration component of the model.

Initially, values of the minor flows are not available for use in the calculations of at-risk populations, and they are set equal to zero. After deriving preliminary estimates of the minor flows, they are fed back into the calculation of at-risk populations. The process continues until the minor flows converge (typically in less than five iterations).

Finally, net foreign immigration is added to the population by assuming a constant 400,000 immigrants per year. Immigrants are allocated to states based on the state of intended residence of immigrants in 1972 and 1973 according to data provided by the Immigration and Naturalization Services (INS) The intended residence is used in ECESIS rather than the residence observed as much as five years later by the census because immigrants revise their plans in part on the basis of economic opportunities. Their reaction to those opportunities is modeled endogenously using the migration equations.

After the state populations by age and sex including foreign immigration have been estimated in the demographic accounts, they are used as inputs in the economic models. After those models are run using the population values, the resulting values of the economic variables are used in the migration models. The new migration levels generally will differ from those initially used as inputs in the demographic accounts because of the feedbacks from population change to economic change to population change. Therefore the demographic accounts are recalculated for the same period with the adjusted migration estimates. The entire process involving the demographic accounts, migration models, and economic models is repeated until population converges.

The Economic Models

Several restrictions were imposed on the state economic models in order to hold the modeling effort to a reasonable size. Each model was to be as small as possible, since 51 separate regions are involved. Yet the models were to contain enough detail to allow the major interregional and demographic linkages to be adequately specified. Also, rather than attempting to model the idiosyncrasies of each state, a common structure for all states was used. This conformity required that the equation specifications be simple and robust. Since only a model specification firmly rooted in economic theory could hope to achieve any degree of success when applied to so many diverse states, emphasis was placed on deriving equations with strong theoretical foundations. (This strategy is consistent with the findings reported by Taylor in chapter 6.)

Each economic model is disaggregated into three sectors: manufacturing, nonmanufacturing, and farming. As an example of how a more disaggregated model might be specified, the manufacturing sector is modeled with considerable detail. The manufacturing sector was chosen for this purpose because that sector comprises 25 to 30 percent of national income and is the largest sector in over three-quarters of the states. Also, the available data for the manufacturing sector are more complete than for any other sector.

Supply and demand factors interact in determining the output of the manufacturing sector of each state. Demand is a function of the state's manufacturing wage and of income in every state weighted by a trade matrix. A production function and the related factor demand equations are key elements in the supply side of each model. Increased demand from outside the state cannot induce increased production unless the factors are available for expansion.

The more utilized the factors of production are, the more costly it is for the manufacturing sector in the state to meet increased demand. An important demographic linkage helps illustrate this interaction of factor supply and output demand. As outmigration increases, the labor force decreases and the unemployment rate falls. Also capacity output of manufacturing falls and the capacity utilization rate increases. The changes in the unemployment and capacity utilization rates both cause manufacturing wages to increase. This higher production cost makes the state's output less competitive, leading to decreases in demand.

The nonmanufacturing sector includes agricultural services, forestry, and fisheries; mining; construction; transportation, communications, and public utilities; wholesale and retail trade; finance, insurance, and real estate; services; and government. Nonmanufacturing is dominated by the trade, services, and government industries, each accounting for approximately 15 percent of national income (although considerable variation exists among states). This rather aggregated sector is treated very simply with reduced-form equations. The farm sector, which accounts for less than 2 percent of national income, is exogenous for all states.

The state economic models are bottom-up in design. No regional variables are determined by disaggregating national variables. Some national variables, most notably manufacturing output prices, are taken to be exogenous in the state models. Although the bottom-up approach is theoretically appealing, it is more difficult to implement than top-down models (Klein and Glickman 1977). The bottom-up design, however, allows ECESIS to be solved independently from a separate national econometric model, thereby avoiding one additional level of linkages that is not the primary focus of this study.

A complete description of all the economic models with estimation results is not feasible in this chapter. Rather, a general overview of the model specification is provided with selected equations from a diverse set of states. A complete list of equations is provided in the appendix. In this chapter, only equations that feature an important modeling philosophy or that demonstrate an interesting linkage mechanism are emphasized. Generally only a quick summary of the estimation results is given. Discussions of data sources or particular data problems are also held to a minimum. In most cases, the equations are estimated using ordinary least-squares with annual data over the sample period 1959 to 1974. Data available from 1974 to the present have been reserved for future use to test the simulation properties of the model. The fullest discussion of ECESIS to date is found in Beaumont (1984).

Manufacturing Output

Manufacturing output in state i (Q_i) is partially a function of the demand for manufactured goods in every other state. The degree of this interdependence is captured in ECESIS by weighting a vector of demands of each state by an interstate trade share matrix. Let Q_{ij} be the amount of state i's manufacturing output that is shipped to state j. Then define

$$r_{ij} = Q_{ij}/\Sigma_i Q_{ij} = Q_{ij}/Q_{.j}.$$

State j's total demand for manufacturing output is $Q_{.j}$. Thus, demand for state i's manufacturing output may be written as

$$Q_{i.} = \Sigma_j r_{ij} Q_{.j}.$$

The r_{ij}'s are estimated from the 1977 commodity transportation survey of the U.S. Bureau of the Census (1980) and are assumed to be fixed. The demand for goods in a state is approximated by that state's real personal income ($YT72$) and $\Sigma_j r_{ij} YT72_j$ is used as a weighted demand indicator for state i's manufactured goods.

Demand for a state's manufactured output should also depend on the

ECESIS ECONOMIC-DEMOGRAPHIC MODEL OF THE UNITED STATES

output price of that state. Since output price data by state are not available, the ratio of the hourly manufacturing wage rate in the state to the U.S. average manufactured output price index is used as an approximation (*WMH/USMP*). The wage bill comprises about 60 percent of the cost of manufactured goods, so the wage rate is a reasonable approximation to production costs. To capture the inertia of the manufacturing process an anticipated demand variable (Q^a) is included in the demand equation.

$$Q^a = Q_{-1}(IP/IP_{-1}),$$

where *IP* is an industrial production index for the United States. Output in state *i* is anticipated to be close to Q^a unless relative prices change or the interstate demand (income) structure changes. The final specification for the manufacturing output equation is

$$Q_{i\cdot} = a_0 + a_1 Q^a + a_2(WMH/USMP) + a_3(\Sigma_j r_{ij} YT72_j). \quad (9.5)$$

The coefficient a_3 is estimated algebraically so that the elasticity of output with respect to income is equal to one. The remaining coefficients are then estimated with ordinary least-squares. Table 9-2 summarizes the estimation results for a small set of states.

Table 9-2. Manufacturing Output Equations

State	Constant	Anticipated Output	Relative Price	Trade-Weighted Income[a]	R^2/D-W
Arizona	−.242	.750	−.140	.369	.93
	(.58)	(4.67)	(.90)		2.31
Indiana	−.632	.474	−1.131	.420	.77
	(.75)	(4.35)	(2.35)		.80
Iowa	−.674	.676	−.455	.293	.86
	(1.67)	(4.23)	(1.73)		1.12
New York	5.986	.479	−4.635	.649	.91
	(7.84)	(6.51)	(9.91)		1.98
Texas	1.842	.835	−3.158	.262	.82
	(.55)	(3.14)	(1.75)		1.41
Washington	−.006	.556	−.520	.460	.34
	(.01)	(2.44)	(1.74)		1.51

[a]No t-statistic is shown for this variable because its coefficient is estimated algebraically before the rest of the equation is solved by ordinary least-squares regression. The R^2 thus refers to the proportion of the variation not explained by the trade-weighted income variable. The terms in parentheses are the t-statistics of the other variables.

Factor Demands

A completely specified macro-econometric model includes a production function and the demand equations for those factors which enter the production function. Since the parameters of these equations are not independent of one another, appropriate restrictions must be imposed on the parameters when these equations are estimated.

The production function, as noted by Coen and Hickman (1970), is a relationship among variables at equilibrium. Usually the economy is not at equilibrium so that these variables cannot be directly observed. Presumably, at equilibrium capital and labor inputs are fully utilized. It is reasonable to assume, since labor inputs may be adjusted quickly through hires and layoffs, that observed labor inputs are fully utilized. For simplicity, it is assumed that the utilization rate of capital is equal to the output capacity rate. Once the production function is specified in terms of desired output and inputs, the implicit desired factor input equations may be derived. Finally, a simple partial adjustment model may be used to adjust actual inputs toward the desired levels.

A Cobb-Douglas production technology is assumed with the factors of production being capital and labor:

$$\log(QC_i) = a_o + \alpha \log(MLFC_i) + \beta \log(MKS72_i) + \delta(PRTR_i) \tag{9.6}$$

where QC_i is capacity manufacturing output in state i; $MLFC_i$ is capacity labor inputs in manhours; $MKS72_i$ is real fully utilized capital stock; and $PRTR_i$ is a measure of average productivity growth to quantify neutral technical progress.

Using a simplified version of a method developed by Klein and Su (1979), capacity manufacturing labor inputs ($MLFC$) are calculated as,

$$MLFC_t = (EM/POP)_t^c (POP_t)(HR_t^c)/(52 \text{ wk/yr.}), \tag{9.7}$$

where $(EM/POP)_t^c$ is the peak ratio of manufacturing employment to total population, POP_t is the current state population, and HR_t^c is the peak hours worked per week. The capacity utilization rate is obtained from

$$CU = Q/QC.$$

Capacity output is not directly observed and must be calculated from $QC = Q/CU$, but CU cannot be calculated until QC is known. The iterative estimation procedure used for equation 9.6 is explained in Beaumont (1984).

Assuming that firms follow profit-maximizing behavior, the desired level of factor inputs will be a function of desired output, expected output price, factor prices, and the parameters from equation 9.6. The desired real capital stock (*MKD*) equation is:

$$MKD = \beta[1 - (1/e)] P(Q/UCC), \qquad (9.8)$$

where *P* is manufacturing output price, *UCC* is the user cost of capital, and *e* is the elasticity of demand (imperfect markets are assumed to exist). The equation for desired labor inputs (*MLD*) is:

$$MLD = \alpha[1 - (1/e)] P(Q/WMH), \qquad (9.9)$$

where *WMH* is the nominal hourly manufacturing wage rate. The estimates of returns to scale ($\alpha + \beta$) from equation 9.6 generally fall between 1.0 and 1.5, indicating moderate increasing returns. The estimates of the elasticity of demand generally fall in the range of two to three, suggesting a moderately competitive climate.

Actual factor inputs are assumed to adjust to desired levels using a partial adjustment model. Labor inputs are estimated as:

$$\log(MLAB) = a_0 + a_1 \log(MLD) + a_2 \log(MLAB), \qquad (9.10)$$

where *MLAB* is actual labor inputs. Estimates of the labor-adjustment rate are quite variable but are usually in the range of 40 to 75 percent. Manufacturing employment is determined from *MLAB* by dividing by hours worked.

Gross manufacturing investment is modeled as a geometrically declining lag structure on past differences of desired and actual capital stock:

$$I = a_0 + a_1 I_{-1} + a_2 (MKD - MKS72_{-1}), \qquad (9.11)$$

where *I* is real manufacturing gross investment. This specification worked well, particularly considering the poor quality of regional investment data.

A summary of estimation results from the production function and factor demand equations is given in table 9–3.

The nonmanufacturing sector is modeled with a reduced-form employment equation. Since the trade, services, and government industries dominate this sector, the local population size should be an important determinant of nonmanufacturing employment (*ENM*). Distance-weighted populations of other states are used in the specification in a manner analogous to the trade-share variables of the manufacturing output equation. The economic base approach is also incorporated by including manufacturing employment in the specification, and the nonmanufacturing

Table 9-3. Summary of Results from Capacity Output and Factor Demand Equations

State	$(\alpha + \beta)$[a]	e[b]	Average lags:[c] Labor	Investment
Arizona	.892	3.79	.79	3.77
Indiana	1.047	2.83	.39	3.38
Iowa	1.201	1.81	.72	3.83
New York	1.323	1.93	1.04	6.56
Texas	1.175	2.05	1.56	3.65
Washington	.993	2.96	.59	2.69

[a] Returns to scale.
[b] Elasticity of demand.
[c] Average lag of adjustment to desired level (in years).

real wage is included with the demand effect expected to dominate. The final specification for *ENM* is:

$$ENM_i = a_0 + a_1 ENM_{i,-1} + a_2(\sum_j (1/d_{ij})POP_j) + a_3 EM_i + a_4(WNM_i/CPI72_i) \qquad (9.12)$$

In many states lagged nonmanufacturing employment was excluded in the specification, and in other states the wage variable was omitted. Estimation results were generally good and are summarized in table 9-4.

Wages and Income

Wage rates are determined using a leading region and leading sector approach. The manufacturing sector is taken to be the leader with the nonmanufacturing sector following. Rather than specifying some state or subset of states as the leading region, a wage transmission variable is constructed that allows all states to have some impact upon the manufacturing wage-rate determination process. This transmission variable DW_i^* is defined:

$$DW_i^* = \Sigma_j \{(1/d_{ij})[(YM_j/YTLPR_j)/(YM_{us}/YTLPR_{us})]S_i\}WM_j,$$

where d_{ij} is the distance between 1970 population centroids of states i and j; the term in brackets is the ratio of manufacturing income (*YM*) to total labor and proprietors income *YTLPR* in state j relative to the same ratio for the United States; S_i is a scaling factor; and WM_j is the manufacturing

Table 9-4. Nonmanufacturing Employment

State	Constant	Lagged Nonmanufacturing Employment	Distance-Weighted Population	Manufacturing Employment	Real Nonmanufacturing Wage	R^2/D-W
Arizona	−419.384	—	.227	3.224	−62.496	.92
	(.85)[a]		(1.36)	(1.66)	(1.25)	.33
Indiana	−2118.396	—	.477	.698	−158.943	.99
	(14.13)		(14.02)	(3.55)	(5.24)	1.01
Iowa	−321.317	.621	.111	.753	−33.589	.99
	(3.21)	(6.73)	(2.67)	(5.84)	(2.03)	1.21
New York	−2088.303	.955	.111	.570	—	.99
	(5.22)	(13.05)	(2.00)	(5.51)		2.43
Texas	−3178.609	—	1.445	2.612	−370.187	.98
	(3.55)		(4.57)	(4.41)	(3.06)	.50
Washington	−446.451	.687	.173	.653	−33.618	.99
	(3.87)	(6.86)	(3.07)	(5.04)	(1.96)	1.43

[a] The numbers in parentheses are t-statistics.

wage rate in state j. Every state's manufacturing wage rate has some influence on DW_i^*, but nearby states and states with large manufacturing sectors have relatively more influence.

Local labor-market conditions and an industry's ability to substitute for scarce resources are also important, so the local manufacturing employment to working age population ratio ($EM/P1864$) and capacity utilization rate (CU) are included in the equation. Inflationary effects are captured by the local consumer price index ($CPI72$). The final specification for the manufacturing wage equation is:

$$\log(WM_i) = a_0 + a_1\log(DW_i^*)_{-1} + a_2\log(EM_i/P1864_i)_{-1}$$
$$+ a_3\log(CU_i) + a_4\log(CPI72_i)_{-1} \qquad (9.13)$$

All coefficients are expected to be positive, but the coefficients on the capacity-utilization rate and employment-to-population ratio are often not significant or only marginally significant, indicating that the local labor market often may not have a sizeable impact on the local manufacturing wage rate. Table 9–5 provides a summary of estimation results for equation 9.13. The CU rate generally performs better than indicated by the subgroup of states shown in this chapter.

The nonmanufacturing wage rate (WNM) is assumed to be a simple function of the manufacturing wage rate and the local nonmanufacturing employment to working-age population ratio. As expected, estimation results show that the coefficient of the manufacturing wage rate is generally slightly less than 1.0 and that the employment-population ratio is usually more significant than in the manufacturing wage equation. The latter result suggests that the local labor market is more important in determining wages in the trade and services sectors, possibly because the market areas of those sectors are usually quite local and national labor settlements may be more important for manufacturing.

Wage income is solved by identity. Additional income equations which complete the personal income accounts are listed in the appendix. Demographic linkages are provided in the proprietors' income and transfer payments equations. The latter includes both direct and indirect population effects and also age distribution effects. The transfer payments equation is specified as:

$$YTP_i = POP_i \left[a_0 + a_1\, PCYT_i + a_2(P65_i/POP_i) + a_3(U_i/POP_i) \right],$$

where $PCYT$ is per capita personal income, $P65/POP$ is the proportion of the state's population that is aged 65 years or older, and U_i is the number of unemployed workers in state i.

Table 9-5. Manufacturing Wage Equations

State	Constant	Composite Wage Variable	Employment Population Ratio	Capacity Utilization	Consumer Price Index	R^2/D-W
Arizona	−.886	.603	.107	—	.464	.99
	(2.59)[a]	(8.66)	(2.87)		(4.20)	2.92
Indiana	−3.010	.415	.096	.142	.964	.99
	(3.89)	(2.40)	(1.07)	(2.10)	(3.22)	2.88
Iowa	−2.415	.470	.247	.039	.880	.99
	(4.28)	(3.61)	(2.96)	(.62)	(4.17)	2.25
New York	−2.501	.905	.285	.055	.53	.99
	(6.34)	(14.77)	(3.59)	(.61)	(3.69)	2.12
Texas	−.854	.480	.276	.104	.590	.99
	(1.93)	(5.37)	(4.56)	(1.67)	(3.93)	2.29
Washington	−.926	.896	.183	.033	.357	.99
	(.90)	(5.21)	(2.19)	(.40)	(1.06)	3.06

[a]The numbers in parentheses are t-statistics.

Labor Force

Perhaps the most direct linkage between the demographic and economic models is in the determination of the labor force. Labor-force participation rates disaggregated by age and sex are estimated. They are applied to the age-sex specific populations derived by the demographic model. The unemployment rate is then calculated by identity. This approach, while theoretically appealing, has the problem that the unemployment rate, when calculated by the identity, is very sensitive to minor errors in the forecast values of the labor-force participation rates. Since the unemployment rate plays such as important role in an econometric model, this sensitivity can create serious problems when using the model for forecasting exercises.

An alternative is to use a stochastic equation to estimate the unemployment rate and then calculate the labor force or the labor-force participation rate by identity. The major problem with this approach is that there is no good way to derive the age-sex disaggregated labor-force variables from the aggregate variable determined by the identity. Another disadvantage is that simulation experiments become more difficult to interpret when the unemployment rate is calculated from a stochastic equation rather than the identity.

Estimation of age-sex specific labor-force participation rates is further complicated because there is no age-sex detail among the economic data. The procedure used in ECESIS to deal with these problems is to model the labor-force participation rates with a two-step procedure and then calculate the unemployment rate by identity. The total labor-force participation rate is modeled as a function of the real wage, per capita property income, and the inflation rate. Of the eight age-sex groups in ECESIS that participate in the labor force, the participation rates of the 5–17 and 65+ age groups for both sexes are taken as exogenous. The remaining participation rates are modeled as ratios of the already determined total participation rate. For example, the participation rate for 18–44-year-old females is modeled as:

$$LFPR1844F = RTOT(a_0 + a_1(LFPR1844F/RTOT)_{-1} + a_2 BRATE),$$

where $RTOT$ is the total labor-force participation rate and $BRATE$ is the birth rate. The participation rates of 18- to 44- and 45- to 64-year-old males is modeled similarly except that per capita property income is used in place of the birth rate. One rate must be calculated by identity and in this case it is the participation rate of 45- to 64-year-old females.

The estimation results from these participation rate equations are not outstanding. Participation rates are always difficult to estimate, particularly when trying to estimate disaggregated rates without disaggregated economic data as independent variables. The total participation rate equation generally works quite well, including the inflation variable as suggested by Simler and Tella (1980).

Economic-Demographic and Interregional Linkages

Three important sets of economic-demographic linkages exist in ECESIS. They are all interrelated. Two are economic consequences of population change—one operating initially through the supply of labor, the other initially through the demand for output. The third is an economic determinant of population change, namely, migration responding to employment change and unemployment. All of the linkages will be illustrated taking as a starting point a change in population. The example could have begun anywhere in the process to be described below—for instance, with an income change.

A change in population leads directly to changes in labor force through the labor-force participation rates. A labor supply increase leads to increases in unemployment because the latter is treated as a residual in the economic models. Capacity output also increases, so capacity utilization declines. The decline in capacity utilization and the increase in unemployment both tend to decrease wages. That decrease may lead to increased output through increased demand for manufacturing output. The increase in unemployment also leads to increases in transfer income, resulting in increases in both manufacturing and nonmanufacturing output.

More direct demand effects of population change occur through the income and output equations. Transfer income, proprietors' income, and nonmanufacturing employment increase directly with population. The additional income also induces increases in manufacturing output. The increased demand leads to employment increases and unemployment decreases.

These changes in economic conditions lead to population change. Both the employment increases and unemployment decreases lead to improvements in a state's attractiveness index, causing increased inmigration. The resulting population change then leads to the supply and demand effects already discussed.

Both the supply and demand effects of population change have an impact on unemployment, capacity and capacity utilization, wages, income, demand, migration, and labor force. These effects are simultaneous, but not always in the same direction. Which effects dominate is an empirical question whose answer will vary with the initial conditions and elasticities of each state. The demand effect may be expected to dominate, except if a state is near capacity output. Then the increased wages could lead to leakages of demand to other states through the manufacturing demand equation.

Interregional linkages, including manufacturing demand, also are important in ECESIS. Other strong linkages involve nonmanufacturing employment, manufacturing wages, and migration. In each case, conditions in a single state affect and are affected by conditions in all other states. Manufacturing output in a state depends on the trade-flow weighted income levels of every state. Nonmanufacturing employment depends on the distance-weighted populations of all states. Manufacturing wages depend on the distance- and size-weighted wages in every state. Finally, migration to and from a state depends on employment change, and unemployment in every state weighted by past migration flows and on the population levels and composition of every state. Thus, regional economic and population changes are not just linked to one another in ECESIS, but they are linked interregionally as well.

Few disagree that these linkages are important from a theoretical perspective. Little is known, however, of their empirical significance. How much more accurately can population be forecast if its economic determinants are modeled? How much more accurately can economic change be forecast if its demographic determinants are modeled? What is gained by including interregional linkages? Due to the relatively high costs of building interregional economic-demographic models, answers to these questions have important implications for regional modeling. For example, if the economic determinants of population change are important, but not its economic consequences, population can be modeled simply by adding demographic models post-recursively to existing economic ones. If all the economic-demographic linkages prove to be of minor importance, models which ignore these linkages may be adequate, or at least cost-effective. Although individual equations or elements of ECESIS may be questioned and the results from one model cannot provide conclusive results, ECESIS provides a framework for carrying out empirical tests of the importance of these linkages.

References

Alonso, W. 1980. Population as a system in regional development. *American Economic Review* 70, 2:405–509.

Beaumont, P. 1984. ECESIS: an interregional economic-demographic model of the United States. Ph.D. dissertation, University of Pennsylvania.

Butz, W., and Ward, M. 1979. The emergence of countercyclical U.S. fertility. *American Economic Review* 69, 3:318–328.

Coen, R., and Hickman, B. 1970. Constrained joint estimation of factor demand and production functions. *Review of Economics and Statistics* 52, 3:287–300.

Engels, R., and Healy, M. 1981. Measuring interstate migration flows: an origin-destination network based on Internal Revenue Service records. *Environment and Planning A* 13: 1345–1360.

Hamilton, H.; Goldstone, S.; Milliman, J.; Pugh, A.; Roberts, E.; and Zellner, A. 1969. *Systems simulation for regional analysis: an application to river-basin planning*. Cambridge, MA: MIT Press.

Isserman, A.; Plane, D.; and McMillen, D. 1982. Internal migration in the United States: an evaluation of federal data. *Review of Public Data Use* 10: 285–311.

Isserman, A.; Plane, D.; Rogerson, P.; and Beaumont, P. 1985. Forecasting interstate migration with limited data: a demographic-economic approach. *Journal of the American Statistical Association* 80, 390: 277–285.

Klein, L., and Glickman, N. 1977. Econometric model building at regional level. *Regional Science and Urban Economics* 7:3–23.

Klein, L., and Su, V. 1979. Direct estimates of unemployment rate and capacity utilization in macroeconometric models. *International Economic Review* 20, 3:725–740.

Rees, P., and Wilson, A. 1977. *Spatial population analysis*. London: Arnold.

Rogerson, P. 1981. Behavioral and aggregate approaches to migration modeling. Ph.D. dissertation, State University of New York at Buffalo.

Simler, N., and Tella, A. 1980. Inflation and labor force participation. In *Stagflation: the causes, effects, and solutions*. Special study on Economic Change, Joint Economic Committee, U.S. Congress.

U.S. Bureau of the Census. 1980. *1977 census of transportation: commodity transportation survey*. Washington, D.C.

Appendix: Specification of Economic Model Equations

Output and Factor Demands

(I.1) Output Demand

$$Q = a_0 + a_1 Q^a + a_2(WMH/P) + a_3(\Sigma_j r_{ij} YT72_j)$$

Q—real manufacturing value added; 10^6 72 \$.
Q^a—$Q_{-1} \cdot IP/IP_{-1}$.
IP—U.S. index of industrial production; 1967=100.
r_{ij}—interstate trade share matrix for manufactured goods.
$YT72$—real total personal income; 10^6 72 \$.
WMH—manufacturing hourly wage rate; \$/hr.
P—U.S. manufacturing price index; 1972=1.

(I.2) Capacity Output

$$QCAP = a_0 MLFC^\alpha MKS72^\beta \exp(\gamma PRTR)$$

$QCAP$—capacity manufacturing output; 10^6 72 \$.
$MLFC$—manufacturing labor-force capacity; 10^6 hr/yr.
$MKS72$—real manufacturing capital stock; 10^6 72 \$.
$PRTR$—productivity trend (function of past productivity growth).

(I.3) Desired Capital Inputs

$$MKD = \beta(1 - 1/\xi)PQ/UCC$$

MKD—desired manufacturing capital stock; 10^6 72 \$.
PQ—nominal manufacturing value added; 10^6 \$.
UCC—user cost of capital.
β—elasticity of capital inputs from production function.
ξ—elasticity of demand for manufactured goods.

(I.4) Desired Labor Inputs

$$MLD = \alpha(1 - 1/\xi)PQ/WMH$$

MLD—desired manufacturing labor inputs; 10^6 hr/yr.

WMH—manufacturing hourly wage rate; $/hr.
α—elasticity of labor inputs from production function.

(I.5) Capital Adjustment—Investment

$$MGI72 = a_0 + a_1 MGI72_{-1} + a_2(MKD - MKS72_{-1})$$

MGI72—manufacturing real gross investment; 10^6 72 $.
MKD—desired manufacturing capital stock; 10^6 72 $.
MKS72—real manufacturing capital stock; 10^6 72 $.

(I.6) Labor Demand Adjustment

$$\log(MLAB) = a_0 + a_1 \log(MLD) + a_2 \log(MLAB_{-1})$$

MLAB—manufacturing labor inputs; 10^6 hr/yr.
MLD—desired manufacturing labor inputs; 10^6 hr/yr.

(I.7) Capacity Utilization Rate

$$CU = Q/QCAP$$

CU—manufacturing capacity utilization rate.
Q—real manufacturing value added; 10^6 72 $.
QCAP—real capacity manufacturing output; 10^6 72 $.

(I.8) Manufacturing Capacity Labor Inputs

$$MLFC = MHC(EM/PTOT)^c PTOT \cdot 52/1000$$

MLFC—manufacturing capacity labor inputs; 10^6 hr/yr.
MHC—capacity hours per week (past peak); hr/wk.
$(EM/PTOT)^c$—capacity manufacturing employment-to-population ratio (past peak).
PTOT—total state population; 10^3 persons.

(I.9) Manufacturing Capital Stock Depreciation

$$MD72 = \delta \cdot MKS72_{-1}$$

MD72—depreciation of real manufacturing capital stock; 10^6 72 $.

$MKS72$—real manufacturing capital stock; 10^6 72 \$.
δ—capital depreciation rate.

(I.10) Net Manufacturing Investment

$$MNI72 = MGI72 - MD72$$

$MNI72$—real net manufacturing investment; 10^6 72 \$.
$MGI72$—real gross manufacturing investment; 10^6 72 \$.
$MD72$—depreciation of real manufacturing capital stock; 10^6 72 \$.

(I.11) Manufacturing Capital Stock

$$MKS72 = MKS72_{-1} + MNI72$$

$MKS72$—real manufacturing capital stock; 10^6 72 \$.
$MNI72$—real net manufacturing investment; 10^6 72 \$.

(I.12) Nominal Manufacturing Output

$$PQ = P \cdot Q$$

PQ—nominal manufacturing value added; 10^6 \$.
Q—real manufacturing value added; 10^6 72 \$.
P—manufacturing output deflator; 1972 = 1.

(I.13) Manufacturing Gross Profits

$$MGP\$ = PQ - YM$$

$MGP\$$—manufacturing nominal gross profis; 10^6 \$.
PQ—nominal manufacturing value added; 10^6 \$.
YM—manufacturing income; 10^6 \$.

Employment

(II.1) Manufacturing Employment

$$EM = MLAB/(MHR \cdot 52/1000)$$

EM—manufacturing employment; 10^3 jobs.

MLAB—manufacturing labor inputs; 10^6 hr/yr.
MHR—manufacturing hours per week per employee; hr/wk

(II.2) Nonmanufacturing Employment

$$ENM = a_0 + a_1 ENM_{-1} + a_2(\Sigma_j d_{ij}^{-1} \cdot PTOT_j) + a_3 EM + a_4(WNM/CPI72)$$

ENM—nonmanufacturing employment; 10^3 jobs.
d_{ij}—distance between 1970 population centroids of state i and state j.
PTOT—total state population; 10^3 persons.
EM—manufacturing employment; 10^3 jobs.
WNM—nonmanufacturing average earnings; 10^3 \$/yr.
CPI72—consumer price index; 1972 = 1.

(II.3) Total Employment

$$ET = EM + ENM + EOTHER$$

ET—total state employment; 10^3 persons.
EM—manufacturing employment; 10^3 jobs.
ENM—nonmanufacturing employment; 10^3 jobs.
EOTHER—other employment (farming) plus jobs to people employed conversion.

(II.4) Average Labor Product

$$APL = Q/EM$$

APL—average labor product; 10^3 72 \$/employee.
Q—real manufacturing value added; 10^6 72 \$.
EM—manufacturing employment; 10^3 jobs.

Wages and Prices

(III.1) Manufacturing Wages

$$\log(WM) = a_0 + a_1 \log(\Sigma_j d_{ij}^{-1} W_j^*)_{-1} + a_2 \log(EM/P1864)_{-1}$$
$$+ a_3 \log(CU) + a_4 \log(CPI72)_{-1}$$

WM—manufacturing average earnings; 10^3 \$/yr.

d_{ij}—distance between 1970 population centroids of state i and state j.
W_j^*—$WM_j[(YM_j/YTLPR_j)/(USYM/USYTLPR)]$
YM—manufacturing income; 10^6 \$.
$YTLPR$—total labor and proprietors' income; 10^6 \$.
$US\ldots$ —U.S. aggregate variables.
EM—manufacturing employment; 10^3 jobs.
$P1864$—state population aged 18 to 64; 10^3 persons.
CU—manufacturing capacity utilization rate.
$CPI72$—consumer price index; 1972 = 1.

(III.2) Nonmanufacturing Wages

$$\log(WNM) = a_0 + a_1\log(WM) + a_2\log(ENM/P1864)_{-1}$$

WNM—nonmanufacturing average earnings; 10^3 \$/yr.
WM—manufacturing average earnings; 10^3 \$/yr.
ENM—nonmanufacturing employment; 10^3 jobs.
$P1864$—state population aged 18 to 64; 10^3 persons.

(III.3) Manufacturing Nominal Hourly Wage Rate

$$WMH = WM/(MHR \cdot 52/1000)$$

WMH—manufacturing nominal hourly wage rate; \$/hr.
WM—manufacturing average earnings; 10^3 \$/yr.
MHR—manufacturing hours per week per employee; hr/wk.

(III.4) Manufacturing Real Hourly Wage Rate

$$WMH72 = WMH/CPI72$$

$WMH72$—manufacturing real hourly wage rate; 72 \$/hr.
WMH—manufacturing nominal hourly wage rate; \$/hr.
$CPI72$—consumer price index; 1972 = 1.

(III.5) Total Wages

$$WT = (YM + YNM)/(EM + ENM)$$

WT—total average earnings; 10^3 \$/yr.
YM—manufacturing income; 10^6 \$.
YNM—nonmanufacturing income; 10^6 \$.

EM—manufacturing employment; 10^3 jobs.
ENM—manufacturing employment; 10^3 jobs.

(III.6) Total Real Average Earnings

$$WT72 = WT/CPI72$$

WT72—total real average earnings; 10^3 72 \$.
WT—total nominal average earnings; 10^3 \$.
CPI72—consumer price index; 1972 = 1.

(III.7) Consumer Price Index

$$\log(CPI72) = a_0 + a_1 \log(WT)$$

CPI72—consumer price index; 1972 = 1.
WT—total nominal average earnings; 10^3 \$.

Income

(IV.1) Manufacturing Income

$$YM = WM \cdot EM$$

YM—manufacturing income; 10^6 \$.
WM—manufacturing average earnings; 10^3 \$.
EM—manufacturing employment; 10^3 jobs.

(IV.2) Nonmanufacturing Income

$$YNM = WNM \cdot ENM$$

YNM—nonmanufacturing income; 10^6 \$.
WNM—nonmanufacturing average earnings; 10^3 \$.
ENM—nonmanufacturing employment; 10^3 jobs.

(IV.3) Nonfarm Proprietors' Income

$$YPROP = a_0 + a_1 YT + a_2 PTOT$$

YPROP—nonfarm proprietors' income; 10^6 \$.

YT—total state personal income; 10^6 \$.
PTOT—total state population; 10^3 persons.

(IV.4) Total Labor and Proprietors' Income

$$YTLPR = YM + YNM + YPROP + YFARM$$

YTLPR—total labor and proprietors income; 10^6 \$.
YM—manufacturing income; 10^6 \$.
YNM—nonmanufacturing income; 10^6 \$.
YPROP—nonfarm proprietors' income; 10^6 \$.
YFARM—total farm income; 10^6 \$.

(IV.5) Property Income

$$YDIR = a_0 + a_1 YDIR_{-1} + a_2(GP\$ + GP\$_{-1})/2 + a_3 PR + a_4 CPI72$$

YDIR—total dividend, interest, and rent income; 10^6 \$.
GP\$—nominal gross manufacturing profits; 10^6 \$.
PR—U.S. average prime lending rate.
CPI72—consumer price index; 1972 = 1.

(IV.6) Transfer Payment Income

$$YTP = PTOT[a_0 + a_1(YT/PTOT) + a_2(P65+/PTOT) + a_3(U/PTOT)]$$

YTP—total transfer payment income; 10^6 \$.
PTOT—total state population; 10^3 persons.
YT—total state personal income; 10^6 \$.
P65+—state population aged 65 years and over; 10^3 persons.
U—unemployment; 10^3 persons.

(IV.7) Social Insurance Contributions

$$YSIC = YTLPR(a_0 + a_1 USSICR)$$

YSIC—social insurance contributions; 10^6 \$.
YTLPR—total labor and proprietor's income; 10^6 \$.
USSICR—U.S. social insurance contribution rate.

(IV.8) Total State Personal Income

$$YT = YTLPR + YDIR + YTP + YRA - YSIC$$

ECESIS ECONOMIC-DEMOGRAPHIC MODEL OF THE UNITED STATES

YT—total state personal income; 10^6 \$.
YTLPR—total labor and proprietors' income; 10^6 \$.
YDIR—total dividend, interest and rent income; 10^6 \$.
YTP—total transfer payments; 10^6 \$.
YRA—residence adjustment; 10^6 \$.
YSIC—social insurance contributions; 10^6 \$.

(IV.9) Real Income Variables

$$Yxxx72 = Yxxx/CPI72$$

Yxxx72—real income variables; 10^6 72 \$.
xxx—*T, TLPR, DIR*, etc.

Labor Force and Unemployment

Notation: $^aX^s$—variable X for age group a and sex group s.
Age groups: $a = 1$: 0–4 yrs.
$\quad\quad\quad\quad = 2$: 5–17 yrs.
$\quad\quad\quad\quad = 3$: 18–44 yrs.
$\quad\quad\quad\quad = 4$: 45–64 yrs.
$\quad\quad\quad\quad = 5$: 65+ yrs.
Sex groups: $s = 1$: male
$\quad\quad\quad\quad\quad = 2$: female
R—labor-force participation rate.
$^aR^s$; $a = 2,5$; $s = 1, 2$ are exogenous.

(V.1) Total Labor-Force Participation Rate

$$RTOT = a_0 + a_1(YDIR/P1864)_{-1} + a_2WT72 + a_3\%CPI72$$

RTOT—total *LFPR*.
YDIR—total dividend, interest, and rent income; 10^6 \$.
P1864—state population aged 18 to 64; 10^3 persons.
WT72—total real average earnings; 10^3 72\$.
%CPI72—percentage change in the consumer price index.

(V.2) LFPR for 18- to 44-Year-Old Males

$$^3R^1/RTOT = a_0 + a_1(^3R^1/RTOT)_{-1} + a_2(YDIR/P1864)_{-1}$$

(V.3) LFPR for 18- to 44-Year-Old Females

$$^3R^2/RTOT = a_0 + a_1(^3R^2/RTOT)_{-1} + a_2BRATE$$

$BRATE$—births per female aged 8–44.

(V.4) LFPR for 45- to 64-Year-Old Males

$$^4R^1/RTOT = a_0 + a_1(^4R^1/RTOT)_{-1} + a_2(YDIR/P1864)_{-1}$$

(V.5) LFPR for 45- to 64-Year-Old Females

$$^4R^2 = {}^4LF^2/{}^4POP^2$$

(V.6) Age-Sex Specific Labor Force

$$^aLF^s = {}^aR^s \cdot {}^aPOP^s$$

(V.7) Total Labor Force

$$LF = \Sigma_{a,s}{}^aLF^s$$

(V.8) Unemployment Rate

$$UR = (LF - ET)/LF$$

IV THE CHALLENGES AHEAD

10 REGIONAL ECONOMIC-DEMOGRAPHIC MODELING: PROGRESS AND PROSPECTS

Jeffrey Williamson

Introduction

It may seem especially inappropriate for me—an economic historian with interests in past, present, and future Industrial Revolutions—to write about forecasting regional populations in currently industrialized nations. But I have three advantages. First, I share an interest in spatial inequality, an interest which surely should motivate most of the debate about regional modeling. Second, I have been sufficiently distant from the literature on regional econometric models that it cannot be said that I have any personal axe to grind! And third, my point of vision on the problem is so different from most regional modelers that there is the distinct possibility that I might offer a fresh idea or two which may provoke useful debate or even suggest future research directions.

In that spirit, let me pose an argumentative question: What's wrong with current models of regional population change?

Clearing Away the Modelers' Underbrush

There is always the danger that a researcher will lose sight of the purpose of the modeling exercise as equations swell in number and an ever-expanding list of endogenous variables spill down the page. The danger also exists that forecasting exercises with large models hide more than they reveal. An additional danger is that the social issues get lost in the econometric underbrush as the modeler struggles with a framework sufficiently complex to supply descriptive detail. Thus, it might prove helpful to clear away some of the modelers' underbrush that has sprung up and begin anew with the basics.

Why Do Regions Matter?

For the moment, let's ignore the fact that planners need future estimates of regional income to project the tax base and regional demographic detail to project social overhead needs. Let's also ignore the fact that regional chambers of commerce would like regional market forecasts to help guide their members' business plans. In other words, ignore forecasting accuracy and focus for the moment on impact multipliers, sensitivity analyses, and policy counterfactuals. Given that focus, why do demographers and economists care about regions?

For me, distributional issues lie at the heart of the answer. First, there are the *endogenous* tales to consider. That is, migration is a central force by which a more equitable distribution of income can be achieved in any society. Migration, after all, is a response to disequilibrium, manifested in part by unequal incomes across space. We need to know more about how that mechanism works, and regional models surely offer one path to that knowledge. Second, there are the *exogenous* tales to consider. That is, what are the forces that create the disequilibrium in the first place? What is the regional incidence of macro-economic-demographic events? Which regions gain and which regions lose from national economic growth? From macrostabilization policy? From OPEC fuel crunch? From demographic transition, baby booms and bust? From trade liberalization and retreat toward protectionism? From technological slowdown? From tax and welfare reform? My own reading suggests that today's models are rarely equipped to handle such issues. That is a pity, since such issues should lie at the top of our agenda.

What About the Spatial Distribution of Jobs?

Surely the spatial distribution of jobs drives the spatial distribution of the labor force. Whether the model clears excess demands in the very short run by wages or unemployment rates is a trivial issue to me. Whether local labor supply is responsive to these labor-market conditions also seems a trivial issue to me. Migration—whether responsive to wages or unemployment rates—is the main device by which these markets are eventually cleared in the medium term and long run. To repeat, the central force driving the labor-market disequilibrium is the unequal rate of job creation across space. If the model is weak at this point, it will never offer an effective explanation of migration response and population redistribution. The more that derived spatial demands for labor rely on exogenous output change—unconstrained by capital, skills, and competitive technology—the weaker the model will be. My own reading suggests that regional models offer only weak endogenous explanations of unequal rates of job creation across space, and that's a pity.

The Time Dimension and Modeling Strategy

The time dimension should dictate modeling strategy. Demand-driven models may be appropriate for regional analysis in the very short run, but it's unclear how relevant the export staple or Keynesian demand-driven models will ever be for the medium term and long run. The analysis of regional growth requires a supply-driven model, where accumulation, capacity expansion, and total factor productivity growth are the central actors. My reading of the literature suggests that demographers are well equipped to handle the purely demographic responses to exogenous economic events, and the economists are far better equipped to handle the short run simply because the properties of demand-driven models are better understood by the regional modeler. That is a pity, since most of the economic-demographic issues of interest to us are manifested in the long run, requiring supply-driven models with careful attention to endogenous economic forces.

Supply-Driven Models, Factor Markets, and Regional Autonomy

If the model is to be supply-driven, how should regional factor markets be treated? I suspect that most of the empirical results of interest hinge critically on their treatment.

Consider the schooling content of the labor force. Are skills primarily endogenous to a region, or can future requirements be satisfied in large part by inmigration? The question is important only if the regional model admits skilled labor as a separate input into production activities; otherwise there is little need to model migration by schooling and experience.

What about capital stocks? Many models view capital as a free lunch; either capacity is determined only by labor inputs, or it is determined exogenously like manna from heaven. But surely regional capacity and the derived demand for labor is constrained by the availability of savings to finance the regional capital stock. Well then, do regional sources of finance seriously constrain capital accumulation, or are national financial markets sufficiently competitive to release regional capital accumulation from that constraint?

What about the provision of public goods and social overhead? Are we only interested in the employment effects generated by the construction and operation of social overhead activities? Surely not in the long run. To what extent is social overhead a direct input into firm production activities, thus influencing firms' per unit supply price and eventually their employment decisions? To what extent does the provision of public goods and social overhead therefore influence regional output and its competitive position vis-à-vis other regions? For that matter, to what extent does the availability of social overhead (public goods which influence spatial amenity differentials) influence *migration* decisions and thus the nominal cost of labor facing employers? Is not national policy toward the regional distribution of social overhead a central determinant of regional capacity, the derived demand for labor, migration, and thus the regional distribution of population? Most models are not equipped to answer such questions. That is a pity since issues of efficiency and equity hinge on the answers.

Two Big Issues in Detail

Let me elaborate on two issues that lurk behind my previous remarks. Both of these are central to the determinants and consequences of regional population change. Oddly enough, they appear to receive almost no attention in most models.

The Limitations of "Partial" General Equilibrium Models

Since the regional models typically take nationwide economic-demographic conditions as given, they tend to ignore the impact of the region in question on other regions with which it competes. For example, the most sophisticated of the models make regional wages endogenous, while nationwide labor-market conditions are taken as exogenous. That is, most assume that future regional employment conditions—including regional inmigration itself—have no impact on the national labor market. To the extent that the assumption is inappropriate, the rate of inmigration is exaggerated and the elasticity of regional labor supply is overstated. Of course, the same might be said of the migration literature. Typically, the partial equilibrium analysis of migration entails the construction and estimation of OLS equations where migration flows are correlated with regional wages and other employment variables. It has always struck me as odd that migration, an endogenous variable, is regressed on the regional wage differential, also an endogenous variable, in such exercises. After all, migration itself has an impact on labor-market conditions in both the sending and receiving regions. Thus, any effort to understand regional population change must explore the interaction among regional labor markets.[1] For long-run analysis, general equilibrium models of a spatially linked national labor market seem like one fruitful direction that future research might take.

Even if each region is believed to be small enough to warrant the elastic labor-supply assumption, what does the forecasting exercise tell us about the forces serving to redistribute population across regions? Every region is, after all, subjected to the same set of nationwide economic-demographic events. What we would really like to know is how these events favor some regions at the expense of the others. Only then can we separate out the impact of nationwide economic-demographic shocks on population distribution and spatial patterns of inequality from those which reflect long-run forces of spatial growth and decline.

One important example from 19th century American history may serve to illustrate the point. Every regional economist knows that the American South lagged behind in the post-Civil War period. Indeed, regional divergence characterized the late 19th century, and regional convergence failed to become an attribute of American growth until well into the second third of the 20th century (Williamson 1965). Why did the South fail up to the late 1920s? Why has the South risen again in the middle third of the 20th century? Most of our explanations dwell on Southern backwardness, social forces endogenous to the region associated with racism, and an agrarian system inconsistent with modern economic growth. But how can we adopt that position without having assessed the impact of macro-economic events external to the South, including national policy? Could international commodity markets and sagging prices for raw cotton have played a role? What about the impacts of balance of payments management and a gradual resumption of the pre-Civil war gold standard? What about a tariff policy which favored Northern industry at the expense of exportables centered in Southern (and Western) states? What about the distribution of the national social overhead which politics served to tilt toward the North and West? It seems to me that we cannot evaluate the historical impact of economic-demographic events on spatial inequality and Southern backwardness in the absence of a general equilibrium model which analyzes the regional incidence of national events, especially federal policy.[2]

If this assertion holds for America a century ago, it surely must hold for the 1970s and 1980s, a period of difficult structural adjustment to profound changes in policy and world market conditions. First and foremost, we would like answers to the following questions: What has been and will be the impact of a productivity slowdown on regional income inequality and population redistribution? What has been and will be the regional impact of the energy crisis on regional income inequality and population redistribution? What about capital shortages in the recent past and near future? What about national tax reform? What about a likely change in American attitudes toward foreign immigration in the face of high unemployment, especially given that immigration now tilts towards America's southern rim bordering on Mexico and the Caribbean Basin? What about the rising threat of world protectionism? Most regional models do not have the structure capable of supplying effective answers even if the questions were posed.

I urge regional modelers to devote more of their future energies toward these problems.[3] I view them to be absolutely central to any forecast of regional income and population change, whether the focus is on America, England, Japan, or even the Third World. They would certainly be central to any effort to assess issues of spatial equity in a world of profound structural adjustment.

Cost-of-Living, Nontradeables, and the Migration Decision

For a long time now, economists have thought it was adequate to focus on nominal income differentials in analyzing the determinants of migration. Indeed, those labor economists favoring the labor-market segmentation thesis have appealed to the abundant evidence of nominal wage differentials and wage gaps for confirmation. Perhaps the most often cited example has been the American South, where nominal wages have remained below those prevailing elsewhere. More recent evidence has suggested that this simplification can no longer be maintained. Cost-of-living differentials matter to the migration decision, and the application of hedonic earnings equations now suggests that regional amenities matter as well. Futhermore, as real incomes have increased everywhere in America, services with explicit prices and amenities without them have all increased in importance in household budgets. In short, there is reason to believe that cost-of-living and quality-of-life differentials have become increasingly important in the potential migrant's calculus. If this interpretation is correct, it seems relevent to ask how regional cost-of-living differentials are determined—if at all—in the models offered today. Since services and amenities tend to be nontradeables, to what extent are regional cost-of-living and amenity differentials influenced by migration and population redistribution itself? In short, it seems to me that the regional modeler should work just as hard exploring the endogenous determinants of regional amenities and living costs as employment demand and nominal wages. They are equally important to understanding the operation of regional labor markets. They are even more important in understanding migration of those retired or only part-time in the labor force.

What do I have in mind? Surely spatial differentials in housing costs should be captured in the modeling exercise, especially given that a handful of cities normally bear the brunt of regional migration flows and that migrants may be increasingly in retirement ages. Rapid inmigration implies housing scarcity, manifested by rising rents and/or dwelling unit scarcity under sticky rent conditions. Rapid inmigration, especially if centered on a few key cities, implies rapidly rising land-site values and future pressure on cost-of-living in the inmigration region. But surely that's not all. What about the availability of schooling, medical facilities, the incidence of crime, pollution, and other attributes of crowding and rising population density?[4]

I urge regional modelers to consider more seriously the endogenous determinants of cost-of-living and quality-of-life differentials. Surely they are central in any effort to assess the welfare implications of national policies which have spatial impacts. Surely they have a profound influence on population redistribution in the long run.

An Example from the Third World: Urbanization and City Growth[5]

It is easy enough to be critical of the work of others. It's quite a different matter to offer a concrete alternative. What I propose to do for the remainder of my remarks is to describe one effort to implement these suggestions.

For some time now, Allen Kelley and I have been developing a computable general equilibrium model of Third World city growth. True, the model is not designed to confront regional issues, but rather only urbanization aspects of spatial problems. In addition, the model was designed to confront recent Third World experience, not that of advanced industrialized societies. Furthermore, the model was not designed for highly detailed, short-run economic-demographic forecasts, but rather for counterfactual and parametric policy analysis over the very long run. Nevertheless, there may be some morals of use.

Multisectoral computable general equilibrium models have grown by leaps and bounds over the past decade. In developed countries, they have been applied to issues of tax policy, international trade, and energy. In developing countries, they have been applied to problems of growth, distribution, balance-of-payments adjustment, and demographic absorption. Their application to spatial issues is more recent, but early experiments look promising, whether the issues are late 19th century American regional development (Williamson 1974) or Third World urbanization in the 1980s.

Let me offer some brief words of motivation on the urbanization issue. Current rates of Third World city growth are enormous, averaging around 5 percent per annum. Pessimists have argued that these rates of spatial population redistribution cannot be sustained, and fear that Third World cities will shortly become unmanageable, environmental disasters, and centers of social revolution. The pessimists offer three sources of an incipient urban crisis in the Third World. First, a savings constraint may bridle the growth of capital-intensive cities. Second, since it has been alleged that city inmigrants have been motivated by unwarranted employment expectations, a labor-market disequilibrium may have made over-urbanization a serious problem of overshoot. Third, and perhaps most important, pessimists have argued that past urban excesses can be traced to the availability of cheap energy (favoring fuel-intensive cities), technological diffusion from the developed world (favoring urban-based sectors), heavy capital inflows (helping finance city social overhead), world trade liberalization (favoring urban-based manufacturing), a drift toward domestic price distortions favoring city output, and unusually rapid population growth. These conditions now show signs of changing. Thus projected high rates of urban growth may not be reached over the next two decades, given further OPEC-induced fuel scarcity, technological regression in urban-based sectors that have borrowed heavily from advanced countries which themselves have recently undergone productivity slowdown, diminished capital transfers due to economic austerity in advanced countries, a retreat toward protectionism in industrialized countries, and retardation in economy-wide population growth rates.

While the pessimists have established a plausible case, no one has offered a quantitative assessment of the importance of these forces over the past two decades. Without such an assessment, debate over future Third World population redistribution toward the cities will be dominated by allegation and anecdotal evidence. Our modeling effort has been motivated by the view that the debate can be better informed by the application of general equilibrium models which include the costs of urbanization so that the "natural limits" to urban growth can be evaluated, and the impact of changing economic-demographic conditions assessed.

Sketching Out a General Equilibrium Model of Migration and City Growth

How might our models of development be revised to better capture the costs of urbanization? This is not the place to expose the technical detail of the supply-driven Kelley-Williamson model, but a few words may inspire a closer look at this work (Kelley and Williamson, 1980, 1982a, 1982b, 1984).

It seems likely that far more insight into the limits of urban growth might be gained by examining various urban costs which influence the migration decision, on the one hand, and rising urban housing and social overhead requirements which compete with conventional capital accumulation, on the other. First among these influences are inelastic urban land supplies. Urban land constraints serve to raise (market or shadow) rents, augment urban relative to rural living costs, and inhibit inmigration to the city. To the extent that rising rents and urban disamenities are both caused by increased density, crowding, and other manifestations of inelastic urban land supplies, then city rents reflect more than simply living costs, but the quality of urban life as well. The importance of these urban land constraints on city rents can only be evaluated in a general equilibrium model which, at the very minimum, admits housing service activities and confronts equilibrium land-use issues.

Second, the housing-cum-social overhead investment requirements of city growth must be confronted. Urban housing and social overhead investment may well take priority over those forms of accumulation which create capacity for future urban employment. In any case, housing and social overhead investment requirements compete directly with other forms of capital accumulation which embody more enduring job creation effects.

Any model of urban growth must deal with these competing requirements since new housing-cum-social overhead requirements may very well serve to check urban growth. Of course, if the housing-cum-social overhead investment is foregone, then housing costs will rise and the quality of urban services fall, further discouraging inmigration to the city. In short, the rise in the relative cost of living in the city may impose a limit to urban growth and/or the rise of urban housing, and social overhead requirements may diminish the rate of productive urban capital accumulation and new urban job creation, and thus limit urban growth.

The Kelley-Williamson model is in the neo-classical general equilibrium tradition. Prices of outputs and inputs are completely flexible, and most are endogenously determined, including location-specific nominal wages and living costs. Firms are driven by profit maximization. Household choices are determined by utility maximization, including their location decision and migration behavior.

There are eight sectors in the model, two regions (urban and rural), and five household types. Five of the sectors are urban-based and three are rural-based. The model distinguishes between tradeables and nontradeables, the latter including various location-specific services. It is hardly the first multisectoral model to recognize nontradeables, but it is the first spatial development model that simultaneously stresses the importance of nontradeables as an influence on migration behavior. The presence of nontradeables results in spatial cost-of-living differentials. Since migrants are assumed to move in response to improvements in expected earnings adjusted by cost-of-living, the latter may exert an important impact on the rate of urban growth.

The model is dynamic, and accumulation is savings-driven. In any period, the aggregate savings pool is generated endogenously from three sources: retained after-tax corporate and enterprise profits, government saving (augmented by financial transfers from abroad), and household saving. This savings pool is allocated to three uses: investment in physical (or conventional) capital, investment in human capital, and investment in housing. It should be emphasized that these three modes of accumulation are competitive and determined endogenously, but institutional and technological features seriously restrict the economy's ability to equate rates of return at the margin. Any dwelling market may be starved for investment funds since the absence of mortgage markets may leave housing investment requirements in excess demand. The immobility of sector-specific capital stocks makes it likely that current investment allocations are insufficient to equalize spatial and sectoral rates of return. Furthermore, firms' demands for skills may remain unsatisfied if the stock of potential trainables is insufficient to meet desired training investment levels. In short, capital market disequilibrium can be a chronic attribute of our economy.

Finally, there are the exogenous variables which help drive the economy over time, and which are alleged to have influenced Third World city growth and population redistribution as a consequence: the nominal value of foreign capital available to help finance the development effort and forestall balance of payments problems; the total unskilled labor force driven by previous demographic events; the sectoral rates of total factor productivity advance, favoring urban-based sectors; prices of imported raw materials and fuels, influenced by the vagaries of OPEC and other world market conditions; and the terms of trade between primary exportables and manufactured importables, twisted by domestic price policy and the political economy of protectionist/liberalization winds in the industrialized nations.

Validating the Model

The Kelley-Williamson model generates predictions for more than 100 endogenous variables. Most of these reflect general attributes of growth, accumulation, income distribution, and industrialization; but three aspects of population redistribution are of special interest here: urbanization, city growth, and rural-urban migration. Table 10-1 presents some results for the pre-OPEC period, 1960-73, where the Third World history being replicated is based on 40 developing oil-importing countries. The first panel of the table reports the pre-OPEC time-series predicted by the general equilibrium model; the second compares the model with history over the decade of the 1960s as a whole.

Panel A suggests that the model reproduces the qualitative dimensions of Third World urbanization fairly well. Urban shares rise over time, and there is clear evidence that the model predicts accelerating rates of urbanization, conforming to the pre-inflection point phase along a logistic urbanization curve so common to Third World time-series (Ledent 1980; Preston 1979). Similarly, city growth rates rise over time, conforming to the trends reported by the World Bank (International Bank for Reconstruction and Development (IBRD) 1976, table 2). Rural-urban migration rates rise over the period as well.

Panel B supplies a more detailed assessment of the model's performance. While Third World city growth rates were 4.6 percent per annum over the 1960s, the model predicts a rate of 4.7 percent, certainly a close correspondence. True, the rate of urbanization is somewhat faster in the

Table 10-1. Third World Migration, Urbanization, and City Growth 1960-73

A. Model's Predictions: Annual, 1960-73

Year	Percent Urban	City Growth Rate	Net Urban Inmigration Rate
1960	32.60%	—	—
1961	33.55	5.56%	2.91%
1962	34.30	4.87	2.24
1963	34.73	3.85	1.25
1964	35.25	4.13	1.51
1965	35.78	4.11	1.50
1966	36.49	4.60	1.98
1967	37.23	4.64	2.01
1968	38.07	4.90	2.27
1969	38.95	4.94	2.31
1970	39.93	5.15	2.51
1971	40.96	5.22	2.58
1972	42.15	5.56	2.91
1973	43.45	5.72	3.07

B. Model's Predictions and History: Decade Averages, 1960-70

Variable	Model	History
1. City growth, per annum (compounded)	4.67%	4.60%
2. Total increase in share urban	7.33	5.30
3. Increase in share urban, percent per annum	0.73	0.53
4. Net inmigrant share of urban population increase	45.0	39.3 to 49.0
5. Net inmigration rate	2.09	1.81 to 2.26

Source: Kelley and Williamson (1984, table 3.13).

model, but it should be pointed out that while the model predicts changes in spatial employment distribution, alas history only reports changes in spatial population distribution. Panel B also reports inmigration rates for the decade as a whole. Once again, the model appears to conform with the quantitative averages generated by Third World history across the 1960s: while the predicted urban inmigration rate is 2.1 percent per annum, the historical estimates offered by demographers range from 1.81 to 2.26 percent per annum. Finally, the model predicts that 45 percent of the increase in city population is accounted for by inmigration. This figure falls between Preston's (1979) low estimate of 39 percent for the 1960s and Keyfitz's (1980) high estimate of 49 percent.

Changes in the Growth Environment After OPEC

The changing growth environment in the aftermath of the OPEC price shock has been significant, manifested mainly in relative prices. Relative to primary product exports from developing countries, the price of manufactures declines at an annual rate of 0.7 percent per annum up to 1973. The rate of decline accelerated after 1973, averaging 1.6 percent per annum up to 1979. In contrast, the relative price of imported raw materials (including fuels) rose by 5.2 percent per annum after 1973, while the same relative price exhibited long-run stability prior to 1973. There were other, nonprice changes in the Third World's economic-demographic environment after 1973: labor-force growth rates rose from 2.54 percent to 2.68 percent per annum, and the rate of expansion in the arable land stock declined from about 1 percent to 0.5 percent per annum. These land and demographic trends were not, of course, OPEC-related and, furthermore, not all of the epochal price trends were OPEC-related either. Nonetheless, in what follows we shall invoke poetic license and label these two epochs as "pre-OPEC" and "post-OPEC."

Structural Adjustment and City Growth Slowdown

As every analyst knows, the world economy is undergoing painful adjustment to the price shocks associated with short-run OPEC policy and long-run raw material and fuel scarcities. One manifestation of the structural adjustment has been the city growth slowdown in the Third World. Or is it? That a modest city growth slowdown took place during the 1970s there is no doubt. The World Bank reports a decline from 4.4 to 4.3 percent per annum for *all* developing countries (IBRD 1980, table 1), while the model predicts a similar slowdown for our 40-country sample. But how much of this modest slowdown is due to exogenous post-OPEC economic-demographic events and how much to the "natural limits" to urbanization?

Table 10-2 summarizes the model's city growth predictions. Panel B of the table offers three predictions: (1) a 1960-73 prediction using the actual pre-OPEC economic-demographic environment, a prediction that has already been compared with history in table 10-1; (2) a 1973-79

Table 10-2. Third World Urban Adjustments in Post-OPEC

A. *Post-OPEC Model Predictions: Annual, 1973–79*

	Actual Post-OPEC Environment			Counterfactual Pre-OPEC Environment		
Year	Percent Urban	City Growth Rate	Net Urban Inmigration Rate	Percent Urban	City Growth Rate	Net Urban Inmigration Rate
1973	43.45	5.72%	3.07%	43.45	5.72%	3.07%
1974	44.45	5.10	2.32	44.78	5.75	3.10
1975	45.22	4.48	1.72	46.25	5.92	3.27
1976	46.26	5.03	2.26	47.80	6.03	3.38
1977	47.05	4.52	1.76	49.46	6.14	3.47
1978	47.85	4.47	1.71	51.22	6.23	3.56
1979	48.58	4.29	1.53	53.03	6.16	3.49

B. *Period Averages, Pre-OPEC vs. Post-OPEC Model Predictions*

Variable	1960–73 Actual Pre-OPEC Environment	1973–79 Actual Post-OPEC Environment	1973–79 Counterfactual Pre-OPEC Environment
City growth, per annum	4.86%	4.65%	6.04%
Total increase in share urban	10.85	5.13	9.58
Increase in share urban, percent per annum	0.83	0.86	1.60
Net inmigration share of urban population increase	47.72	41.34	57.50
Net inmigration rate	2.35	1.91	3.48

Note: The 1973–79 counterfactual results assume the 1960–73 dynamic parameters to prevail after 1973. See Kelley and Williamson (1984, table 5.3).

prediction using the actual post-OPEC economic-demographic environment discussed above; and (3) a counterfactual post-OPEC prediction. The third of these predictions simply allows the pre-OPEC environmental conditions to continue beyond 1973. The counterfactual experiment makes it possible to assess what urbanization experience would have been like in the absence of the post-OPEC epochal shocks.

The results are informative indeed. Any analyst comparing the pre-1973 and post-1973 record predicted by the model in Panel B of table 10-2 might well have concluded that the OPEC price shocks mattered little to subsequent urban performance. After all, the rate of city growth declines only modestly over the period as a whole (from 4.86 to 4.65 percent per annum), the percent urban continues its climb, and inmigration rates, although somewhat lower, still remain at high levels. True, but note the unambiguous evidence of retardation in Panel A (Actual)—the rate of inmigration and city growth lose their steam quite dramatically. More importantly, in Panel B compare this predicted actual post-OPEC experience with the counterfactual 1973-79 experience assuming pre-OPEC environmental conditions: while the actual city growth rate for 1973-79 is 4.65 percent per annum, the counterfactual rate would have been 6.04 percent per annum! Furthermore, without these shocks in the late 1970s, the counterfactual rate of inmigration would have risen to 3.48 percent, rather than suffer the fall to 1.91 percent as it in fact did.

Isolating the Sources of City Growth SlowDown

It seems quite clear that exogenous economic-demographic conditions had a powerful impact on Third World urbanization experience during the 1970s. Can we isolate the most important of these influences? Table 10-3 reports an effort along these lines, (although additional research has pushed forecasts forward to the year 2000). There are nine counterfactual simulations reported in table 10-3. Each of these generates a history across the 1970s (1973-79), but the table only presents one of the model's predictions—the per annum rate of city growth. Each of these counterfactual cases should be compared with the actual 1973-79 performance reproduced in the first column (which repeats table 10-2). For example, the fuel-abundance counterfactual in column 3 maintains all of the exogenous conditions underlying the actual in column 1 *except* fuel price behavior: while the relative price of fuels rose by 5.2 percent per annum between 1973 and 1979, the counterfactual assumes no change in that relative price as was indeed the case up to 1973.

What were the main forces responsible for the Third World urban slowdown? It certainly had very little to do with agricultural land expansion or aggregate population and labor-force growth. Rather, it appears that prices were doing most of the work. Furthermore, and in spite of all the attention which it has received, rising fuel scarcity was nowhere

Table 10-3. Sources of a City Growth "Slowdown"? Some Counterfactuals Applied to 1973-79

		OPEC Watershed Counterfactuals, 1973-79				Other Counterfactuals, 1973-1979			
		Fuel Abundance Pre-OPEC	World Markets Pre-OPEC	Land Expansion Pre-OPEC	Population Pressure Pre-OPEC	Stable World Markets	No Population Pressure Developed Countries	Foreign Capital Austerity	Technological Slowdown
Year	Simulated Actual 1973-79	Total Pre-OPEC Environment	$P_z^* = 0$ Only	P_M^* Only	R_A^* Only	$(L^* + S)$ Only	$P_M^* = 0$	Rate	$F = 0$	
	(1)	(2)	(3)	(4)	(5)	(6)	(7)	(8)	(9)	(10)
1973	5.72	5.72	5.72	5.72	5.72	5.72	5.72	5.72	5.72	5.72
1974	5.10	5.75	5.35	5.59	5.09	5.06	5.95	4.46	5.21	5.10
1975	4.48	5.92	4.91	5.67	4.51	4.50	6.46	4.03	5.66	4.27
1976	5.03	6.03	5.28	5.90	4.95	4.96	6.51	4.37	4.37	4.60
1977	4.52	6.14	5.13	5.91	4.47	4.48	6.64	3.72	4.33	4.22
1978	4.47	6.23	5.05	5.96	4.36	4.36	6.63	3.68	4.21	3.93
1979	4.29	6.16	4.83	5.79	4.27	4.28	6.76	3.57	4.24	3.82
Average	4.65	6.04	5.09	5.80	4.61	4.60	6.49	3.97	4.67	4.32

Note: Each entry refers to the per annum rate of city growth, and the bottom row supplies the average growth rate for the period 1973-79 as a whole. The ten cases make the following assumptions about six key exogenous variables, where * denotes growth rates:

Variable	1	2	3	4	5	6	7	8	9	10
P_z^*: Fuel and raw material prices	5.2%	0	0	5.2%	5.2%	5.2%	5.2%	5.2%	5.2%	5.2%
P_M^*: Domestic price of manufactures	−1.6	−0.7%	−1.6	−0.7	−1.6	−1.6	0	−1.6	−1.6	−1.6
R_A^*: Agricultural land stock	0.5	1.0	0.5	0.5	1.0	0.5	0.5	0.5	0.5	0.5
$\overline{(L+S)}^*$: Population (or labor force)	2.68	2.54	2.68	2.68	2.68	2.54	2.68	0.9	2.68	2.68
F^*: Foreign capital inflow	←——— F such that $F/GDP = 3\%$ ———→								$F = 0$ ↑	
TFPG: Productivity growth (economy-wide)	1.8	1.8	1.8	1.8	1.8	1.8	1.8	1.8	1.8	1.0

Source: Kelley and Williamson (1984, table 5.5).

near as important a source of city growth slowdown as was the accelerated decline in the relative price of manufactures. Obviously, this finding supports the view that any future trend toward protectionism in the industrialized countries will play a very important role in shaping Third World city growth over the next two decades. The same might be said, of course, for the mix of internal policies which may twist the relative price of manufactures in the future. This position is reinforced by the counterfactual experiment under stable world markets where the relative price of manufactures is held fixed across the 1970s. Under these more favorable price conditions for manufacturing, the model predicts city growth rates of 6.49 percent per annum in contrast with the actual rate of only 4.65 percent per annum.

Table 10–3 reports three other counterfactuals which are extremely suggestive. While a sharp decline in the rate of population growth would certainly have diminished the rate of city growth in the Third World, column 8 suggests that this influence has been grossly overdrawn in the popular literature. The counterfactual explores the impact of a spectacular reduction in population pressure, from the actual rate of 2.68 percent per annum to the far lower rate which prevailed among the industrialized countries, 0.9 percent per annum. Even under this enormous diminution in population growth, the rate of city growth in the Third World would still have reached almost 4 percent per annum for the 1973–79 period as a whole. While rapid population growth certainly has contributed to the spectacular city growth rates we observe in the Third World, our experiments suggest that it is *not* the central force driving Third World urbanization. Table 10–3 also suggests that a shift to foreign capital austerity would not matter much to Third World urbanization either.

Note, however, the sensitivity of Third World urbanization to productivity slowdown. For a plausible retardation in the economywide rate of total factor productivity growth (TPFG) from 1.8 to 1 percent per annum, city growth rates decline quite a bit, and the impact seems to show signs of cumulating over time.

A Plea for Future Research on Regional Population Redistribution

I am not about to urge regional modelers to restrict themselves to a general equilibrium paradigm like the one illustrated by the Kelley-Williamson model. Nor am I suggesting that urbanization and city growth should take precedence over other regional aspects of spatial population redistribution.

But I *do* strongly urge that modelers focus on multiregional interaction, which makes it possible to assess the impact of nationwide economic-demographic events—*especially* policy—on unequal job creation across space, and that modelers take regional cost-of-living and quality-of-life differentials more seriously. If that plea has struck a responsive chord, then I shall be pleased indeed.

Notes

1. For an example applied to 19th century regional and international labor markets, see Williamson (1974, ch. 7).
2. For example, see Williamson and Lindert (1980, part III).
3. These comments do not necessarily apply to the entire literature on regional forecasting. See, for example, Ballard and Wendling (1980), Milne, Glickman, and Adams (1980), or Adams and Glickman (1980).
4. The classic example of disamenities generated by crowding is mortality differentials. These were important determinants of labor-market behavior and location choices driving 19th century rural-urban migration. See, for example, the application of hedonic wage equations to the British Industrial Revolution in Williamson (1981).
5. This section draws heavily on Kelley and Williamson (1982b, 1984).

References

Adams, F.G., and Glickman, N.J. 1980. *Modeling the multiregional economic system*. Lexington, MA: D.C. Heath.

Ballard, K.P., and Wendling, R.M. 1980. The national-regional impact evaluation system: a spatial model of U.S. economic and demographic activity. *Journal of Regional Science* 20, 2: 143–158.

International Bank for Reconstruction and Development. 1976, 1980. *World tables, 1976 and 1980*. Baltimore, MD: Johns Hopkins University Press.

Kelley, A.C., and Williamson, J.G. 1980. *Modeling urbanization and economic growth*. Laxenburg, Austria: International Institute for Applied Systems Analysis.

_____. 1982a. The limits to urban growth: suggestions for macromodeling third world economies. *Economic Development and Cultural Change* 20, 3: 595–623.

_____. 1982b. What drives Third World city growth? Paper presented to the Conference on Urban Processes and Policies in Developing Countries, University of Chicago, May 10–13.

_____. 1984. *What drives Third World city growth? A dynamic general equilibrium approach*. Princeton, NJ: Princeton University Press.

Keyfitz, N. 1980. Do cities grow by natural increase or by migration? *Geographical Analysis* 12, 2: 142–156.

Ledent, J. 1980. *Comparative dynamics of three demographic models of urbanization*. Laxenburg, Austria: International Institute for Applied Systems Analysis.
Milne, W.J.; Glickman, N.J.; and Adams, F.G. 1980. A framework for analyzing regional growth and decline: a multiregion econometric model of the United States. *Journal of Regional Science* 20, 2: 173–189.
Preston, S. 1979. *Patterns of urban and rural population growth*. New York: United Nations, Population Division.
Williamson, J.G. 1965. Regional inequality and the process of national development: a description of the patterns. *Economic Development and Cultural Change* 13, 4, Part II: 1–84.
———. 1974. *Late nineteenth century American development: a general equilibrium history*. Cambridge: Cambridge University Press.
———. 1981. Urban disamenities, dark Satanic mills and the British standard of living debate. *Journal of Economic History* 41, 1: 75–84.
Williamson, J.G., and Lindert, P.H. 1980. *American inequality: a macroeconomic history*. New York: Academic Press.

11 INTUITION, SCIENCE, AND THE APPLICATION OF REGIONAL MODELS

William Alonso

In this chapter I address some long-held concerns of mine: (1) the matter of scale and boundaries; (2) time; (3) some relations between theory and observations; (4) the importance of historicity; and (5) the uses and purposes of regional projections in policy.

Scale and Boundaries

A duality exists in regional work between the concepts of continuous and bounded space. Classical location theory, for instance, deals with continuous space, but most of regional economics (such as the many versions of multipliers) deals with a social unit in bounded space. These two ways of thinking about space, distance, and region cannot be easily reconciled in our theories. They stand somewhat as the wave and quantum theories of light did in physics; both are useful, and sometimes we make use of one and sometimes of the other according to the occasion, but we find it difficult to unify them.[1]

The concept of bounded, or regionalized, space is most useful for the consideration of complex interactions in a functional region such as a labor-market area, where we may wish to balance labor supply and demand and take account of multipliers, externalities, comparative price advantages, etc.

The notion of such a region, in our intuition, is not really that of a sharply bounded piece of territory: rather the boundaries will be fuzzy in our mind. How far do externalities extend, where does the labor market end, what is the range to which prices or wages apply with precision? In fact, our intuitive notion of such a region is a mix of bounded and continuous space. We might accept some pragmatic boundaries, but we recognize that these are a procrustean trimming of our real meaning.

The statistics with which we will study the situation will not conform to this intuition or meaning. Some may be available at a finer geographic detail, and some for larger areas (such as states when we consider metropolitan areas). Some might even coincide exactly with the pragmatic boundaries we have set for our region, especially as these boundaries are likely to have been chosen with an informed regard to the availability of data. But the statistics will not truly conform with our intuition of the region because in each case they will refer to sharply bounded areas.

Why is this? The reasons lie in the nature of mathematics and bureaucracies. The data are gathered of necessity by bureaucracies, which must produce them by a set of definable and well-specified procedures of identification and measurement, which amount to the operational definition of the category. The space within which things are to be counted or measured must also be clearly bounded. This Weberian requirement of bureaucratic rationality is matched by the nature of set theory, which underlies counting and measurement: an element is or is not a member of a set; the set is bounded; counting is matching the elements of this set to that of the positive integers; and so on. Thus the nature of mathematical theory and of the bureaucratic social processes results of necessity in something very like that Bertrand Russell called "misplaced specificity." The boundaries of our conceptual categories, and those of the social systems we are trying to represent, are fuzzy rather than knife-edged: what is the exact geographic boundary of a market area? What is a wage? Who is unemployed? What is capital?

And just as the data have harder edges than reality does, so do our mathematical models, which use functions and equations also based ultimately on set theory, and on which the handling of the statistical error term is only a modest convenience not adequate to handle the larger issues I worry about here. Thus, when we do regional models we should recognize that we are always trimming and cutting here, stuffing some extra there.

These consideration should always be on our mind, of course, but most particularly when we make hard demands on the data or on the models, in the form of drawing sharp conclusions about optimizing conditions or about the meaning of derived quantitative data such as the parameters of the equations.

An apparently simple but profoundly difficult problem deserves special mention: the area definition of a system across time, as might arise in tracing a metropolitan area. If the definition of area is preserved unchanged from one period to the next, it will be under- or overbounded in periods other than that chosen as the reference. If the area is allowed to change from period to period, it becomes quite unclear what is being caught within this net. Thus the fundamental problem of regional definition is not only one of fuzzy functional boundaries at any given moment but of their shifts in time.

Comparable problems of core and boundaries, of intuitions and procedures, and of changes in meaning in time are the root of very practical data problems. Consider only the technical questions about how migration data are produced by various methods: residual, retrospective sample, continuing survey, or administrative sources. A few moments' thought will begin to reveal the parallels.

Having data available by finer and finer disaggregation does not do away with these problems, whether it be by industrial or geographic detail, or by age, sex, race, or education. The basic reason for this is that the functioning of systems at higher levels does not normally proceed by the simple aggregation of lower level elements, anymore than a crowd at a theater does when each person tries to make for the exit at the cry of "Fire!" Since this point is well developed in much of the literature, I will not dwell on it here.

Time

Time is relevant to regional models in various ways: in models stressing dynamics and models based on comparative statics, in lagged variables, and in technical issues having to do with the frequency of data. Censuses, samples, administrative records, and panels each have their own rhythm and punctuation in time and their own issues of categories and continuities. Each "regionalizes" time by its own logic and characteristics.

As with geographic data, having finer and finer temporal data would not solve our problems. Just as we need to aggregate geographic, industrial, or demographic data to the right scale for proper analysis, so we need to organize information about time.

Time, in our intuition, is a continuous variable, as is space. But also in our intuition we divide it into loosely defined chronological regions: day-night, infancy-youth-maturity-old age, the Middle Ages, the Agricultural Revolution, the 1973 recession, the little Ice Age of the 1830s, the Great Depression, the Eisenhower years, the school year, summer, and fiscal years. Even if we had the time of every event down to the second, in order to use it we would have to organize it into categories, and thus again we would overspecify and mask detail.

Implications: What To Do

These thoughts do not imply either that statistics or the models built upon them cannot be improved. Surely they can, and all the chapters of this book are part of that effort. My point is rather that the intrinsic problems of statistics and of modeling to which I have called attention need greater recognition than they usually receive. Too often our research and findings are presented as if they were truer reflections of reality than they in fact can be—considering the mismatch of intuitions, formalizations, data, and time.

Rather than laying claim to hard certainty or statistical magic (so many models have R-squares of over 0.9, when the basic data surely have at least 10 percent noise), my suggestion is that, for scientific work, we become more aware of something like a Heisenberg principle, and present and discuss findings in more conditional and contextual ways. Later I shall make some comments about work intended to inform policy.

Theory and Observation

There were at the ASA/Census conference some lively moments, indeed quite a flap, as to the relation and validity of theory and observations. It was held by some that observations without theory are worthless.

It is undoubtedly true that observations systematic enough to be recorded must have, even if unacknowledged, a basis in some sort of organizing theory. It has often been the fate of the social sciences to be considered fakey, flaky, wordy, and unscientific. One can clearly see that much of social science is defensive and minds its skirts against such accusations and, for reasons which escape me, particularly against that of lacking theory. It can strike terror in the heart of a social scientist (especially if he is a junior faculty member in search of tenure) to have a righteous finger pointed accusingly at him for having no theory. This situation, I think, goes back to the nefarious influence of Karl Popper on the social scientists at Chicago two generations ago, but I will not dwell on this speculation.

At any rate, if a scholar in our insecure sciences ventures to describe some apparent factual matters which seem interesting, he is likely to be smitten by label of "atheoretical."

This practice seems to me wrong and wasteful. Goodness knows that in many areas we have a surfeit of explanations for a paltry collection of facts. Contributions which establish sturdy facts are very valuable.

James B. Conant proposed many years ago a distinction that seems to me admirable. There are theories of fact and theories of explanation. Both types of theory are important. For instance, a theory of fact was that combustion was a weight-gaining process. Establishing this fact was the result of brilliant experimentation by Lavoisier. Once the theory of fact is established, how does one explain it? There were two principal competing theories of explanation, phlogiston and oxidation, and in time oxidation won. Whichever theory of explanation succeeded, the question had been posed by the theory of fact.

To my mind, one of the fascinating aspects of geographical analysis, under the label of one or another discipline, is that there seem to be so many "facts" and regularities such as distance decay, rank-size rules and many other scale effects, substitutions of seasonality for distance in agricultural crops, the concentration of migration destinations by oldsters in post-industrial circumstances, and many others. Therefore I am an enthusiast of theories of fact, much as I am a skeptical adherent of theories of explanation. I am quite impatient of players of the bead-game who berate for lack of theory those who point to interesting and instructive facts.

Regional and Migration Theory and Facts

Much of the substantive and theoretical concern with the projection of regional economies and populations has centered on the migration among regions. For the most part models have assumed that migration is largely economically based, i.e., in search of jobs and higher wages, and the econometric findings have generally supported this perspective.

But here we come again to the fact that facts are only perceived through some organizing theory. There is a theory lurking through several of the models in this book, and elsewhere in the comparable literature, that the free mobility of factors in an open economy (such as that of the United States) will shift these factors toward those sectors and locations where they can maximize their returns. For our purposes this theory implies that the returns to labor (allowing for human capital and other factors) are everywhere the same. Therefore, according to this theory, the observed wage differences are artifacts of, on the one hand, differences in the cost of living, and, on the other hand, of amenities and disamenities at the various locations. In other words, by theory, the return to labor of various kinds is everywhere the same, and therefore the observed differences in wages (after allowing for cost of living) are shadow prices for the unobserved amenities and disamenities.

This theory has produced in recent years a lively literature which, by econometrically estimated hedonic pricing, attempts to tell us what a winning baseball club or a certain crime rate are worth in dollars and cents. It has thereby been influential for estimating costs and benefits of projects and policies.

Here we have then a "fact"—the dissimilarity of wages or incomes—filtered through a "theory"—that factor mobility has homogenized factor prices—and therefore a conclusion: that the observed differences reflect compensatory payments. This conclusion creates a set of new facts: the presumed compensatory payments. These then can be used as "prices" to be estimated against the characteristics of places.

Although this "disamenities" theory has not been explicitly prominent in regional models, it has become a substantial stream within the applied economics literature.

What if we were to take it seriously? Then, obviously, there would be no clear meaning to the wage, unemployment, and other local variables of migration attractiveness which feature so prominently in many of the regional models. Indeed, they should appear only as noise because of the unmeasured local amenities and disamenities. Rather, although economic self-interest would motivate the individual at the micro-level, it would be totally unobservable at the macro-level. The general patterns of migration would be based on "noise" from the point of view of standard economic theory: people trying to get close or away from relatives, life-stage migration, and so forth.

Unless geographic changes in the demand for labor were radical, local projections of the demand for labor would be sufficient for projecting the local labor force: increases or decreases could be accomplished by skimming the directionless noise migration.

In a longer run, of course, nicer places would need to pay less to workers, and thus would have a comparative advantage in labor costs. This advantage would raise their demand for labor and, depending on one's temperament, one could view the eventual outcome as that of an overall shift of population to nicer places, or as a transfer of population just sufficient to ruin the nicer places to make them comparable to the older ones.

At any rate, if this theory is subscribed to, there is no point in studying migration as such for the purpose of regional analysis and projection, because at the level of regional systems migration would only be background noise.

For myself, I think this theory of substitutions of wages and amenities is very partially true at best. My skepticism is based largely on theoretical grounds, which I will not elaborate here, and partly based on common observation: San Francisco has higher wages, after all requisite adjustments, than Fargo.

But this skepticism is only my own, and many serious scholars do seem to suscribe to the theory of equality of real wages. I think it important that this theoretical issue be resolved in the near future. Until this is done, regional analysis and its usefulness will suffer greatly from this internal contradiction. I must add that resolving this issue may not be easy because what is involved is some fundamental thinking about the nature of equilibria and steady states.

Historicity

It is the style of models such as those presented in this book to be ahistorical: that is to say, there are no wars, no changes in the patterns of world trade, no great social changes such as the move to the post-industrial economy or the stunning rise in the labor-force participation of women, no oil shocks, no shifts from Great Societies to Reaganomics, and seldom any economic cycles. The style of the inquiry is to find functional forms and parameters which shall be timeless.

Where the historical events of a particular period are in question (which is seldom in these models), there is strong bias to impersonal economic explanation. Thus Ledent's contribution (chapter 3) displays sharp movements in time for the parameters of migration within Canada.[2] Ledent was somewhat apologetic about this instability, presumably because parameter stability is to be cherished, as in the law of gravity. Some participants suggested linking the parameter shifts to economic cycles. Yet, when one looks at Ledent's Canadian data, it is clear that the strong parameter shifts coincide with the Quebec separatist initiatives and with the Anglo reactions. The point is that regional histories and futures are richer by nature than the set of variables built into these models.

Purposes

Why have the models presented in this book been built? Does the purpose matter? I think it does. Surely the purposes should determine the questions that the model is prepared to answer, and therefore its form and dimensionality. My strong impression is that the majority of the models skirt this issue. Indeed, in most cases it is impossible to tell what questions the modeling exercise was meant to answer: the model was presented as its own justification, somewhat like a Fabergé egg.

Are the models advancing science? Are they projections or predictions, however conditional? Mostly, I think the builders of the models would view their contributions as scientific ones, an addition to the understanding of our past and the structure of relations. Yet, the significance of almost every model is to the future; whether explicit or implicit, there is a projection. In most cases some sponsor paid for the researcher's time, his colleagues and assistants, computer costs, and some travel and secretarial costs. I would guess that the sponsors did not care mostly for modeling the past, but rather that they paid for studies of the past as means of understanding possible developments in the future.

Let me grant immediately that scientists want to advance their scientific understanding much of the time, whether or not it has practical results. Such is the distinction between basic and applied science. Equally, public and private sponsors range in their willingness to support basic science and in their patience for applied science and its results.

Still, the origin of the conference underlying this book, as I understand it, was that of applied science: there was a federal need to project local populations, and this conference was meant to advance the state of the art. Let me therefore speak to that purpose, granting that there are others at least as valid.

First, for policy, what is needed is not a projection which is by nature unalterable, but a model into the future that has both control variables (things one can do) and evaluation variables (things that tell you whether possible outcomes are good or bad). A model that includes control and evaluation variables may range from difficult to impossible, but the

INTUITION, SCIENCE, AND APPLICATION OF REGIONAL MODELS

intellectual frame for developing it is different from that of the models described in this book.

Second, in the making of policy it is normal to consider things such as the chances of going wrong, the benefits and hurts to particular client groups, and the peculiar calendar of elections, fiscal years, and other institutional regionalizations of time (such as the requirement to provide small-area population and economic projections some decades into the next millennium). A model's significance will usually depend on its being able to speak to these specifics.

Third, the previous points clearly imply that in order to play a significant role, technical or scientific work must interact with the political process and be responsive to the particularities of its timetables and its questions; it must give a sense of how reliable its answers and how large the risks are; and it must be as understandable and transparent as possible.

The cost of active participation in public policy can be high and may be unacceptable to many researchers. Quite properly, most will decide that they want to stay in science rather than move into policy analysis, but for those who wish to contribute to informing public issues, there is a need to find different and more effective modes of using science for regional analysis and projection.

Note

1. It is interesting that this duality is only bridged by the exotica of the discipline in the form of map generalizations, of which population and other forms of potential are the most common.

2. *Editor's Note*: Alonso's reference is to a much different, earlier version of Ledent's paper. The results mentioned by Alonso are not found in chapter 3, but this passage was retained because Alonso's point should be clear to the reader and its relevance extends far beyond Ledent's paper.